The
COMPLETE
IDIOT'S
GUIDE TO
Dating

by Dr. Judy Kuriansky

alpha
books

A Division of Macmillan General Reference
A Simon & Schuster Macmillan Company
1633 Broadway, New York, NY 10019

International Standard Book Number: 0-02-861052-0
Library of Congress Catalog Card Number: 95-083356

98 97   8 7 6

Interpretation of the printing code: the rightmost number of the first series of numbers is the year of the book's printing; the rightmost number of the second series of numbers is the number of the book's printing. For example, a printing code of 96-1 shows that the first printing occurred in 1996.

Printed in the United States of America

Publisher
Theresa Murtha

Editor in Chief
Megan Newman

Editor
Nancy Mikhail

Production Editor
Lynn Northrup

Copy Editors
Charles K. Bowles II
Noelle Gasco
Lisa Gebken
Maureen Schneeberger
Michael Thomas

Cover Designer
Michael Freeland

Illustrator
Judd Winick

Designer
Kim Scott

Indexer
Gina Brown

Production Team
Heather Butler, Angela Calvert, Tricia Flodder, Erich Richter,
Christine Tyner, Christy Wagner, Karen Walsh

Contents at a Glance

Contents

Introduction

This book is intended for anyone who is looking for love—whatever your age, background, dating history, or sexual intentions.

In the search for love, many people display their deepest fears—that they are unlovable, or that there is something wrong with them. I offer this book to reassure you, to give you hope that your quest will be successful! Your dreams can come true—but first you must be clear about what you are really looking for. And most of all, you must feel good about yourself.

This book is a guide to dating—from meeting and starting a relationship to making a commitment. It contains facts, corrections of myths, tips, and plenty of simple as well as sophisticated how-to's and exercises that you can immediately put to use. It also includes valid psychological principles, which will help you understand your own personal dynamics on a deeper level. The more you know about what makes you tick, the better prepared you will be when approaching potential loves.

Many people in the dating game are in the dark about human behavior. Men and women alike ask me, "Why did she say that?" "What does he mean by that?" "How can she do this to me?" When you understand what motivates and immobilizes people, as I help you to do in this book, you'll feel more empowered and in control. In addition, as you increase your self-esteem through self-knowledge, you'll improve your chances of dating success.

How to Use This Book

Treat this book as a good friend who supports you at any time and in many situations, who calms you down and peps you up.

➤ Keep it by your bedside to read before you go to bed.

➤ Discuss it with your friends.

➤ Refer to it before a date.

➤ Read sections and do the quizzes *with* a date.

Use it as a great conversation opener, or a means of learning about one another in a non-threatening way. Blame the book for making you ask some tough questions: What are we each looking for? Are you into commitment? When should we have sex?

In the front of the book is a reference card with some dating pointers. Tear it out and keep it in your pocket. Refer to it when you want a boost and a reminder that I'm always there with you in spirit. I'll always remember the first acting class I ever took, where the coach told us, "Take your biggest fan with you on an audition," (meaning, imagine them in the audience). So, imagine me cheering you on as you set out on a date!

To help you get the most out of this book, you'll see the following information boxes scattered throughout:

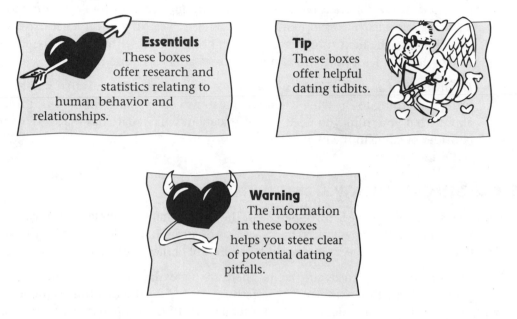

Essentials
These boxes offer research and statistics relating to human behavior and relationships.

Tip
These boxes offer helpful dating tidbits.

Warning
The information in these boxes helps you steer clear of potential dating pitfalls.

Throughout the book, you will encounter the three A's: *acceptance*, *appreciation*, and *adjustment*. The three A's are guideposts; when you're feeling confused about a person, or are having trouble remembering what you're after, the three A's can help restore your focus. You'll find them helpful in all kinds of situations—whether you're ready to make a commitment or trying to resolve an argument.

Mastering dating and mating is a metaphor for mastering your life. Here are some metaphors about dating that can also be helpful to you:

➤ *Love is art*. You start out with an empty canvas, a tabula rasa, then you layer on the shapes and colors. The details are all of your choosing.

➤ *Life is a play*. As Shakespeare said, "All the world's a stage and we are but players on it, who strut and fret their hour upon the stage." Realize that you create your own play of your love life. You select the leading lady or man, and you cast them in your story line. You have a script in your mind, even if you're not aware of it. What have you been putting on your love screen—a romantic drama where man and woman fall deeply in love and live happily ever after, or an action adventure where they encounter violence, enemies, and end up alone?

➤ *Dating is about selling.* Forget the cynicism; the truth is that, in dating, you're selling yourself to others. So follow certain tried-and-true rules of selling. Go after your prospects. Make cold calls (without formal introductions). Don't be discouraged by a "no," but see each as an opportunity to get to a "yes." If you can't get to "yes," go quickly on to the next "no," since that will bring you closer to a "yes" merely by the rule of odds (at least nine "no's" may be necessary before one "yes").

➤ *Dating is like a deal.* Forget any unromanticism of this; the truth is that you each bring something to the table when you meet. As you evaluate your assets, think about what you think you need, and think about what a date has that you would consider of value in the merger.

Being Single Today

These days, one out of every three people in the United States is single. That means there are about 50 million singles age 20 to 55 across America. That's a lot of people to reassure you that you are not alone, and that there are a lot of choices out there for you!

The U.S. Bureau of the Census shows that there are increasing numbers of singles these days, and that the estimated age of those getting married for the first time is higher than in recent years (26.5 for males and 24.4 for females in 1992, compared to 22.6 for males and 20.2 for females in 1955). The proportion of men and women in their twenties and thirties who have never married has grown substantially since 1970. Among women age 20 to 24, two-thirds had never been married in the 1990s, compared to just over one-third in 1970. About one-third of women in their late twenties and early thirties, and about 20 percent of women age 35 to 39, were unmarried. These proportions tripled and doubled over the past 20 years. Similarly, 80 percent of men age 20 to 24 and nearly half of men age 25 to 29 had never been married, and about one-third of men in their thirties were unmarried in the 1990s—this number tripling over the past two decades.

Though strong in numbers, singles unfortunately are not equally strong in attitude. Facing the perennial question "Why haven't you found anyone?" many wonder, "What's wrong with me?" I am painfully reminded that my mother's generation dreaded being the "old maid," and even in my college days, you had to graduate with an engagement ring and an "MRS." degree or you were looked upon askance. Times have changed; in the past 20 years, more and more people spend their 20s and 30s focusing on career goals rather than commitment goals. But they still need their self-esteem to catch up with their choices. And society's attitudes and laws need to offer support to validate these choices.

My Philosophy of Life

I hope you come away from this book trusting that you can have what you need in life. This message came across to me powerfully during a recent trip to India's Taj Mahal, where our guide ended up taking me to a carpet store. Initially, I had no desire to buy Indian carpets, but the owner spread them out, inviting me to appreciate the art. I ended up buying several rugs to the tune of several thousand dollars, and asked him, "How did you get me to buy these when I had no intention of bringing carpets back to America, much less spending so much money?" What he said rings in my ears, in his Indian accent: "Whatever is yours will come to you." It seemed a wise message for life and love: The love that is yours will come to you.

Of course, not all is fate. You are in control by your thoughts and actions. Remember one of my favorite phrases: Whatever you believe and conceive you can achieve. And then you must take steps to realize your dreams.

The fundamental message in *The Complete Idiot's Guide to Dating* is that the key to success is to be happy with yourself. Happiness is not just the fulfillment of needs; it's how you choose to think and feel every second. So make each second count by thinking good thoughts and feeling good about yourself!

While other guides may tell you to play games in dating (to hold out, or maintain mystery), I do not believe in game-playing. Real love comes from being appreciated for who you are—not who you pretend to be. And finally, because I am on my own course to be completely authentic and more spiritual in life, I encourage you to consider dating as simply meeting kindred souls, teaching and supporting each other in life's journey. Useful in this is the Sufi principle: Show up, pay attention, tell the truth, and don't be attached. Trusting and valuing yourself, with few demands or expectations on others, will bring you a purer love.

Acknowledgments

This book is the result of sharing from thousands of amazing and cherished callers to my radio show, "LovePhones"; letters from newspaper columns, guests and audience members on innumerable TV shows; men and women in lectures and seminars I've led; and precious friends. I've heard thousands of stories, revealing so many open hearts. For sharing them on "LovePhones," much heartfelt love to my loving and talented co-host Chris Jagger, my producers Sam and then Fuzzball, the LovePhones' Mousie, Piechick, and to P.D. Steve Kingston, for the magical mix of humor and healing.

This book—and I—have been blessed with the enthusiasm, wisdom, and love of my trusted and cherished assistant, Alissa Pollack. From day one, Alissa offered the most perfect and tireless inspiration, support, devotion, and even some wonderful anecdotes!

Then cabinetry master, Brian Courtney, brought light, as well as sex-role equality, literally and spiritually, onto the subject. And in the final hours, some perfect enrichments from buddy Evan Fairbanks. Cheers to my *Long Island Newsday* editor Barbara Schuler for her continual support and inspiration, and to Tony Leroi who saw it would all happen.

Honor to the cosmically connected Al Lowman, whose ideas are always an infusion of turbo energy and love, as well as to the entire editorial, sales, and management team at Alpha Books, who were enthusiastic about this book from the first, including editor in chief Megan Newman; editor Nancy Mikhail; copy editors Charles K. Bowles II, Noelle Gasco, Lisa Gebken, Maureen Schneeberger, and Michael Thomas; and production editor Lynn Northrup. Their hard work was invaluable and their contributions brilliant.

As always, gratitude to my angelic loved ones consistently glowing lights for me: my mother Sylvia, soulmate Edward, Brother Robert, "cosmic sister" Voltage, Rhea Ross, Edie Hand, Susie Viebrock, and Laurie Sue Brockway. Their devotion, love, belief, prayers, wisdom, and predictions make me soar and inspire me to pass on the gifts.

Part 1
Dating 101

Look at dating as a valuable learning experience. Dating gives you the opportunity to meet new people, learn about yourself, and, if all goes well, experience love. To help you reach that success, here are some tips to keep in mind:

➤ *Meet as many people as you can*

➤ *Let people know you're available*

➤ *Decide on your "love criteria"*

➤ *Don't be afraid of rejection*

➤ *Go places and see things that you enjoy*

➤ *Boost your self-esteem and mates will flock to you*

➤ *Remember that you have the power to get what you want*

➤ *Always have hope—you can meet someone special anytime and anywhere*

➤ *Be ready and open for love*

Who Is Ms./Mr. Right?

In This Chapter

➤ The meaning of attraction

➤ Making a love deal

➤ Your chances of finding a partner

➤ Do nice guys really finish last?

➤ Test your compatibility

"It ain't gonna be no pickle man!" —Amy Irving's character in "Crossing Delancey"

Of course you want to fall in love, but, like many singles, you despair of finding that "right" one. You may have some idea of your perfect man or woman—he should be good-looking, rich, and powerful; she should be beautiful, sexy, and smart.

One single guy I know says, "In real estate you look for three things: location, location, location. But in the dating market, a lot of women look for three things: cash, cash, cash." In a culture where the free love of the 1970s has emerged into high commercialism, love has been reduced to the "BBD"—the "Bigger Better Deal." But when it comes down to it, the "right" person might just be the pickle man, or the person who seemed quite plain at first, but who turns out to love sports, be a terrific cook, or the best lover you ever had.

The Mystery of Attraction

In many ways, attraction is a mystery, but there are some guideposts to help you understand the process. First off, I'd like to introduce you to my concept of "The Mirror Law of Attraction," which I refer to frequently throughout this book. According to this principle, we attract and are attracted to those people who have something we desire or wish to defy. For example, people who have commitment problems (but deny it) frequently attract unavailable types who wear their noncommittal status like a badge. Or people who are insecure about their looks are often compelled to date the most attractive people they can find.

We are also all equipped with a "love antennae" that help us tune into certain types of people. But beware, your love antennae may be improperly programmed, leading you to make choices that end up making you unhappy.

Your love antennae gets tuned by your particular "love criteria"—things you think you must have in a partner. But on closer examination, those qualities may not be essential, and you may have to change your criteria to find someone more suitable. Along those lines, many of us also keep an "eligibility score," in which we assess our "market" worth, and that of potential mates. Assess each quality from 0 (= zero) to 10 (= hero).

For example, if you rate yourself a "9" in looks but a "4" in intelligence, you might pick someone who ranks a "4" in attractiveness but a "9" in smarts—so your scores even out to a similar number. If you feel you have a quality "covered," you may find yourself going after someone who offers something that you don't quite have.

What Is Chemistry (and Does it Exist?)?

You spot him across a crowded room and you just *know* he's the one. It's the dream of a lifetime. You feel that chemistry, the thrill cursing through your body. Your heart pounds, and you feel that the two of you are meant to be together. Books, songs, movies are replete with these scenarios. These stories fuel hope, and we despair when it doesn't happen to us.

But just what is "chemistry"? Love, attraction, or lust—call it what you will—does trigger physiological reactions. In a heightened state of arousal, our bodies release a number of hormones and chemicals. One of these, adrenaline, triggers the "fight-or-flight response" that explains symptoms such as sweaty palms, palpitations, and weak knees—similar to anxiety symptoms triggered by a final exam or the near-miss of a traffic accident. Other chemicals include oxytocin (the "cuddle chemical"), phenylethylamine (the "natural high chemical"), and endorphins (the "pleasure chemicals").

The feeling of being magnetically attracted to someone may also have to do with the bioelectric fields that surround our bodies. A cycle is created: When we are aroused, our bodies release chemicals, which in turn stimulate the smooth muscles and sensitize the nerve endings. This makes us even more sensitive to pleasure and more emotionally responsive. As you interpret your body signals to mean you are "in love," your enthusiasm escalates.

Essentials

Research indicates that the brain plays a large role in our experience of love. A study of youngsters who underwent surgery for the removal of pituitary tumors found that these individuals were later able to form friendships, but didn't seem to be able to fall in love. The pituitary gland releases hormones essential to "mating" behavior. Scientists think that during surgery, crucial pathways were blocked, preventing the hormones from reaching their proper receptor sites in the brain.

Making Your Love Deal

Picking a mate is like the art of the deal. There are qualities you definitely want in a mate ("deal points"), conditions that you won't accept or live with under any circumstances ("deal-breakers"), and points you are willing to negotiate.

List the qualities you want in a mate. While I've only made room for five, list more if you wish.

1. _____

2. _____

3. _____

4. _____

5. _____

Now go back over your list and circle the qualities that are non-negotiable—the real deal-breakers. Put a question mark next to the ones that are negotiable—things you are willing to compromise on, or could learn to live with or without. Next, put an "x" next to the points that continually cause you trouble in relationships—these may be things you should consider dropping from your list or giving up on when looking for a mate.

Essentials

Research indicates that eight out of ten men still consider looks their primary "deal point." In comparison, women rank personality characteristics tops, such as sensitivity and caring. Yet research shows that physical attractiveness does affect how people react. In one study, people at the controls of a vibrating chair that created pleasurable sensations gave more vibrations to the people in the chair they rated as more attractive looking.

Love Scripts

Chemistry and deal points are just part of the reason we choose the people we do. We also use a "love script." This is a fantasy that tells us how we'd like our love lives to go. Think of it as a movie of your love life, and you are casting a partner for the leading role. Our love scripts are based on our emotional needs, experiences, beliefs, and desires.

Our love scripts often lead us to people who offer us some measure of emotional protection. For example, Geoffrey told me that he had "a special thing" for women over 200 pounds. "If they're not that fat," he said, "I won't date them." Terribly insecure about his own underdeveloped body, Geoffrey convinced himself such full-figured women would never reject him, so he felt safe. To find out why you are attracted to a particular trait, ask yourself: What meaning does this have for me? How does being with a person like that make me feel (safe, protected, important, powerful)?

Of course, our early childhood experiences also play a role in why we pick certain partners. For example, when we dug deeper into Geoffrey's background to find the sources of his attraction to large women, we discovered he had had a frail mother who never hugged him. This helped explain his distaste for slim-framed women, whom he expected would be as cold. A very overweight aunt came to visit infrequently, and her arms around him were his only fond memory of nurturing—making him pleasantly predisposed to other women like her.

Conditions That Enhance Attraction

In one study, men who had exercised vigorously found a pretty woman even more appealing than those who had exercised for only 15 seconds. In another study, men coming off a narrow, swaying footbridge, 230 feet above the rocks, asked a female research assistant out on a date more often than men walking across a low concrete span. The explanation: Arousal from fear (pounding heart, pumping blood) can be interpreted as excitement, making the men more susceptible to attraction.

Experiencing grief or loss stimulates a desire to reaffirm life, bringing people together in the face of tragedy. Sometimes these relationships flower beautifully. For example, Susie lost her fiancé to cancer, but at a memorial service, she met Kurt. Although an unlikely pair (she was a banking executive in New York, and he was a pilot living on a farm in Idaho), they bonded with memories of their cherished friend. Despite their differences, they discovered emotional similarities, and by transcending their shared pain, found a new love that was deep and lasting.

Warning

While Kurt and Susie's relationship worked out, there is a danger in forming bonds based on temporary need. After Lance broke his arm playing football, he ended up in physical therapy three times a week. Finding solace in the sweet physical therapist who carefully bandaged his arm and exercised his fingers, Lance felt he was falling in love. But once on the mend, Lance called his nurse less and less often, until he finally felt no desire to see her at all. When his need diminished, the attraction faded.

Many people have had the experience of falling for a co-worker or fellow cast member in a play, only to have the relationship fall apart at the end of the project. Mutual endeavors are very erotic, but don't guarantee lasting love. If you fall for someone during an intense project at work, or while you are both performing in a community play, don't be surprised if the relationship fizzles after the common bond dissipates.

Opposites Attract

You know the old saying, "opposites attract," and we have all seen this adage in action. But over time, differences that were once appreciated can become sources of irritation. Renée called my radio show, "LovePhones," to say that her boyfriend loves country music and honky-tonk bars. At first she was captivated by this because she's more the alternative music, pierced belly-button type. But the novelty was beginning to wear thin. If Renée and her boyfriend want to keep the relationship going, they both have to learn to accommodate their differences.

To this end, I suggest that couples keep in mind the three A's: acceptance, appreciation, and adjustment. New York mayor Rudy Guiliani and his wife, TV reporter Donna Hanover, are a good example of how opposites can attract and make a wonderful match. They seem to have put the three A's to work! She loves country music, he loves opera; he's into football, and she loves baseball. Joking about these differences helps them appreciate each other all the more.

Common Dating Myths

When you become depressed about dating, it might be because your mind is telling you discouraging thoughts. Many of these are blatantly untrue! Here are some common misconceptions, and the truth about them.

MYTH: There is no one for you. All the good ones are taken.

REALITY: Negative thoughts create negative outcomes; positive thoughts allow positive realities. Remember, the world is full of possibilities. There is a cover for every pot. Even the gloomy forecast years ago that single women over 35 had as much a chance of finding a man as being attacked by a terrorist was subsequently proved misleading. Instead of worrying about your chances, look at dating as a series of separate events: All that matters is what happens to *you*. In the movie "Dumb and Dumber," Jim Carrey falls hard for Lauren Holly and asks God what his chances are. "One in a million" is the answer. Carrey then cheers, "I have a chance!" Even if it's true that you have a one in 7,397,685 chance of winning a multimillion-dollar lottery, someone has to win it—and it could be you!

You always have a chance. Be encouraged by Nilly's example. "I'm not attractive," he admitted, "and I fell for this gorgeous girl and thought she'd never look at me twice, but I won her heart. We started out as friends and we got to talking. She told me she had been abused when she was younger, and that I made her laugh. Now she says she never felt as comfortable with anyone in her life."

If you do need statistics, be heartened by these, shown in the following chart. The U.S. Bureau of the Census reports show there are more single men for women than you might think (especially for those under 40 years of age).

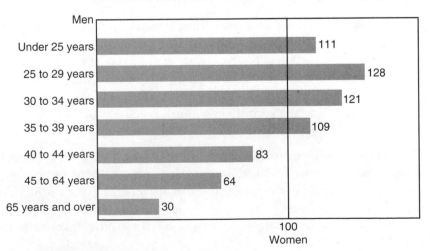

Ratio of Unmarried Men Per 100 Unmarried Women by Age: 1992

Age	Ratio
Under 25 years	111
25 to 29 years	128
30 to 34 years	121
35 to 39 years	109
40 to 44 years	83
45 to 64 years	64
65 years and over	30

Source: U.S. Bureau of the Census, March 1993

Tip

Chronic pessimists may have only themselves to blame! I've found in years of counseling singles that women and men who insist they can't find anyone are often afraid, unwilling, or not ready to commit themselves. Overcome this problem, adjust your too-rigid criteria, or tune your love antennae to whir for the right kind of date.

Rather than looking for "the one," be open to "dating around." Make the most of every date, not in terms of success or failure, or ridden with expectations or desperation, but as an adventure, a way of enjoying and learning about yourself and others. Beat any man (or woman) shortage odds: Instead of insisting on a certain height, salary, or status, be open to possibilities of who might be good for you.

For example, consider white-collar/blue-collar unions: Princess Stephanie of Monaco had two children by her bodyguard before she married him; Elizabeth Taylor married carpenter Larry Fortensky; Roseanne divorced her producer-husband Tom Arnold to marry her chauffeur-bodyguard. More secure women today consider repairmen, chauffeurs, and bodyguards, not fearing "marrying down" but welcoming the man's love and support.

Also consider May–December and December–May (age gap) relationships. Research shows the ideal relationship was once considered to be the man being three-and-a-half years older than the woman (anthropologically, younger fertile females were desirable to propagate the species). But today's trend of older women with younger men (made popular by Cher, who in her forties dated twenty-something lovers) can be a successful coupling. The younger man has grown up respecting independent, mature women and is more comfortable with equality than many older men. Lots of guys, including my "LovePhones" co-host Chris Jagger, answer proudly to losing their virginity to the "Mrs. Robinson" (from the movie "The Graduate," in which Dustin Hoffman had an affair with a woman old enough to be his mother), revering the sexually confident "teacher."

Differences in culture, race, and religion can seem insurmountable. C.J. is black and attracted to a Pakistani Muslim girl. Abe's girlfriend is Lutheran, but he's Jewish. Parents and friends warn and object, causing these couples to argue. Get past your own and society's prejudices. Be prepared for life changes, understand each other's background and perspective, and agree on important lifestyle decisions. Understand the reason for the attraction: for the person or what that person can do for you (protect, nurture, provide)?

I maintain that any difference can be overcome if you truly appreciate each other and work out major lifestyle decisions (about kids, careers, family visits). If others' objections get to you too much, they are triggering your own hesitations or doubts that you should examine. Are you worried that your attraction is a rebellion, an escape, or a challenge? Declare a moratorium on the worries and spend time strengthening your relationship so it can withstand objections.

MYTH: There is only one person right for you.

REALITY: There are many fish in the sea. There is no one and only Mr. or Ms. Right, and no perfect person—only real people, with real imperfections. It's totally true that finding love means being open to many possibilities and making compromises.

MYTH: It's impossible to find someone to love.

REALITY: Love can come in unexpected places and times, and in unexpected partners. For example, Jeannette was morose in her search. She told all her friends to be on the lookout, went to all the "right" parties, and joined all kinds of clubs, but seemingly to no avail. Finally, while visiting her sister in another state, she went to a museum exhibit. As she stood in front of a painting, a man with a small child asked her what she thought of the work. As she wandered to the next painting, and then the next, he seemed to follow her. Finally, he asked her to join him for lunch. They've been painting the town together ever since.

MYTH: Finding the right person is simply a matter of "fate"—being in the right place at the right time.

REALITY: As Jeanette's story shows, fate and timing are important, but you have to be open, receptive, and ready!

You may not be able to ensure that any one activity or place will manifest love (in fact, you should not have any expectations), but when you are open to possibilities, feeling good about yourself, and going about your life with joy, more people are bound to be drawn to you.

MYTH: All the "good ones" are taken. There are no good men or women left.

REALITY: Even if many "good ones" are taken, it only takes one. You may even know that good person now and just need to open your eyes.

So Who Is Ms./Mr. Right?

A few years ago I wrote a book, *How To Love A Nice Guy*, because I found that people were constantly drawn to lovers who were wrong for them. Unfortunately, things haven't changed enough in the five years since then, and men and women still need to be wary of dream lovers and learn to appreciate the "nice" guy or gal. He might be a cook or a carpenter instead of a CEO, or she may be a Plain Jane instead of Michelle Pfeiffer, but that person might be exactly who you need for a lifetime of lasting love.

Fortunately, as women become more emotionally, financially, and sexually secure and independent, they increasingly choose men who treat them well instead of those who are thrilling, "hot," or who fill some inadequacy in their lives. My own research shows that the top three qualities women want in a man are sensitivity (expressed as understanding, kindness, caring), intelligence, and a sense of humor; while men still go for looks. Undesirable qualities in men include arrogance, dishonesty, and selfishness. Both sexes say a sense of humor is a winner.

Nice Guys Don't Have to Finish Last

The lament of the nice guy is a common one that I hear a lot on my radio show. Vincent echoes the troubled refrain of many guys: "Why is it that girls stay with guys who treat them poorly but nice guys get stepped on?" Vincent is right—many women are attracted to "bad guys." As Christie says, "I like exciting guys. I know they're jerks and I'd like to like another guy I know who's sweet, but I can't help it. The rats just turn me on." Some women, like some men, in this trap of being torn between two loves—one nice and one "exciting"—are addicted to a challenge. They need to prove they are desirable. They can only escape this trap when they feel secure within themselves and find their own life exciting.

Like Vincent, Billy is similarly befuddled: "I spared no expense romancing this girl for two weeks, opening doors for her, taking her horseback-riding, buying her gifts. But she said I was too nice and left me for some guy who acts tough and treats her rough. What's wrong with me?"

What's wrong with Billy is that he opened his bank account and his heart too fast. Showering someone with gifts does not ensure her approval. But before he jumps to conclusions that being nice isn't worth it, Billy has to examine what else he might be doing wrong, such as choosing a woman who is unavailable and unattainable, who only wants a challenge in a man, and who may have such low self-esteem that she can't let herself be loved.

Following my "Mirror Law of Attraction," if you're always attracted to unavailable, unattainable dates, look at why you need to have partners who don't appreciate you. It might be to prove that you're okay (because of low self-esteem; if so, value yourself as you are); or because you need to prove that all people are hard to please (look at your history and see why you resent men or women); or because you are really afraid of commitment (so you pick partners who would never want to settle down either).

"Nice" used to be the kiss of death, implying doormat, nerd, or wimp. But the *new* nice (male or female) can be good-looking and exciting. The one thing the nice guy or gal may lack is mystery or elusiveness—in its place is sensitivity, caring, sincerity, and reliability.

Nice people are there for you in an emergency, give even more than they take, and listen when you need to talk. They're your best friend, the ones you call to complain about all the others who treat you poorly. Like Harry in the movie "When Harry Met Sally," or the pickle salesman in "Crossing Delancey," they love you for *you*. And they'll probably remember your birthday. They may not show up like fireworks, but they'll warm your heart by the fire. One guy I met on a talk show in Boston, Craig Sutton, started a club for nice guys, with dances and T-shirts that read, "This is what a nice guy looks like."

I'm often asked, "Where do I go to meet someone nice?" The nice guy or gal often shows up as somebody's good friend. So look right under your nose. Ask friends, relatives, and co-workers to introduce you to their best friends. The nice guy may be the one who lets you out of the elevator first in your office building or the one who offers you a seat on the bus. The nice gal's the one with the smiling face at your coffee shop. Once you've determined that "nice" is the one quality you won't compromise on, your "love antennae" will be attuned to that type of person and he or she will show up in your life.

The Good Friend Test

I always marvel at how people accept things from lovers that they would never accept from a friend. As Zenia says, "My boyfriend cheats on me, he lies, he always forgets to call me...but I still love him."

Before you set out to find your ideal date, think about what friendship means to you. After all, you want your lover to be your friend, don't you? List the things that are important in a friend (steadfastness, honesty, reliability), and then consider whether your current or past lovers have these qualities. If anything, you can be a little more lenient with friends, but should compromise *less* when it comes to a love partner—where you have more to invest and more to gain or lose.

Expecting Change

Part of love is supporting each other to become your best. But if you choose partners with the expectation of changing them, you're courting serious disappointment. Tara learned this the hard way. As she explained, "I've been seeing Ben for six years. He's really smart, but he's lazy. He's been working on his dissertation for years and just can't finish it. I keep encouraging him because I know he's talented, but now I feel like I'm just pushing him. Lately he's said that he's not interested in a career—that he'd rather do something simple. I'm afraid he'll never make anything of himself."

While it is wonderful to be a partner's cheerleader and inspiration, if you both have decidedly different goals, it might be time to either accept your mate or cut your losses. Eventually, Tara decided she could never be happy being a constant nag, nor could she be happy with someone who wasn't as ambitious as she was, so she and Ben parted ways.

Compatibility Test

Let's close this chapter with a simple compatibility test that helps you gauge if a relationship is going to work. If you're not seeing someone right now, remember to turn back to this test when you start dating. Compatibility is essential if a relationship is going to work. Ask yourself these questions:

➤ *Do the two of you have similar values?* Research shows that shared values are crucial in keeping a relationship together.

➤ *Can you resolve your differences?* Every couple has arguments, but can you resolve them, respecting one another's opinions and needs? If you argue more often than you agree, you're in trouble.

➤ *Do you have similar needs for closeness or separateness?* If one person wants to be inseparable while the other feels suffocated with too much togetherness, you're in trouble.

➤ *Do you have similar sex drives?* Sex doesn't have to be on top of the list for every couple (and keep in mind sex drives can ebb and flow), but in most happy relationships, partners have similar feelings about sex.

➤ *Do you have similar lifestyles and goals?* Some differences can be worked out (he's an early riser while she comes alive late at night), but others can tear couples apart (she wants children and he doesn't).

A "no" answer to any one of these questions could spell trouble. Since each one of these can determine whether your relationship is happy and lasting, concentrate on how you may differ and make efforts to apply the three A's: acceptance, appreciation, and adjustment.

Before jumping to conclusions about any relationship, make sure you observe your partner over time. Follow my "three-month observation period" guideline—this is the minimum amount of time necessary to truly assess someone's character (trustworthiness, security, reliability, kindness). Falling too fast leads to trouble, so take things slow. You don't want to cast someone into your love script without *really* knowing that person.

The Least You Need to Know

➤ Attraction seems to be a mystery, but can actually be explained (by your experience, physical reactions, and the situation).

➤ We often seek in others what we wish for in ourselves.

➤ It is possible to open yourself up to fall in love with different types of people.

➤ Ultimately, the best partner is someone who is secure and who really cares about you. Pick the woman idolizer instead of the womanizer.

➤ Remember, you always have a chance.

➤ Treat dating as an adventure.

Chapter 2

The Hunt For Ms./Mr. Right

In This Chapter

➤ The best hunting grounds

➤ Improving your chances of meeting someone

➤ Where the single men and women are

"Where do I go to meet someone?" This is the MOST common question that single men and women of all ages have asked me over the years. If there is one lesson you learn from this book, let it be the following: Don't worry about where you go, just *go*! You don't always have to do something special or go out of your way to meet your future mate. In fact, you can meet her this morning while waiting for the train, at lunchtime while standing in line for your grilled chicken sandwich, or even this evening while riding the elevator. The point is to get out, enjoy your life, and start sending out vibes that you're happy, open, and available!

Rule 1: Get Going!

When the energy is right, people will come into your aura without any huge effort. It happened to Janey. Desolate and depressed, she turned down many invites so she could stay home and feel sorry for herself. Then one day an electrician came to rewire her apartment—and now he is igniting her passion as well.

Research shows meetings are conducive in places close to home where people feel comfortable and safe to talk to strangers. You become attractive when you are going about your normal activities because you are unself-conscious and you are being *yourself*—which is after all, what everyone really wants to be loved for! So, shop at the supermarket, go to the cleaners, and visit the health club—and keep your love antennae tuned.

Tip

More singles today are finding themselves new and alone in town because of job transfers or break-ups after following lovers to different cities. To help make new friends, talk to neighbors, attend local events, and check out local newspapers, tourist magazines, and pamphlets that cover what's going on around town.

Rule 2: Be Proactive

Although it's not necessary to travel far and wide to find a mate, you can improve your chances of meeting someone by being proactive in your search. There are three strategies to this plan:

➤ *Do something you enjoy.* This maneuver has a number of benefits. First of all, when you are actively engaged in something that interests you, you automatically become excited and emanate sex appeal. Secondly, you'll meet people who have similar interests as you—one of the best foundations for a relationship. Meeting through a common interest provides both an instant bond and ice-breaker for that dreaded first conversation.

Write down three interests you have and where you would go to pursue them:

Interest	Where to Go
1.	
2.	
3.	

Use the following table to help you with this exercise.

If Your Interest Is:	You Might Meet People Here:
Spiritual exploration	Holistic health expos, encounter group meetings, weekend getaways, trips to holy places
Sports	Health clubs, tennis lessons, pool halls, teams at local schools, Y's, sports bars
Dancing	Parties, dancing lessons, clubs, weddings
Art	Classes, museum exhibits and courses, art supply shops
Music	Classes, concerts, record stores, music stores
Health	Health clubs, retreats, health food stores

➤ *Choose places to go and things to do based on your personality style.* For example, if you are a quiet person who loves to spend time reading or listening to music, go to a bookstore—preferably one of the superstores where you can discuss your favorite novel or CD over a cappuccino. Or attend lectures where authors speak—during a break, you can talk to people who like the book or author.

If you're more adventurous, go where the action is—amusement parks, sporting events, and concerts. Places like these give you the freedom to release your inhibitions. Excitement tends to get you "pumped up," causing your heartbeat to race and your blood pressure to rise—all of which make you and others more turned on and more likely to fall in love.

➤ *Go to places where the type of mate you're looking for might be.* Vinny wanted to know where he could meet a classy girl. The key to finding your ideal person is to pretend that you are that person. If you were a classy girl, where would you go? Maybe to a health club, a fancy restaurant, or an art history class. If you're looking for a wealthy person, you might try a golf course, stock exchange, charity ball, or chic vacation spot. If you're looking for a sports nut, go to a football game or sports bar. Pretend that you are your ideal mate.

Tip
The best time to meet working people is early in the morning, at lunchtime, after work, and during weekends. The best time to meet freelancers is during midday hours.

Always be ready—you can meet that special some-one at the most unexpected times and places. Dawn went on a fishing trip with her friend even though she hates to fish, and met James, an avid fisherman, who hooked her line and sinker!

Make up an activities calendar of places to go and things to do for the week, for fun and singles scouting.

	Mon.	Tues.	Wed.	Thurs.	Fri.	Sat.	Sun.
9 a.m.							
Noon							
7 p.m.							
10 p.m.							

Do Your Homework!

Remember what it was like to do a term paper? At first, your mind was probably blank. But as soon as you began to research the topic, ideas popped into your head and your creative juices started flowing. Trying to meet someone is like writing a term paper. At first you may be void of any clues of where you can meet him, but once you do a little research of your own and brainstorm, you might come up with fresh ideas as well. For now, use the following sources to begin your research:

➤ Yellow pages for clubs and groups

➤ Local or neighborhood newspapers—special sections on activities and events

➤ Magazines for special interests

➤ National newspapers for travel ideas

➤ Friends and other singles

➤ Newspaper gossip columns that cover upcoming events

➤ Chamber of Commerce listings and pamphlets

➤ "Around town" books and pamphlets found in hotel rooms and lobbies that describe where to go and things to do

➤ Mailing lists—various clubs and party promoters use mailing lists to produce new events

Dating Networks

Think of trying to find a partner like trying to find a job. Besides doing the obvious, like going through the want ads or visiting employment agencies (or going to bars, clubs, or singles parties), you also have to do the not-so-obvious—and that's *network*. I'm sure you know people who got their jobs through a friend or contact they met at some business function, or a chance meeting.

Now ask yourself how many couples do you know who met through a friend, co-worker, or at the gym? The point is that many means can work, so in order for you to find your prey, you have to be willing to search every hunting ground—whether that be a class, concert, or restaurant. And during your search, you'll meet other people—networks—who can introduce you to more people and maybe your Ms./Mr. Right!

The Little Black Book

Once you develop your network, you have to keep track of it. Remember the infamous "little black books"—those "hands-off" address/ratings books that men used to keep of women? Well, as you begin your hunt, you need your own "track record" of who you meet. Think of your black book less as a record of dates, and more as a working list of possibilities. In sales, it's called a *prospecting list*, but I call it a "dating networking list." Include people you haven't yet met but who you would like to date (your "wish list"), as well as people you can call on for other possibilities (for example, as an escort for an upcoming event).

A Little Help From Friends

According to numerous surveys, friends are the number-one source for finding a mate. The more dangerous life becomes, the safer people feel being introduced to someone by friends. Friends can offer a ready-made character reference, as well as a ready ear for feedback about the relationship.

"Do I have a girl for you!" Who hasn't cringed at the thought of Aunt Abby setting you up, or your mother wanting you to meet the son of one of her friends. However, don't cut off any possibilities—open your heart, mind, and spirit to *all* possibilities. Frank's "Aunt Abby" was right on target, and he ended up marrying her referral.

Distant Co-Workers

Although love affairs at the office are often too close for comfort, look beyond immediate co-workers and partners. For example, you may find potential mates in other departments and working other shifts.

Also consider attending industry-related workshops and seminars. Conventions are a hotbed for contacts. With everything from social hours and exhibition halls, they offer lots of opportunities to mingle. Billy met Patty Sue at the jalapeño-eating contest at their district advertising convention. And when Candace stopped by Cal's booth at the annual gift show, he offered her free samples—and dinner. Plan your schedule to stay that extra day for the golf tournament, party, or tour.

Classroom Connections

Tip
When you do finally take a class, don't immediately take a seat. Instead, stand by the door or wander around until you spot someone you want to sit next to.

Who hasn't fallen in love with someone you met in class, in a club, or in the cafeteria? School provides a fertile meeting and mating ground for all ages. Where else can you take an interesting class in history or photography, and at the same time meet like-minded people? Use local newspapers, school newspapers, and special-interest publications to find out what kinds of courses are being offered. You might also find listings and free publications at bookstores, music stores, newspaper stands, convenience stores, health food stores, doctors' offices, school lobbies, popular nightspots, and libraries.

Religious and Community Groups

What's a safer and a more common-ground place to meet than in a religious institution? Most churches and synagogues have special singles' clubs that sponsor evening events and trips where you can meet other singles trying to find that special someone, while strengthening their ties to religion. You don't always have to be a paying member to attend. Stop in and pick up a listing of lectures, discussion groups, dances, holiday services, and parties. Also, volunteer to be a speaker at events so that you are the center of attention—drawing others to you without any effort.

Because connecting on familiar home territory can be comfortable and less awkward, also consider joining a community group. Here you can meet someone as you lobby for mutually-important issues or plan block parties.

Cafes, Restaurants, and Shops

Tip
Don't be afraid to go places alone. If you like, bring along a conversation tool like a magazine or your favorite book.

Because food is already a symbol of love, eating can easily set the stage for romance. Additions such as fireplaces and piano bars in restaurants, and coffee bars in bookstores, have made finding opportunities to chit-chat much easier. Theme restaurants for sports, movies (such as Planet Hollywood), and music (such as the Hard Rock Cafe) feature all sorts of memorabilia that can be used as ice-breakers.

Believe it or not, supermarkets are also great spots to meet someone. They offer a safe environment and easy opportunities to strike up a conversation with someone: "Do you think this cantaloupe is fresh?" or "I recommend this brand of spaghetti sauce because..." You can also observe a person's eating habits by taking quick glances at his shopping cart or food basket. Good single shopping hours are between 6 p.m. and closing, particularly in the frozen-food aisle!

Picking up people in specialty shops is a tried-and-true trick. Men should go to the Women's Wear floors in department stores and ask for help in choosing a gift for mom or sis, and women should browse in the Men's Wear department (because single guys have to buy their own clothes). Different stores cater to different ages and types, so your prey comes presorted. Women should also hang out at electronic and hardware stores, and new or used car lots.

Laundromats

With the addition of coffee stands, video games, and other diversions, laundromats have given singles opportunities to socialize while they wash their duds. You can be creative and discuss detergents or help someone fold their sheets. You also have an opportunity to examine someone's lifestyle through her wash load (Is he washing mostly dress shirts? Did she throw in lots of workout clothes?).

Parties

Meeting people at parties is easier for more confident and adventurous souls, but even shy people can grow from the challenge of throwing themselves into party-type situations. There are many types of parties: small friendly gatherings, special-event parties (such as birthdays, art openings, and weddings), singles parties, and formal events. Some singles parties have ice-breaker techniques; for example, write on a card what your interests are and find someone in the room who has the same interests.

Tip

It's easier to approach someone who's alone rather than in a pack. In roping a steer, a cowboy isn't supposed to throw his lasso into the herd, but coax one selected animal aside. When Patty goes skiing with her girlfriends, she always gets on the singles line for the ski lift so she can pair up with another single for the ride up the mountain.

You should adopt certain strategies when at a party:

➤ Place yourself in a strategic position so you're easily seen, or "cruise" the room to get comfortable with your environment (a good way to reduce anxiety before a speech, for example, is to survey the room beforehand). Also, strike up a conversation by asking a DJ or bartender for help in finding a pay phone or restroom. Adopt an inviting "look."

Tip Many organizations hold social events for gays and lesbians. Check local and specialty newspapers that are distributed free in many stores and on college campuses. Also, check the phone directory for clubs and organizations listed under "Gay" and "Lesbian."

➤ Have a positive attitude. Don't feel embarrassed or ashamed to be there ("I'm a loser") or think of past failures ("I was always a wallflower in high school"). Instead, think positive thoughts ("I'm attractive" and "I'm having a good time"). At the very least, distract yourself from negative thoughts by observing the color of the room and the food being served.

➤ Amuse yourself. Survey the crowd for someone who interests you. Be aware of the superficiality of such attractions, but enjoy playing mental games by yourself, fixing on someone and imagining what that person is like. Become aware of what makes your love antennae whir and what makes it wilt (such as hair length, style of clothes, and certain postures).

Self-Improvement Workshops, Retreats, and Expos

Last year, I returned to the granddaddy of all "new-age" retreats—Esalen—on the Big Sur. Esalen became famous in the 1960s for self-awareness seminars (and hot tubs) where you could "let it all hang out." As soon as I stepped foot on the grounds again, I felt myself opening up, relaxing, breathing easier, and smiling to everyone who walked by. "How nice it would be," I thought, "if I could bring those feelings back home with me to the rat race and shark waters of New York City!"

Besides getting in touch with yourself, being in an atmosphere where people expect to spiritually grow and meet others facilitates confidence, communication, and openness. Because everybody comes to a self-improvement workshop with the intention of being open, half your work is done, and half your fear is erased. Women will be especially glad to meet the more sensitive men who are drawn to these experiences. Activities usually last for a day, a weekend, or even longer. They also usually consist of group mealtimes, and classes with built-in exercises designed for interaction and group activities, which are instant structured ways to get to know other people.

Seminars on money management, financial planning, time management, and general management skills are also great places to meet men and women climbing up their career ladders. These seminars are usually held at hotels or other rented meeting rooms. Many are run by professional organizations that can charge several hundred dollars, but some are offered by networking clubs for $20 or so. You can even find a few free seminars that serve as introductions to a company's service. Refer to listings in newspapers and newsletters. Also call brokerage firms and financial companies and ask if they're offering any seminars.

You can also find someone with similar interests at expos that are advertised in publications and booklets distributed free of charge in various stores and street vending boxes. Popular health expos include the New Life Expo and the Whole Life Expo held in cities around the country several times a year. They feature lectures and exhibit booths on everything from clothes and jewelry to "magnet mattresses" (to balance your energy) and powdered health potions. You can get a Reiki massage, remove ear wax with candles, and find your soulmate.

Tip
Single parents can attend any one of these activities. You can go alone, or bring your children along (kids can be company and great conversation pieces), as long as you make it obvious that you're single.

Health Clubs and Health Stores

In the past decade, health clubs have become the hot spot for singles to meet. Pumping up your muscles also pumps up your self-esteem. Making conversation is easy, with built-in ice-breakers about workout routines, help on using machines, and nutrition. You can even "spot" someone who's weight training. Many clubs offer classes in everything from karate to ballroom dancing, and trips for sports and socializing.

Health enthusiasts hungry for love can also frequent health-food stores and check out customers while buying soybean milk. Men should take health-food cooking classes, which are usually loaded with women. Refer to health newsletters to find out where health nuts hang out.

Political Campaigns and Volunteer Organizations

Politics make not-so-strange bedfellows, because strong competition can spark an attraction between two opponents. (Remember the marriage between Republican party member Mary Matlin and Democratic party leader James Carville?) On the other hand, when two people team up against a common enemy, they grow to protect and value each other—making political volunteering a good hunting ground. Be prepared, though. Don't walk in blindly; instead, make sure you know the issues of the candidate you are working for. Besides, being informed and committed offers you an even better chance to get into an impassioned conversation with someone.

Volunteering as a way to meet people is rewarding because you are contributing to the world in a worthwhile way. Remember that unselfishness is a top quality valued in the mating world, by both men and women. By volunteering, you are likely to meet others who are also giving and have similar values as you.

Pick a cause that you feel strongly about and that has some meaning in your life. For example, if your sister has multiple sclerosis, work for an M.S. charity. If you love animals, volunteer at the local zoo. If you enjoy reading, raise money for the local library or literacy foundation (they have major celebrity fundraisers with the likes of Liz Smith and Barbara Walters). Jill found the man of her dreams by working at a bachelor auction. Ivy and Dino hooked up working the table for Lifebeat (the music industry's fight against AIDS). Will and Gina bonded over planning a Greenpeace demonstration. The possibilities for good Samaritans are endless.

Tip

A good way for single parents to meet other single parents is to go to children's events (many are listed in local newspapers), children's activities (dances, sports, classes, and rehearsals), and single-parent clubs, meetings, or events (listed in local newspapers and singles newsletters). While their kids were watching the puppet show at the Renaissance Fair, Al and Francine started talking about the puppet shows they used to put on when they were kids, and found a common interest in drama and each other.

Concerts, Museums, and Cultural Events

Jackie was marveling over Janis Joplin's 1969 painted Porsche in the Rock-and-Roll Hall of Fame. "Can you believe it really only cost $3,500 back then? I'd sure love to own one now," she said, half to the display case, and half to the guy next to her—who ended up offering her a ride home in *his* Porsche.

Jeannette and Larry both lingered over a Degas until they ended up going through the rest of the art exhibit together. There are an infinite number of museums, art galleries, and dance and theater groups that you can get involved with by taking classes or attending special showings or performances. Barbara met Kent while she was playing the lead in a community play he directed. She's a magazine editor and he's a doctor; they probably would not have met had they not both decided to pursue their amateur theatrical interests.

If you've ever been to Woodstock, a rock concert, or even a karaoke or piano bar, you know how music can bring people together. Feeling at one with a large group of people can create an open spirit, facilitating communication between strangers. Music causes chemicals to flow in the body that physiologically creates a feeling of relaxation or excitation, making you more open to fall in love. You won't have to worry about what to say when it's so easy to talk about the song and what it sounds like—or to dance and let your bodies do the talking!

> **Tip**
> A good guide for singles is *How to Meet A Mensch in New York* by Robin Gorman Newman (City and Company, New York, 1994).

Conventions

Conventions are a great way to meet people, because they usually draw huge crowds. Check with the local Chamber of Commerce, the concierge at local hotels that often host such events, and the large convention and concert halls in your area for their schedules. Sometimes admission is not restricted, and you can just pay to get in. For example, the Nassau Coliseum holds a Magic convention that is open to the public.

Busy Spots: From Malls to Your Building Lobby

Research has shown that people form relationships more quickly in crowded places. So go where lots of people are—for example, to shopping malls. Most feature food courts, scattered benches, entertainment, and even art galleries, all of which can facilitate your hunt.

People also feel more comfortable close to home. Try to hang out in your lobby, in the laundry room, or around your mailbox (repeated encounters also breed familiarity). Also keep your eye on local papers for lists of festivals, arts and crafts shows, and street fairs in your neighborhood. Even public parks have become great places for people to meet while they jog, play Frisbee, or walk their dogs.

Sporting Events

If you're an active participant—whether in softball or scuba diving—get out there! Sports, especially team sports, easily bring people together who share a common interest. Most clubs team you up with others, so you don't have to worry about making your own contacts.

If you're more of an observer, go to sporting events. Talk to people sitting around you. Don't spend halftime in your seat, but wander in the memorabilia shop, or wait on the food line and strike up a conversation about the game with someone. Also attend tournaments (like golf and tennis) where you can wander around instead of staying put in your seat. Stand next to an interesting stranger and talk about a player's great line drive or an incredibly fast serve.

Instead of watching games at home, go to sports bars that have giant-screen TVs, electronic sports games, and lots of food and drinks. You'll have a chance to mingle with other fans while watching your favorite sport.

Support Groups

Although they're divorced now, Elizabeth Taylor once fell in love with unlikely match Larry Fortensky at a rehab center. The bonding makes sense; when you've seen each other at your worst, there's nowhere to go but up. Sharing your deepest, darkest feelings and your fears with someone establishes a strong connection and is the key to intimacy. There are support groups for everything from dealing with pet loss and overcoming shyness to conquering alcoholism and other addictions. Refer to your local hospital or telephone directory for local 12-step self-help ("Anonymous") programs that offer regular meetings.

Openings and Fundraisers

There are innumerable public events in every town, from free openings of museums, community centers, and health organizations to invitation-only galas and expensive fundraisers. Make sure you make it to the cocktail party where the real mingling takes place, or you'll be stuck at a table. Call the organizer beforehand to arrange to be seated at a table with interesting people.

Marathons are popular big events these days—from Walk-a-Thons to Dance-a-Thons. You'll find many singles who've come to raise money for their various charities. Because you don't have to be an expert in the activity, you'll meet all kinds of people with shared spirits, "do-gooder" attitudes, and interests in being active.

> ### Essentials
>
> Surveys of towns across America have found that cold Northwestern states—such as Alaska and Washington—have impressively high percentages of single men to women.

Travel

If you've got the time, the money, and the interest, traveling to some exotic spot—for a weekend getaway or a longer journey—can be the perfect setting for possible romance. Just as places that are close to home facilitate comfort for meeting strangers, the escape from daily life and excitement in a new adventure can allow just the right freedom (from stress or old patterns) and sex appeal for romance. The thrill alone of chance meetings in romantic settings can create sparks.

Most people feel safer having a companion or friend along on a trip, but going alone can afford just the open space for you to befriend others on your trip, talk to strangers, or spend time with someone you might meet.

Some people feel more comfortable going on a singles' trip arranged by an organization. Other more adventurous souls might take off by themselves. I'll never forget the year I had an unexpected week off from work. Because no one could take the same time off with me, I simply called United Airlines and told them to book me a ticket to the farthest place they could fly me. I ended up in Australia where I made lots of new friends—whom I still have and probably would never have met had I not gone alone.

When planning trips, pick destinations that are known for drawing singles or that have things to do for singles (such as clubs and shows). Do some research on airlines and travel organizations that book vacations, tours, camps, cruises, and trips for singles to resorts, sports outings, and exotic destinations. Consider all-inclusive packages such as those offered by Club Med, where you don't have to worry about what to do and where to eat, since they provide instant playmates and meal companions.

Tip
You don't always have to travel far. Be a tourist for a day and take a tour of your local city. Stacy met John on a Rock-and-Roll bus tour of New York City, while Pam fell for Larry on a behind-the-scenes tour of Madison Square Garden.

Also know the type of vacation you want: Do you want to loll around the beach all day, or be active and go horseback riding or scuba diving? There are all kinds of organized outdoor singles trips that feature special interests, such as hiking, biking, rafting, safaris, archeology, and more.

Consider spiritual trips to sacred destinations where you are ensured that even if you don't meet your soulmate, you can get more in touch with your own inner soul. Outward Bound-type trips have become popular in the past decade; while embarking on a journey for survival, you discover yourself as well as bond with others. Who isn't familiar with the fun and camaraderie of camp as a child? Look into adult camps, such as Club Getaway, where you can recapture those experiences.

Buying a share in a summer house is a popular way to cut costs for a vacation and to increase your social contacts. Everyone chips in for food, so dinners can be parties, and there are always new people dropping by to visit friends.

Essentials

Pittsburgh and Seattle have been rated as the most livable cities, while Rochester, N.Y., East Lansing, Mich., and Nashville, Tenn. scored as the most kind. Although New York and Los Angeles have been rated as the rudest cities, big urban cities generally offer a wider variety of people to meet.

Amusement Parks

When fun and fear mix, they create arousal and open the doors to falling in love. Based on this theory, and my research at Universal Studios Florida, I've developed what's called "Theme Park Therapy." It's easy to meet someone special or spice up your love life at an amusement park, theme park, state fair, or the like, because of the magical mixture of the four F's:

➤ Feelings (allowing yourself free expression)

➤ Fear (getting "scared" on rides, while knowing you're safe)

➤ Fantasy (suspending reality in imaginative settings and rides)

➤ Fun (experiencing uninhibited glee reminiscent of childhood)

In addition, four chemicals flow in the body as you get excited on a theme park ride. Besides the physiological high, there are psychological benefits, such as returning to the joy of childhood. These benefits put you in a positive and open mental state to fall in love.

Going to a theme park is also a good way for single parents to meet someone and at the same time entertain their kids. Or you can take a date and allow your child to get to know the new person in your life in a fun and nonthreatening way.

Life is full of interesting and fun things to do and places to go. As you explore all of these possibilities, you're bound to meet new friends, and some relationships may blossom into love. At the very least, you'll be enjoying your first love and number-one date—yourself!

The Least You Need to Know

➤ You can meet that special someone simply during the course of your daily life.

➤ To increase your chances of finding someone to love, get involved in an activity you enjoy doing.

➤ Think of where your ideal person might be, and then go there.

➤ Go where lots of men (sports events, loading docks) or women (dance lessons, cosmetic counters) are.

➤ Keep a "dating networking list" of contacts and possibilities.

➤ Be open to all possibilities.

Chapter 3

Matchmaking Services

> ### In This Chapter
>
> ➤ Services to meet your match
>
> ➤ Honesty is the best policy, and creativity too
>
> ➤ Making connections in cyberspace
>
> ➤ Checking out a service

In ancient days, marriages were arranged to ensure fiefdoms and obtain dowries. Over time, matchmaking became somewhat nobler and less opportunistic, with good-natured relatives and friends pitching in to make two people happy. In recent years, matchmaking has become big business, with dating services charging big bucks for the promise of love.

In this chapter, I talk about various services to help you meet your match. Each has benefits, drawbacks, and limitations. I encourage you to give these services a try, but don't be overly optimistic. Also, check Appendix B in the back of this book for more suggestions and details about these services.

Personal Ads

One of the least expensive matchmaking services, personal ads are carried in a tremendous number of publications, ranging from local newspapers and singles newsletters to national magazines. Before placing an ad, think carefully about the type of person you are trying to reach. Study the contents of the publication and try to assess the readership so that you get the kind of responses you are looking for. For example, someone advertising in *Screw* magazine would probably not have the same intentions as someone placing an ad in *New York Magazine*.

Remember, when you submit a personal ad, you are an advertiser selling yourself. As such, you want to "break out of the clutter" (one of my favorite phrases), meaning stand out from the crowd. You also want to attract the desired "customer" to your "product." Remember, the goal is not the *quantity* of responses, but the *quality*.

In writing your ad, be honest, creative, and descriptive about what you offer and what you want. Make sure your personality shines through. For example, a funny person might say, "Why can't Miss Piggy count to ten? For the answer, call me." Or a spontaneous person might say, "Want to fly off to Bali tomorrow?" Or a romantic might say, "Come sit by my fire and share dreams..."

Essentials

I'm always encouraged by success stories. My cousin placed an ad in which she described her love of cats, Baudelaire, and Bach. Her passionate descriptions drew her now-husband to her ad and the altar. Another friend met his wife through the personals by describing himself this way: "36-year-old dancing psychiatrist likes ballet and sports, prefers nonsmoker 25–35. Hopes for lasting relationship and family."

If you have trouble describing yourself, ask a friend to help. Also, have a friend help you go over the responses to get an objective perspective.

Personals do have a downside. It takes time to get responses, and you can count on some people being less than truthful in their advertising.

Answering Ads

In answering an ad, the same rules apply: be honest, creative, and descriptive. Use the guidelines for good communication and listening; besides telling about yourself, respond to the specific points the person wrote about, with comments or questions (just as you would in a good conversation).

Do a background check. Investigate this stranger, just as you would a job prospect. Get as much information as you can.

Ask for a photo—not just to see if the person is your type, but to try to get a "sense" of the person. "Read" it: is his posture open or closed (arms crossed, hands hidden)? Is she stern or smiling? What's the setting: a stark background or warm surroundings? Kathie sends a picture of her hugging her puppy, and not surprisingly she wants a guy to snuggle with. Paul is standing by his Harley; you can imagine he has a wild streak.

Be cautious about getting together. Be sure that you have several phone calls before you meet for a date. During the calls, interview the person, asking direct questions. Meet during the day, in a public place, preferably with a friend.

If the date doesn't work out, or if there is no spark, don't waste time dragging it out. You can simply say, "It was nice meeting you, but I guess it wasn't a match made in heaven."

Tip

Most personal ads have voice mail as an added feature. A lot of people prefer it to a written response because it is more immediate, and they like hearing the person's voice. If you decide to try it, write out your voice-mail message before you record it. Be creative. Instead of saying "Call me" and leaving your number, respond as if you were giving your own personal ad. Remember, as in advertising, you have to stand out from the crowd, so add intriguing details (talk about interests, your dreams, your ambitions, your desires).

"900" Numbers

Telephone party lines were popular in the early 1990s, when ads for these services flooded late-night cable TV. The premise is simple: by dialing a certain 900 number, you gain access to a public phone line with other callers who want to talk or make dates. These lines tend to cater to young people. While 900 numbers may seem inexpensive, they can be costly—you are charged per minute, and when you are chatting on the phone it's very easy to lose track of time. Be wary of using these!

Video Dating

Remember, the more senses you can use to get an impression of a stranger, the easier it is to determine whether you are simpatico. Seeing a person and watching how he moves and talks gives you much more information than a written personal ad, and saves time and energy, though not money (video ads are more expensive).

Video dating involves joining a private club, filling out a computerized personal profile, and making a videotape. Your profile, photo, and tape become part of the club's library, available to other members. You, in turn, can look at the library offerings, and if you see someone on video you would like to meet, submit a meeting request. If the person is interested, she can screen your video. If both are in agreement, phone numbers can then be swapped.

Video dating boomed in the 1980s, but like all other means, is being overshadowed somewhat by the 1990s flurry over computer dating services.

Cyberdating

It's the latest craze in the dating game, the next generation of personals and dating services: modem mating. All you need is a computer and a modem (so you can access the Internet), then you enter different chat rooms (I have my own on AOL, keyword: DrJudy), write messages and send them via e-mail.

Tip
America Online, Prodigy, and CompuServe are among the best-known services for getting on the Internet. But you can also "surf" the World Wide Web. Once you're there, you'll find bulletin boards and "chat rooms" where people discuss everything from politics to sports to health. If you meet someone in these free-for-all discussions, the two of you can go into a different "room" to continue your own private chat.

It's a bit like being a computer pen pal—you create instant intimacy with complete strangers in cyberspace. It's cheaper than dating services, takes less time, is more convenient, and provides instant gratification. Geography and demographics instantly melt as fingers tap out greetings and typists tumble into cyberlove. Time stands still, as you can computer-connect 24 hours a day, seven days a week, in any weather, wearing your worst outfit—and even while having a bad hair day.

There are some advantages to cyber-connecting, but also some compromises. On the upside, you vastly expand your universe of contacts. This method of communication gives you some insight into how articulate and expressive your love interest is. You are also relating with someone whose physical characteristics are a mystery—which some say makes the connection "purer." Without the burden of having to physically interact, many people gain confidence, which helps them over the next hurdle—the actual face-to-face meeting. The "practice" time and safety makes it great for shy people.

For women who have complained that there aren't enough men to go around, the electronic age has solved that problem. With men generally more into electronics and gadgets, computer dating holds great odds for females, with the ratio of male-to-female users well over five to one. Some services report 70 percent male users.

Computer communicating may even be producing better male lovers. At last, men have to express themselves, and focus on something other than looks! It accomplishes my sly suggestion that men who are obsessed with looks should try going out with a bag over their head—so they see women with their hearts instead of their eyes! Of course, this cerebral lovemaking works the other way, too, giving the poetic but unsightly Cyrano de Bergerac a fair chance.

For all the convenience, there is also a downside to cyberspace. It has been argued that cyberlove junkies use the Internet to escape real relationships. On-line minutes easily become hours, replacing troublesome, in-person love and sex with safely-at-a-distance electronic eroticism and Netsex. As with other personals, you can hide behind the anonymity of the words, making up stories about who you really are or what you really look like.

In Cyberspace or Ad Space, Be Safe

Whether you are using a personal ad, a video dating service, or cruising the Net, always make sure you thoroughly check out a person before meeting him or her. Here are some additional pieces of advice:

➤ Be honest about yourself. If you get to the point of meeting the person, you'll have a lot to explain if you've been less than honest about any aspect of your life, from your looks to your livelihood.

➤ Don't reveal too much about yourself until you know the person better.

➤ Be respectful of the other person's privacy, without expecting or demanding too much.

➤ If you are using the Internet, don't give your real name or other information until you have become familiar with the person over a period of months, and until you have some hard evidence that you can trust that person. Talk on the phone; ask for a photograph. You might even ask for a résumé or other materials, as if you were interviewing that person for a job.

Warning
As recent news reports attest, perverts do prowl cyberspace, with the aim of soliciting unsuspecting youngsters for sexual exploitation. While there are investigators on the Net looking for these kinds of problems, there aren't enough to prevent this kind of exploitation every time. It is up to parents and other individuals to make sure that children are well supervised while on the Internet.

35

➤ For those on the Internet, unless you're in a private chat room, be wary of "lurkers"—people who read along during a discussion without contributing.

➤ Be wary of life stories that are too fantastic, glamorous, or dramatic.

➤ Temper your expectations. People tend to be on their best behavior when chatting on the computer or while expressing their desires on a video. You really can't judge compatibility, nor see a person's real personality, until you get to know him face to face.

➤ If you decide to get together, meet during the day, in a public place where there are other people around.

➤ Take a friend along for safety, moral support, and an independent assessment.

Professional Matchmakers

Like Yentl of "Fiddler on the Roof" fame (a perfect example of a "yenta" who loves to fix people up), matchmaking has a long tradition, especially among certain ethnic groups. Many matchmakers are fixtures in a given community, and spend considerable time really getting to know the singles. Their matches are based more on intuition and experience rather than on answers to a prescribed set of questions.

Many people like the personal touch that matchmakers provide. And some matchmaking services are as difficult to get into as some of our nation's finest schools. For example, one matchmaker puts a whole team of professionals on your case, including a handwriting analyst, private investigator, psychologist (for a battery of tests), and an image consultant (for fashion and make-up advice, as well as for advice on weight reduction and plastic surgery). Costs can range from the reasonable hundreds ($250) to the stratospheric thousands ($5,000).

Dating Services

Warning
To avoid rip-off or fly-by-night dating services, investigate what you're buying. Check prices (some limits are set by law) for membership and matches. Ask how long they've been in service, who owns the business, and the number of clients. Stick with busy, reputable businesses.

These services run the gamut, with some offering parties, socials, and other singles events, and others sticking to simple picture and questionnaire introductions. Some specialize in fixing up successful professionals, others say they cater to the sports-minded, and others are for specific religious groups. Call several to get information and recommendations. Ask for success rates and feedback from customers. Don't feel obligated or pressured. Read all the fine print about what you get for your money, including how many dates you're entitled to and over what period of time. Be sure you're provided with a member-services coordinator as your contact person, and call often with questions or to ask for advice.

Dining Clubs

Some restaurants and clubs sponsor events, such as wine-tastings or movie screenings, designed to bring singles together. These events can provide a comfortable meeting atmosphere, reducing pressures and expectations. A well-known franchise that I've written about over the years is the "Single Gourmet." Now franchised in various countries around the world, the Single Gourmet offers dinners as well as day, weekend, or week-long trips. Most of the members have an interest in food and wine.

Essentials

Hats off to the innovative Japanese for coming up with this unique dating service: on-site matchmaking at major corporations! These "matrimonial" companies act as commercial *nakodo* (go-betweens) for *omiai* (marriage interviews), introducing prospective brides and bridegrooms. Some boast about a 50 percent success rate. Granted, the need is there: Japanese workers spend most of their waking hours on the job. By contrast, American companies tend to actively discourage office romances.

The Least You Need to Know

➤ There are endless options for finding a date, from the low-tech to the high-tech.

➤ Whatever your method of contact, always be honest about yourself.

➤ Keep your expectations in check and be on the lookout for stories that sound too good or too wild to be true.

➤ Put potential dates and services through strict, extensive questioning.

➤ Exercise caution when getting together with strangers.

WANNA SEE MY PEZ COLLECTION?

Chapter 4

Opening Lines

In This Chapter

➤ How to break the ice when you first meet

➤ Pick-up lines that charm or bomb

➤ How to keep the energy between you going

Hot on the heels of "Where do I go to meet people?" is the next, related question: "How do I let him or her know I'm interested?" Many people who've asked me where to go to find that special someone have later admitted not knowing how to approach someone or what to say after they've said hello.

My best advice is: Be yourself. You can put on an act for the short run, but if you really want something worthwhile to work, you have to be accepted and appreciated for who you are. Remember, everyone is in the same boat as you—looking to be loved. So approach life and love with a positive attitude and expect the best. Realize that others have the same fears and needs as you.

Quiz: Guess Which Lines Work

While being yourself, keep in mind that different people will react differently based on their personalities, tastes, and experiences. For example, many guys approach my attractive assistant, Alissa, using different openers. Just on the basis of their first sentence, how do you think she rated the following three men?

Guy 1: "Uh, what's your name?"

Guy 2: "Those are great dangling earrings. I wouldn't mind being that close to you."

Guy 3: "Your smile lit up the room here, so I had to come over."

Alissa thought Guy 1's approach was typical, but a little too simple for her. As a result, she feared he could be too shy and not as much fun as she would like. He might be nice to talk to and she might give him a chance, but he didn't get a base hit with her on the first swing.

Although Guy 2's remark was creative, it was a little too close for comfort and forward for her. Alissa was concerned that he could be too much of a fun-loving player. Although she might consider going out with him, she would proceed with caution in case he was too cocky or not serious enough.

Essentials
When you approach someone for the first time, keep in mind that what you say only communicates about a third of your message. The other two-thirds is communicated by your body language—how you stand, move, and react.

Alissa rated Guy 3 as the best possibility. "He seems like a nice guy with a sense of humor—certainly worth a smile, and probably a date."

Of course, everyone has his or her own comfort level regarding different approaches. Just "hello" or "what's your name?" can be fine. What is too dull for one person may be sweet to another. Everyone deserves more of a chance than just an opening line. But often, we judge people that quickly; so think about how what you say reflects who you are and affects how others react.

You Know What to Say!

Although the idea of approaching someone for the first time may seem terrifying, it's really not as difficult as you might think. You don't have to be a poet or a writer to intrigue and attract someone. Simply say exactly what's on your mind or in your heart. The basic point that I want you to remember from this book is that it's important to *be yourself*. There is no perfect pick-up line. The best line is whatever is real for you at the moment. Remember these points:

➤ Charm and sex appeal come from genuineness—being open, honest, and yourself. Whatever is in your mind and heart will come out naturally and sincerely, and that's going to be far more appealing than some contrived set-up.

➤ If you *are* yourself, the other person is either going to like you or not. If they like you, great; you know they really like *you* when you're being yourself. If they don't like you, you haven't wasted any time or energy. (Remember, dating is like one of the rules of sales: don't waste time on rigid "no's" or people who aren't willing to hear your reason or change their minds.)

Essentials
You have only a short time to make that important, and sometimes lasting, first impression. Surveys show people size you up on first glance, which can be as fast as 15 seconds. Then, they make their overall assessment of whether they like you in a minute and a half.

Tip

Don't try to play games. If you pretend to be someone other than yourself and the other person ends up liking you, the relationship will be built on lies. If you slip up (and you will) and your partner finds out that he or she really doesn't like you after all, you've both ended up wasting time.

If you play games successfully and then get dumped anyway, you'll never know what could have happened if you were the real you. Playing games reaps only potential short-term gains, but also long-term heartaches.

➤ Never worry about being rejected. Thinking about the outcome only makes you self-conscious, which can make you clumsy and awkward. Step up to the plate and take your best swing with confidence.

Bold or Subtle?

Should you get right to the point and say something like, "I like you. Would you like to go to the movies tomorrow?" Or should you throw out bait and see if the person bites: "I hear you love movies. Did you see…? I'd like to see it. Maybe we could go one evening or some weekend, maybe this Saturday afternoon if you're free? What are you up to?"

The key to your approach is to go with your instincts. There are no rules. The direct pitch may be music to one person's ears but static to another. A lot rests on both of your personalities and the mood at the moment.

Essentials
Even the best baseball players strike out more than they get hits; a batting average of .300 is spectacular in the game. The great Babe Ruth holds the record for the most home runs—and also for the most strikeouts.

One good rule to keep in mind is to be creative. Ambiguity can create intrigue, where the other person tries to "read" an approach sprinkled with some hesitation. Personally, I favor creative approaches that also give the other person "space" to stay or stray away comfortably and without insult or hurt. For example, after a moment of sensuous eye-locking, switch the mood by saying something off the wall like: "If a UFO landed now, what would the aliens say about this party?" or "Wouldn't it be great to rent motor-bikes along the beach in Bali? Short of that, I guess we could go roller-blading in the park. Do you feel like it?" or "I missed being at the Superbowl—let's go throw some footballs Saturday afternoon." One LovePhones caller reported doing something I love: he goes up to women and gives them a recipe for chicken nachos. A sure way to either engage an equally fun-loving mate, or turn away someone who wouldn't be compatible anyway.

My Favorite Pick-Up Line Story

Another key to success is to first capture the other person's interest while making sure she feels safe and secure about who you are and how free she is to react or turn away. Women these days are wary about strangers being serial killers, so you have to reassure her that she's safe.

One night, I was eating a sizzling steak alone in a booth in a trendy restaurant when a good-looking guy leaned over my shoulder, ostensibly looking at my plate, and crooned, "It looks good, it smells good, and I bet it tastes good." His provocative glance suggested he meant more than the sirloin. I had to compliment him for how bold and clever he was—even though I wasn't into company and I didn't invite him to join me.

Years ago, when times were more innocent and fears (about strangers and sex) less rampant, pick-ups were easier. In these days of caution, people are wisely more wary about strangers, so you have to work harder to win them over, revealing more of yourself to show you can be trusted.

While eating my sirloin, I overheard a pick-up line in the next booth. The guy was telling a woman, "My name is Tom. I live in the neighborhood and come in here often." (Good, I thought, knowing where he lives should make her feel safer.) "I also do my laundry across the street," he offered. (Possible good sense of humor she might appreciate, I registered.) "What's your all-time favorite food?" he asked. (Good next step, I thought, he's engaging *her* to talk, especially about what she likes.) The guy won; he was soon sitting beside her, and I noticed they left together.

The moral of this story is to be yourself, take a risk, get over your shyness, and let your best self shine through, while knowing that not everyone is going to "take" to exactly where you're coming from at that moment. Be sensitive to what others might need to know or feel to respond to you; and be engaging, but nonthreatening.

Sample Openers

Okay, I know I said you shouldn't worry about using pick-up lines. And you shouldn't. Remember, it's important to just say what's on your mind and not to obsess about the outcome: it either flies or dies. You can always laugh it off. However, I want you to read these sample approaches for the following reasons:

➤ To give you an idea of how many kinds of openers you can use

➤ To help you see that an opening should suit your own personality

➤ To get your own creative juices flowing about how to break the ice

Years ago, I was a regular on a live TV show called *Good Morning New York*, and I did a segment on flirting. ABC-TV weatherman Spencer Christian was the host, and I'll never forget the cute line he offered as an opener:

> "Before I came to talk to you, only God and I knew what I was going to say. But now that I'm standing in front of you, only He knows!"

Since then, I've done many shows about meeting people on the radio, TV, and the Internet. The following are some other suggestions people have shared, used, or just brought up for fun.

Tip
Remember, anything you say has to "fit" your personality. However, feel free to experiment because meeting people is an opportunity for you to enjoy, express, and expand yourself.

Charming Romantic Openers

Being charming and romantic is an alluring, attractive quality. The effort to please and enchant is almost guaranteed to work. Admittedly, some of the following one-liners border on being corny, so say them with a glint in your eye, acknowledging that it's a "line." You're bound to at least amuse someone—remember, a sense of humor is the quality that most attracts men and women today!

> "I'd buy you a drink, but I'd be jealous of the glass."

> "Do you believe in love at first sight, or should I walk by again?"

> Check his jacket label. When he says, "What are you doing?" answer, "Checking to see if you were made in heaven."

"If I could rework the alphabet, I'd put 'i' next to 'u.'" (A personal favorite of my LovePhones co-host Chris Jagger)

"Can I have directions?" ("Where?") "To your heart."

"I had a bad day and it always makes me feel better to see a beautiful girl smile. Will you smile for me?"

"Why do you want to go out with me?" "Because the alternative is unthinkable." (said on one of my favorite TV shows, *Highlander*)

"If I could be one thing in the world, I would be a tear born in your eyes, living on your cheek, and dying on your lips."

"Are you okay? That fall from heaven must have hurt."

"Quick, gimme a shot of insulin because you look so sweet, I'm going into sugar shock."

"Ever thank your parents for making you so beautiful?"

"Did heaven open up, because I think I see an angel."

"God may have made all men equal, but He made you without equal."

"Are your feet tired, because you've been running through my mind all night."

"Excuse me, do you have a quarter I could borrow?" ("Why?") "Because I promised my mother I'd call her as soon as I met the girl of my dreams."

"Your father must have been a thief—he stole the stars from the sky and put them in your eyes."

Hand someone a simple but sweet gift like a rose. Then say something like "I wanted to show this rose true beauty." I once read that FDR used this "gift technique" when he was on a political mission. It also worked for Hosea, a "LovePhones" caller from Houston: "When I was stationed in South Carolina, I met a girl who was stationed at the same base. I walked up to her, gave her a rose, and said welcome to Beaufort. That next day, she looked for me on the base to tell me how sweet I was and we ended up dating."

Self-Disclosure One-Liners

It's always a good idea to start off flattering someone you covet (using the openers presented earlier in this chapter). A totally different technique—but also a useful option—is to reveal something about yourself up front to ease the pressure of what you're feeling and to give the other person an insight into who you are. This approach also works best with people who are embarrassed by compliments or uncomfortable with the focus on them.

> "This is the first time I've been here. Do you know anything about this place?" (Inviting help engages compassionate souls.)

> "I feel funny because I don't know anybody here. Do you?"

> "I always feel more comfortable in small groups or one-on-one. I never really liked crowds. Do you?"

> "I'm normally uncomfortable going up to someone I don't know, but somehow I felt you'd be friendly." (This disarms the other person and makes him or her less inclined to act rudely.)

Tip
Share what you feel (excitement, shyness). If you're self-conscious, admit it; hiding it makes you come across clumsy. For example, Dave is 22 years old, but he looks younger. "Women avoid me because they think I'm too young," he complained. I advised him to say up front, "I know I look young, but you might like that when I'm 80, and anyway, I'm really older and mature."

Classic One-Liners

There are some questions that have become standard in first encounters. They have the advantage of being simple and nonthreatening, but run the risk of coming across as uninteresting and trite. (For example, asking "What's your sign?" has become a parody.)

> "Do you come here often?"

> "What's your name?"

> "What do you do?"

> "Where do you live?"

Sexually Suggestive Lines

What to say to indicate your sexual interest in someone is usually a dilemma. Many people are uncomfortable being direct. It's always best to just let things flow. But the following lines are suggestions people sent or told me. I suggest only considering them once you really know someone, when you are both ready to take your relationship to an intimate level, and when you want to spark some humor into your seduction.

> "Is it hot in here, or is it just you?"

> "Would you like gin and platonic, or do you prefer scotch and sofa?"

"I miss my teddy bear. Would you sleep with me?"

"I may be no Fred/Wilma Flintstone, but I sure would like to make your 'Bed rock.'"

"I'm interested in having breakfast with you. Should I call you or nudge you?"

"That outfit looks good, but do you know what would look better on you? Me."

"I've been thinking about you all day, so get out of my head and into my bed."

"Do you sleep on your stomach?" ("No.") "Can I?"

Remember, personal style prevails. A young man in a mosh pit at Buzzardfest in Cleveland once asked me, "Will you marry me and have my children?" and handed me a ring. I smile about it to this day, and occasionally wear the ring as a reminder of his sweetness. Wild Pontiax rock singer Mitch Kashmar reportedly tried to romance O.J. prosecutor Marcia Clark after a performance with the line: "Don't sit too close to me darlin', I'm wet as a pack mule and twice as ornery."

Bold and Seductive One-Liners

Keep in mind that these lines are for shoot-straight-from-the-hip types. Some of these lines can be offensive, but they can be funny if you know that the person to whom they're directed can recognize the good humor and won't be insulted.

"Are those mirrors on your pants, because I can see myself in them."

"Levis should pay you royalties."

"My face is leaving in fifteen minutes; are you on it?"

"I really like what you're wearing, but I would like it even better on the floor of my apartment."

"Would you be my love buffet so I can lay you out on the table and eat what I want?"

"My name's xxx—that's so you know what to scream."

"What would you do if I kissed you right now?"

Pure Obnoxious One-Liners

When we asked about opening lines on one "LovePhones" show, these were among those called in or faxed to us. As expected, there are always pranksters and jokesters ready with quips. You might be amused by these, but I wouldn't advise using them!

"You cost how much?"

"I got something wrong with my car; want to come take a crack at it?"

"Hey baby, I love every bone in your body—especially mine."

"The word is legs—let's go to my place and spread the word."

"Ashes to ashes, dust to dust, if it weren't for women, my thing would rust."

"How about sitting on my lap and seeing what pops up?"

Many "lines" sound just like that—lines. If so, you can make them sound more appealing and natural by prefacing or ending them with an acknowledgment, such as "Isn't that quite a line?"

Tip

To sound more natural, adapt your approach to the setting and the person's situation. For example, someone used the following with Michelle, a waitress in Houston:

Customer: "Can I get anything on the menu?"

Michelle: "Sure you can."

Customer: *Throws menu on the floor.* "Then will you stand on that please?" (Implying that she's on the menu and that he'll have *her*)

Good Stand-Bys

If the previous approaches are simply not your style and don't spark any creativity, here are some other excellent ahd sophisticated ideas for easy openers:

➤ *Talk about current events.* Watch TV news or read *USA Today* to get an idea of how stories are told quickly, succinctly, and compellingly.

➤ *Cut out interesting or odd stories from newspapers or magazines.* My stepfather used to clip all kinds of wacky stories that I could use on my radio shows—like the one about the government being criticized for wasting money on studies about the mating behavior of African fruit flies.

➤ *Talk about the weather.* This is no longer considered a silly topic due to innumerable earthquakes and other natural disasters, as well as the advent of the Weather Channel.

➤ *Talk about common-ground topics.* Whether it's a big issue (like whom to vote for) or just an annoyance (like not being able to read the fine print on a menu or being frustrated a train is late), everybody likes to know someone else shares a similar feeling or is having the same experience.

➤ *Talk about common interests.* Research shows that like often attracts like, at least in initial attraction. Discover something you are both interested in (old movies, animals, music). It gives you something to talk about and makes you feel more at ease and accepted.

➤ *Find something in common in your background or lifestyle.* Did you go to the same school? Visit the same place for vacation? Read the same book? Be observant. Paula noticed Steve used the word "agreement" and discovered they both attended the same workshop years earlier. While riding the bus, Pat pointed out a vacation poster to Leila and they discovered they both dreamed of going there.

Essentials
People become sexier as they talk excitedly about something. Haven't you ever sat at a table across from someone you didn't think was very pretty or handsome until that person started talking about something interesting? Didn't you suddenly find that person attractive?

➤ *Use the "Opening Story."* Keep a journal of the most interesting things you've done, read, or heard about. Talking about something you are passionate about immediately communicates sex appeal because you are at your most attractive when you are involved in what you are saying.

➤ *Talk about a pet passion or pet peeve.* Positives are always better than negatives, but passion supersedes all. Remember: *She or he who is passionate, attracts.* What's your dream: to save the rain forest, travel on the Concorde, write a book?

A Smile Goes a Million Miles

Once when I was in a club, I watched a guy smile broadly at girls until they smiled back. When he approached me, he boldly put his fingers on my mouth to form a smile, and

Essentials
The old saying is true: Smile and the whole world smiles back at you. Research shows that babies smile more in response to their mothers' smiles. The same response is with us all our lives.

said, "There, that's better." Though I was understandably put off at first by his touching me, after I smiled, I agreed with him—it *was* better! A safer but similar tactic one guy used: put a smiley face on a napkin and hand it to her!

You'd be amazed at how powerful a smile can be in the dating game. Smiling makes you look your most attractive (despite the pouty expressions popular on models). In one survey, women were asked to rate physical characteristics— physique, eyes, smile—in order of importance. They rated smiling first. Smiling shows that you're friendly, warm, and open. A smile can even suggest you're richer than you are: In one study, people who made $50,000 a year were found to smile more often than those who made $15,000. Smile, and you're bound to get a smile in return. I'm always surprised when people say to me, "Why aren't you smiling?" As soon as I crack a smile, it changes my mood.

Practice finding a smile you like. Look in the mirror and make different mugs until you find one you think looks inviting and feels good. Purposefully make a smirk and turn up the corners of your mouth into a smile. (One of my favorite actresses, Meg Ryan, has this kind of smile.) You'll feel your face, and your mood, lift!

Essentials
Science has proven that smiling improves your immune system by reducing stress, and can make you happy, even if you're not. The muscles used to make a smile trigger mood impulses that are located in the pleasure centers of the brain.

Using Your Voice

Voices are very important to those of us who work on the radio. A voice that is full of energy is likely to get more attention. My "LovePhones" co-host Chris Jagger is infamous for hanging up on people whose first two words sound faint or too hesitant. Brutal as this may sound, people do this all the time in real life. So make the most of your first impression by using a powerful voice.

Say this sentence aloud: "What a pleasure to meet you." Notice where your voice is coming from—probably your throat. Now take a deep breath and repeat the same phrase, but this time make your voice come from your chest. Repeat the phrase again, feeling your voice come from your stomach and then from your groin.

Full-bodied voices are also sexier. A "LovePhones" caller once asked, "My boyfriend says he loves how the sound of my voice is so much deeper and sexier after we make love. Why is that and how can I make it like that more often?"

It is common that a huskier and more resonant sound comes into the voice after experiencing pleasurable lovemaking or an orgasm. Called the "postcoital voice," it can be explained by the physiological changes that occur in the body at the culmination of the sexual response cycle, including release of muscle tension leading to general relaxation of various muscle groups all over the body, including those involved in speaking: the vocal cords, throat, and diaphragm. Confidence that comes from a satisfying sexual encounter also leads to more firm and direct communication during sex—and even after—that further enriches the voice quality.

In her seminars and book, *Fine Art of Erotic Talk*, Bonnie Gabriel recommends the following exercises to help develop a sexier voice:

➤ Relax your vocal cords by opening the mouth and back of the throat as if yawning, and speak from that position.

➤ Open the back of the throat and yawn, then keep the lips together, exhale, smile, and push the air out as if silently laughing, and then begin speaking.

➤ Open your mouth wide as if starting to yawn, then count aloud from 81 to 89, punctuating each count with a breath of air.

Breath-enriched sound makes the voice sound more erotic, with the added pay-off that heavy breathing intensifies sexual arousal. Experiment with different sounds on your own, and with your date, but keep in mind that the most appealing voice comes naturally when you are relaxed, confident, and secure in expressing what you want to an accepting, loving partner.

Putting It All Together

So far you've learned about a number of different ways you can approach someone. You also discovered the importance of smiling and speaking in a confident and powerful tone. Now how do you put everything together? For starters, you should smile first and make a comment about your common surroundings. Then you could ask a simple question (not personal, but on a neutral topic) and add something about yourself. This technique accomplishes several goals. It lets the other person get a sense of who you are, makes her feel safe, and helps her decide if she likes you. It also gives her something to respond to—taking the pressure off having to think about what to talk about.

For example, imagine you are in a music club. Smile and say something like: "This seems like a fun club" (a neutral statement about a common environment). "I've never been here before" (self-disclosure). "Do you know when the band starts?" (neutral question). "I usually like hard-rock music, but I hear this group has a country sound, and I've been to several clubs in Texas that I like" (leaving a few openings: she can respond to different music styles or to traveling, or turn away!).

Keeping the Gab Going

Now that you've learned everything you need to know about starting a conversation, how do you keep the rapport going and not run out of things to say? Here are a few helpful hints:

➤ *Self-Disclosure.* Recall this technique from opening approaches. Share interesting things about yourself. You emanate sex appeal when you passionately talk about something that interests you. Even if the person is not interested in what you are saying, he can still be captivated by the way you are talking about it.

➤ *The "Tell."* Everyone has a *tell*—their Achilles heel or spot of vulnerability. Once you find this spot and discover what your love interest is really touched by or likes talking about, he will, at the very least, enjoy talking to you and, hopefully, become quite attracted to you. In successful sales, it's called "developing the prospect."

To help you find a person's tell, look for clues in his actions or facial and verbal expressions. After working out in the gym, Leigh became accustomed to how guys who body-build stand with their chests puffed out. So when she noticed Tommy's erect posture, she smiled and said, "You look like you work out; can I touch your arm muscle?" Tommy smiled back proudly and offered up his biceps—and his interest.

➤ *Say how you feel.* Communicate how you feel about yourself, the setting, and the circumstances—I feel excited, happy, uncomfortable, and so on.

➤ *Ask provocative questions.* Barbara Walters is famous for this. For example, she once got flack for asking Katherine Hepburn the following question: "If you were a tree, what kind of tree would you be?" Some other questions include:

Tip
When conversing with someone, use that person's name. Saying someone's name makes her feel noticed, acknowledged, special, and compels her to pay attention to you. One of the best ways to remember a person's name is to say it several times during the course of a conversation.

Warning
Regardless of how good of a storyteller you are, know when to *stop* talking; you don't want to bore your potential mate. My friend, ABC-TV reporter John Stossel, told me that you should be able to tell a story within 3–4 minutes (the length of a typical TV feature), starting out with an attention-grabbing opener.

"If you were a figure in history, who would you be and why?"

"If you were an animal, which one would you be and why?"

Make sure to make sense of the *why* to reveal some characteristic of the person. For instance, here's a question and two possible answers to the question; each one says something about the speaker:

"If you were a piece of furniture, which one would you be and why?"

Essentials
The 1995 Virginia Slims Opinion Poll found that the biggest complaint women *still* have about men is that they don't talk enough about their feelings.

"A chair, because people would sit on it and I like to support others. I'm always the person people lean on."

Or

"A rug, because people are always stepping all over me and taking advantage of me."

Now that you have some suggestions about what to say, practice! Overcome any shyness. Nothing beats "just doing it" and then doing it again, to improve your dating skills.

The Least You Need to Know

➤ Like the first few lines of a book or the opening sequence of a movie, the first thing you say will make you stand out or fade away; you may get a second chance, but make the most of your first impression.

➤ Don't play games; be yourself.

➤ Smile and it's more likely that the world will smile back at you. Remember, smiling makes you feel good!

➤ Take note of interesting stories and practice telling them to become a good conversationalist.

➤ Reveal things about yourself, but also ask open-ended questions to learn about the other person.

Chapter 5

The Art of Flirting

In This Chapter

➤ The six rules of flirting

➤ How to show you're interested and read the reaction

➤ Using body talk to your advantage

➤ A 12-step plan to overcome flirter's block

Which approach do you use when you're trying to meet someone? Are you a good talker, engaging others in interesting conversation, or do you sit back and wait to be courted? Do you "come on" strong with sexual signals, or more subtly "flirt"?

Getting someone's attention in whatever way you're comfortable with involves *flirting*. Flirting was a popular '80s term for trying to get someone's interest in a more subtle way than coming on strong. Unfortunately, flirting has received a bad rap, and these days is usually part of a complaint: "I saw my boyfriend *flirting* with another girl." However, flirting should be treated as fun and a good way to practice social skills and make yourself and your targets feel good.

The Six Rules of Flirting

Besides just being a fun thing to do, flirting can be an effective method for getting to know a person. Remember the following anagram—*FLIRTS*—to help you get the most out of flirting:

F is for Flattery. The fastest way to a person's heart is to find something you truly appreciate about the way that person looks or acts and then compliment it. However, make sure your compliments are sincere (there's no sense saying "You have beautiful eyes" when they're obviously not).

L is for Listen. Get him to talk about what he really cares about and listen attentively. The most powerful aphrodisiac is your undivided attention.

I is for Interest. Find a common interest. Remember, similar tastes and interests are the best foundations for a good relationship.

R is for being Responsible. Be truthful, careful, and clear about your interests and intentions. Don't hurt or lead anyone on or choose inappropriate flirting partners, such as your friend's boyfriend or girlfriend.

T is for Trusting yourself. Believe that you can do it, survive it, and come out winning friends and feeling good about yourself.

S is for a winning Smile. I discussed the importance of a smile in Chapter 4, so you should be practicing this already!

Benefits of Flirting

Believe it or not, you can derive many benefits from flirting. For example, flirting can:

➤ Help eliminate loneliness by enabling you to meet people.

➤ Heighten your appreciation for what you're doing and where you are (both the specific place and in your life in general).

➤ Boost your ego.

➤ Exercise your technique for meeting people.

➤ Give you feedback about how you come across to others.

➤ Help you make new friends.

➤ Activate your adrenaline and nervous system. When this body system is switched on, it causes your blood flow to increase. This in turn makes you more alert and aroused, more able to concentrate and take action, and more sensitive to touch. It also stimulates the limbic center of the brain, which creates pleasurable feelings.

The Flirting Hall of Shame

Although it has many advantages, flirting has unfortunately earned a bad name. In fact, people who do flirt have been stereotyped as being too forward and too sexually aggressive. For instance, saying "She's a real flirt" sometimes translates into "She's a slut." Although this shouldn't be the case, the following shameful flirts perpetuate this bad reputation:

➤ *Blatant flirts*. They come on too strong, too fast, and overdo it—making the other person feel extremely uncomfortable ("Ooh baby, you're sooo hot…").

➤ *Confusing flirts*. They give one message, but mean another: "Yes I might like you, but no, I'm not interested in going out."

➤ *Egotistic flirts*. They are the Don Juans and Don Juanettes who always check themselves out in the mirror and need to make everyone in the room drool over them. They can make you feel like a million bucks, but only to flatter their own ego.

➤ *Controlling flirts*. They flirt just to tease the other person. (They make you think they're interested when they're really not.) These flirts enjoy watching others squirm, and manipulate others into doing things that they wouldn't ordinarily do.

Showing That You're Interested

One key ingredient to effective flirting is to show interest in your potential mate. Let's face it—everyone loves attention and being noticed. Two ways you can show interest is by giving compliments and by asking thought-provoking questions.

Delivering the Compliment

Paying someone a compliment is not as easy as you might think. Simply saying, "That's a nice shirt" is not enough to spark an engaging conversation. To deliver a compliment successfully, that is, to open the door for a promising conversation, follow these steps:

1. Take note of the details. Do this by:

    ➤ Picking out something that the person is wearing. This can include a piece of clothing, jewelry, or even hairstyle.

➤ Noticing something about the person—her smile, her eyes, or his physique.

➤ Paying attention to what the person is carrying. ("That's a beautiful leather case.")

2. Pay attention to what the person is doing. ("You play a great game of pool" or "I notice that you're careful about what you buy.")

3. Follow up with a question. ("Where did you find such an interesting piece of jewelry?")

Tip
When asking a question, listen attentively to the answer, instead of worrying about what your next question will be.

Because I have a habit of dressing unusually and wearing funky clothes, many people are always noticing what I wear. When people compliment me on my fluorescent orange boots with the glow-in-the-dark soles, by saying "Those are really cool boots, where did you get them?" they engage me in a conversation about the store I shopped in (which leads to talking about how everyone hangs out in malls these days, how my conservative mother hates them, how they glow in dark clubs, what clubs I go to, and so on).

Asking Intriguing Questions

What is most people's favorite topic? *Themselves.* So, ask them to talk about themselves. You've got five W's to consider:

➤ *Who.* Who's your favorite actor/relative/friend?

➤ *What.* What's your favorite thing to do?

➤ *Where.* Where is your favorite place to go?

➤ *When.* When was the last time you treated yourself?

➤ *Why.* Why did you come here?

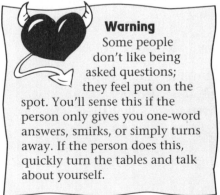

Warning
Some people don't like being asked questions; they feel put on the spot. You'll sense this if the person only gives you one-word answers, smirks, or simply turns away. If the person does this, quickly turn the tables and talk about yourself.

Avoid answering a question negatively. Let's look at an example. Chester asked Elena if she goes to the movies often. She replied, "No, I don't," and the conversation came to a dead end. Instead, Elena could have answered, "I prefer to hang out at my friends' houses, so we rent videos instead," setting a more positive tone to the interaction, and giving Chester the chance to ask about her friends, which videos they rent, and so on.

When the brain hears a negative answer—no matter what it's about—it creates physiological responses in the body and mind of a defensive, protective, and shut-down nature. "Yes" boosts deeper and easier breathing, more even blood pressure, and calmer heartbeats that make for better health and a more positive frame of mind.

> **Tip**
> Ask open-ended questions rather than ones requiring one-word answers like "yes" or "no." By doing this, you get more revealing insight into the person and more of a chance to assess what he is really like.

The Flirting Flamenco

Dating is like a dance—a matter of synchronizing your rhythms (but not backing someone into a corner). Sometimes you can't tell if a person is totally uninterested or just shy or reserved. Make your approach using what I call the "Flirting Flamenco." It has three steps:

1. *The Approach.* Make your boldest move to gain the other person's attention. This should last a few minutes.

2. *The Retreat.* Back off (sip your soda, dig in your pocketbook) to take the focus off the flirtation and to give the person a chance to assess you.

3. *The Re-approach.* Test the waters. If your target responds, fine. But if not, definitely move on after three tries.

Body Talk

Researchers have estimated that more than half of communication comes from body language—gestures and movements that we make that reveal what we think or feel. So let your posture, facial expressions, and eyes do the talking for you. One cue is often not enough, so to send or interpret a message, combine several cues.

Eye Contact

The eyes are the window to the soul. When you look at someone, you are saying that you are willing to see and connect with them, and you are willing to be seen yourself. You have only to watch new lovers in a restaurant gazing across the table into each other's eyes to know how powerful eye contact can be.

But how much eye contact is too much/too little/the right amount? Research shows that a constant stare makes people uncomfortable. However, a short gaze may mean that the person is shy, insecure, or insincere. The most effective eye contact is one where you glance, linger, look away, then reconnect—holding each other's gaze for at least 60 percent of the total time you are together.

Once you've made eye contact, longer looks usually work. Use what I term the "Driver's Eyes." You look straight at the person (like you're watching the road), while occasionally glancing right and left (like you're looking at the side-view mirrors) for relief.

Tip
A playful wink is also a good flirting tool.

Touch

Touch is comforting and also stimulating. Flirt by touching yourself lightly in a nonsexual, safe way. Primp or preen yourself, smoothing your hair or stroking your own hand, neck, face, or leg. Use an interesting trick based on the psychological principle of *modeling*—touch yourself wherever you would like to focus attention or where you imagine the other person touching you.

There are many sensitive nerve endings in the skin surface. When they are touched, they set off impulses to the brain that trigger chemical releases and signal pleasurable feelings.

Tip
Women have a head start in touch flirting and can be more forward because men are less threatened by being touched.

Once you've become comfortable with each other, you can straighten his tie or her necklace, or brush a speck off the shoulder of his jacket. Advance to touching a body part: first covered parts, like the back or shoulder, then hair, and then exposed skin on "safe" areas like on the arm, hand, or cheek. Back off if the person winces or withdraws.

Body Positioning

Research on kinesiology (the study of moving bodies) shows that posture and movement communicates messages. Read and interpret caution or unwelcome signs if the body and head are turned away. Crossed arms could mean he's nervous or closed off. Uncross those arms and see how much more open—and vulnerable—it feels! Better to do that if you want to give the message you're more approachable! Lean in, extend a hand, nod (to signal approval), or puff out your chest or tilt your hips (to show interest). Legs crossed with the top leg nearer the other person signals that you are creating a barrier between you.

Vigorous leg-shaking is a sign of nervousness (a turn-off), while slight movements are stimulating (and a come-on). Mannerisms such as hair-flicking or tie-tugging can be distracting and a sign of discomfort. Also, if someone's hands or mouth are hidden (hands in pocket, or covering mouth), he may be hiding something.

Mirroring or Getting in Sync

When people are in tune with one another, they copy each other's body movements, so one's posture or movements seem like a mirror reflection of the other. Watch how this works—you'll be amused! Observe a couple who seems "into" each other, and notice that if he leans on one elbow, she'll likely do the same thing. If she rubs her lips, he'll reach for his, too. Without even realizing it, people in the seduction mode copy each other.

Body Boundaries

How far away do you stand? Respect each person's "PD"—safe personal distance—measured by an arm's length, usually about two to three feet. Then test the waters: wait to see if she gives you clues to come closer (body touches, smiles, open body position). Also give clues yourself. Then do the "distance duet": move in closer to show you're interested and then withdraw to give her "space" to advance and to show return interest.

Make sure your touches are welcome by "reading" the person's receptivity. Make a gesture first and see if the person resists (moves away) or moves closer or smiles invitingly.

Tip
Purposefully copy your prey's posture or movement, to give the subliminal message that you're interested and on the same wavelength. If she rests her chin in her hand, do the same. If he puts his hand on his hip, you do that, too.

Nonverbal Ways to Tell Him You're Interested

You can also show that you're interested in someone and sense if a person is interested in you without using any words at all. Nonverbal cues of interest consist of what I call "the four P's":

➤ *Presenting.* Present yourself in a sexy and alluring manner. For example, lick your lips, trace the outline of a scoop-neck top, or run your hand down your leg.

➤ *Preening.* Take pride in yourself; show that you know you're appealing. Straighten a tie, smooth or toss your hair.

➤ *Parading.* Stay close to your prey. Show that you're checking her out (think of an animal circling around its prey). For example, Barry had his eye on Jessica at a party.

She, however, was being pursued by so many men that she was unlikely to notice him. But while others courted her and drifted away, Barry always reappeared in her line of vision, until the end of the night when he offered her a ride home—which she took!

➤ *Posturing.* Nibble at food or play with the rim or stem of a glass suggestively. How you stand, sit, and even walk says a lot about you. For example, tilting the head implies vulnerability, extending an arm is inviting, cocking a hip is seductive.

Reading Mixed Signals

Lots of people are confused about whether someone's *really* interested:

Tara: "I go to bars a lot and I've had lots of guys come on to me, but when push comes to shove, they walk away. What's wrong with me and what am I doing wrong?"

The odds of hitting a home run in dating (especially in bars) are as high as hitting one in baseball; you are most likely to strike out. Don't wipe yourself out over it. But think about whether you're showing enough interest in return. Sometimes people act a little aloof, especially when they've been repeatedly rejected.

As you flirt and as others flirt with you, I suggest that you test the waters, so to speak. Use the "Flirting Flamenco" and rule of three advances: Put your foot in the water three times while giving the other person breathing space in between to decide how to react to your advances.

To read someone's reaction and to be really good at seduction, you have to become good at tuning in to what a person is doing, thinking, and feeling. Some people are good at it intuitively, and others need more practice. You'll be better at it the more you are not consumed with your own fears, such as worrying about how you're coming across ("Do I look good?" "Is what I'm saying okay?" "Does he like me?"). When you focus on yourself too much, you can't possibly read the other person.

Flirter's Block

Many singles tell me that they often see someone they'd love to meet but are too afraid to approach. Why? They're afraid of being rejected and feeling like a loser or a fool. You must overcome these feelings. Remember: nothing ventured, nothing gained. Risk being the first to say hello; the other person is probably just as nervous as you.

Check off the risks you fear:

➤ *Embarrassment.* Are you afraid to say what's on your mind for fear of being perceived as silly or foolish?

➤ *Shame.* Are you afraid that you'll be disgraced or humiliated and that others will judge you poorly?

➤ *Guilt.* Do you feel you're doing something bad or wrong and that you will be punished for it?

➤ *Rejection.* Are you afraid of being turned down?

> **Warning**
> Self-conscious-ness comes across as insecurity, making the other person more likely to be turned off.

My 12-Step Plan for Dealing With Flirter's Block

If you have trouble flirting with someone, don't despair! You *can* overcome your shyness and inhibitions. Just follow these steps:

1. *Identify and express your resistance.* Realizing that you have flirter's block has won you half the battle.

2. *Review your past patterns with flirting and rejection and reframe your experience.* See what you can do differently this time. For example, think, "The last time I tried talking to a girl, she sneered and walked away. If this happens again with another girl, I'll assume that she's in a bad mood rather than that I'm a dud."

3. *Forget your past.* Don't relive each rejection you ever had. Come to each new experience with a fresh attitude.

4. *Stop making overgeneralizations.* For example, don't say, "*Every* time I try to meet someone, it doesn't work out," or "*All* pretty girls/good-looking guys don't like me."

5. *Identify your faulty or self-defeating negative conclusions.* Don't say things like "I can't meet someone I like," or "The way I look, I'll never find someone." Expecting negative outcomes predisposes them to really happen.

6. *Think positive thoughts.* Make more enjoyable predictions. Tell yourself, "I will enjoy this encounter," or, if you are rejected, "It's his loss, not mine."

> **Tip**
> Expect rejection; everyone goes through it. If you expect the worst, there's nowhere to go but up.

7. *Eliminate expectations.* Change your intention about flirting from "scoring" (a date, job, or marriage) to simply being an innocent social interaction to establish a friendship. This reduces anxiety (about failure) and disappointment over an outcome.

8. *See things from the other person's point of view.* The reason for someone's non-response may have nothing to do with you. The person may have low self-esteem, or be distracted about losing a job, or be involved with someone else. I remember the time I met a top executive and felt hurt that he didn't talk to me. Imagine my relief when my friend told me that he told her, "I can't talk to Dr. Judy now, I just ate garlic and my breath smells terrible!" Here I had wasted my time feeling slighted, and he was worried about being slighted himself!

9. *Reassure yourself.* "I am a (good/interesting/fun) person." Positive self-talk and affirmations boost your self-esteem and chances for success.

10. *Identify the emotional charge on your resistance.* "I feel like a failure," "I am a loser." Simply state what happened without the emotion: "I approached her, and she wasn't responsive." Don't add how horrible you felt about it or the negative conclusions you came to about yourself.

11. *Identify the true meaning of the fear—that will often reveal its insubstantiality.* For example, shame is a feeling that you have done something wrong or foolish and that others will think less of you. Decide instead that there is nothing foolish about your actions, and that others either aren't that focused on what you've done, or that their opinion doesn't matter.

12. *Mentally practice flirting so that when the opportunity arises, your actions will flow.* Imagine how you would like the encounter to go. Rehearse it over and over, as if you're watching a movie in your head. The more you practice, the more likely you'll behave that way in real life. For example, imagine you're crossing the street and you see a terrific guy. You step up to the curb next to him and make a comment about how much traffic there is today. Or, you're at a card store and you spot a beautiful woman, so you pick out two birthday cards and ask her which one she would prefer getting.

The Least You Need to Know

➤ Besides being fun, flirting can be an effective way of getting to know a person.

➤ One key ingredient to effective flirting is to show interest in that person.

➤ More than half of communication comes from body language.

➤ To become successful at reading people, practice tuning into others' actions, thoughts, and feelings.

➤ To overcome flirter's block, forget past failures, reassure yourself, and anticipate having a good time. Remember, the other person is probably just as nervous as you.

Chapter 6

Building Confidence and Self-Esteem

In This Chapter

➤ The steps to building self-esteem

➤ A plan for reaching your dreams

➤ Developing body confidence

➤ Talking yourself into self-love

➤ Getting over the need for approval

"Girls don't seem to like me."

"I can never get a boyfriend."

"I'm not ugly, but I'm not great-looking either. How will I ever find somebody?"

Do you engage in negative thinking? Are you constantly dumping on yourself and imagining the bleakest future possible? Right this minute, make a commitment to stop it! Replace self-dumping with self-pumping and images of a bright future—one where you really dig yourself. What happens when you constantly imagine the worst, and put yourself down in front of other people? As my mother always warned, what you say will come true, and everyone around you will believe either the complimentary or derogatory things you say about yourself. So you might as well fill your own, and others' thoughts, with positive images. Practice these affirmations—after a while, the sentiments will come naturally.

Question: "Who's the best date?"

Answer: "Me!"

Question: "Whose company do you enjoy the most?"

Answer: "My own."

Give Yourself Permission to Like Yourself

What will you gain as you gain self-confidence? Sex appeal! People are drawn to self-confidence. I'm not saying you should be an egotistical, selfish narcissist, but neither should you be so humble or self-effacing that you fade into the background or put yourself last. Love yourself enough to be self-confident; this will draw others to you and give you a solid foundation from which to appreciate and love others.

Self-esteem comes from three A's: acceptance, appreciation, and adjustment. Love yourself with the same unconditional love that a mother (ideally) gives a child. That means love yourself regardless of your IQ, your wardrobe, your job, or your looks.

Self-esteem—or the lack of it—is often the result of experience. If your parents and those around you are mindful of the three A's, you stand a better chance of liking yourself. But ultimately, self-esteem has to come from within. It has to be a flame that glows from inside you that says, "I am wonderful. I am lovable. I enjoy me."

You are your own best date and most entertaining companion. Too many people seek dates or mates because they are bored with themselves. If you bore yourself, there is little reason to think that someone else will be thrilled with your company. Consider the following truisms:

➤ You'll never be happy with or truly love anyone until you're happy with and truly love yourself.

➤ People are drawn to those who like themselves. Everybody wants to be around someone who is having a good time. Self-confidence screams sex appeal.

➤ Sometimes, being with someone you feel no connection with can be lonelier than being alone.

➤ Most people don't think highly enough of themselves.

The conclusion? The key to happiness, whether you find a mate or not, is to love yourself.

Your goal is to give yourself permission to like yourself, appreciate yourself, and give yourself the time and attention you would give a lover. Remember the Army's advertising slogan: "Be all that you can be." Do all that you can do, and you'll have all that you can have.

Embrace Your Individuality

A caller to my radio advice show, "LovePhones," once told me: "I've been dating a woman who lately has been treating me like crap. She criticizes me constantly about everything from my clothes to the way I hold my fork. But I can't bear to think of my life without her."

If you find yourself with people who don't appreciate you or who are overly critical, walk away. You deserve more. Learn to train your love antennae to pick up on positive signals, and people who will treat you with the respect and love that you deserve.

One night I stood at a club watching a really cool female punk band, the Lunachicks. The kid to my right told me that he was wild for the guitarist, and that he'd even hung out with her and kissed her once. A few minutes later, the guy to my left said, "I can't stand that short girl playing the guitar," and described how he had met her also and been really turned off by her antics. Same girl, two guys, two opinions. Should she change so that guy number two changes his opinion of her? Should she punish herself because some guy finds her undesirable? Heck, no.

Always remember one person's poison is another's aphrodisiac. The very characteristic or behavior that turns one person off may turn another person on. There's the ultimate proof of this point in the story of Rudolph the Red-Nosed Reindeer, whose nose, you'll remember, made him the butt of the other reindeers' jokes, but was beloved by Santa, who gave him a prime spot at the front of the sleigh. So, if you think your nose is too big, your chest too hairy, or your breasts too small, love yourself anyway. Someone will appreciate you for those qualities!

Exercises to Help You Build Self-Esteem

Building your self-esteem is like having an exercise program to keep your body fit. You have to focus on certain activities and repeat them in order to change your bad habits, improve your outlook, and maintain the benefits. The following exercises will help.

Morning Wake-Up Call

Be your own perfect parent. Think of how you would wake up a child in the morning, with a smile and a cheerful, "Good morning, honey!" If you usually start the morning with a sneer, slamming the alarm, cursing your reflection in the mirror, and dreading the day, use what seer Roberta Herzog calls—the "cosmic erasure." Say aloud, "Cancel, cancel." Then use your mental TV clicker and change the program in your brain and in your behavior. Look in the mirror and say, "I love you" or "I've got something to make you happy today." Every day, think of one fun or challenging thing you can do, and use that as a motivator as you bounce out of bed. You may feel silly at first, but soon this will come as natural and feel as refreshing as brushing your teeth.

Smile

When you look in the mirror, whether you're shaving, brushing your hair, or checking your reflection in your car's rearview mirror, don't frown and point out your various flaws. Change the program in your brain and smile instead.

Essentials

As soon as you smile, your facial muscles alter your brain state to a calmer frequency, lifting your mood. Remember throughout the day to turn your lips into a smile even if you don't feel much like smiling. The physical "set" of your muscles will actually create a more buoyant emotion.

Be Your Own Cheering Section

Like sports players need a coach and cheering squad, you need ongoing pep talks to spark up your energy to do your best. When you feel your security waning and your shyness escalating, picture an angel on your shoulder goading you on: "You can do it!"

Self-Pump (Instead of Self-Dump)

Whenever you feel down or afraid to approach someone for a date, remind yourself of all your wonderful qualities. If you tend to focus on the negative (I'm too short and chunky, my nose is too big, I stutter when I'm nervous), refocus your energy on the positive.

Try this exercise. Quick, tell me five great things about yourself and list them in the first column of the following table (I'll get to the other two columns later).

	Up the Ante 1×	Up the Ante 2×
I am: _____	_____	_____
_____	_____	_____
_____	_____	_____
_____	_____	_____
_____	_____	_____

By writing down your assets, you fix them more firmly in your mind. Next, get a tape recorder and record the same information. Before you go to sleep at night, play the tape—the semihypnotic pre-sleep state makes thoughts stick more in your mind.

Try a visualization exercise where you picture your biggest fan making a speech about how great you are. Also, save complimentary notes from friends and colleagues, and take them out when you need a lift. I have to smile when I reread my mother's birthday cards where, being a master of superlative adjectives, she describes me as "the most wonderful, beautiful, gracious, creative, thoughtful, independent, energetic, stimulating, loving daughter"—I pause on each adjective and drink in how it feels to be that way.

If you have similar cards or letters, put the messages on a small card and keep them in your wallet. Refer to the card while you're on hold, in an elevator, on the subway—whenever you have spare time. Or put these words of praise on tape and carry the tape with you to play in your portable tape player. As you hear the words over and over, they'll become part of your self concept. Don't feel embarrassed or silly doing this. Take these in as honest truths about yourself.

Another exercise is to blow your own horn. Brag about yourself. Describe your triumphs enthusiastically and extensively. Don't worry about being humble, or acting too full of yourself. People find it sexy and attractive when other people are pleased with themselves.

Now you're ready for the exercise I call "Pump It Up." I love this exercise, and use it all the time at my college lectures and other workshops. Go back to your asset list and get ready to fill in columns two and three. "Up the ante" on each asset—the next highest level of that quality, and then the next level after that. On my "LovePhones" radio show, for example, I sometimes start out the show saying "Do you feel good? Say you feel good...now better...now GREAT!"

For example, if you wrote *funny* in column 1, write *hysterical* in the second column. Up the ante again in the third column, writing *side-splitting*. If you wrote *smart* in the first column, write *most intelligent* in the second column, and then *brilliant* in the third. Now, say "I am" and call yourself aloud the qualities in the third column.

Self-Talk

All of us have a running monologue going on in our heads, as we comment on situations, feelings, and moments in our day. Sometimes the monologue is filled with negative messages ("How could you be so stupid? He really hates you now. You'll never find someone."). Negative thoughts deplete self-esteem and create self-sabotaging actions. We turn people away by the "vibes" we send out.

You can get rid of negative thoughts in two ways. First, picture a street sign in your brain that reads "No dumping allowed." Next, go into the computer program in your brain, print out the negative program (the one that says, "You're a jerk, you blew that, no one loves you"), then use the cosmic erasure. Say aloud, "Cancel, cancel," press the delete button and type in a new program, one that says "I'm a neat person," "I am a lot of fun to be around," "I have so many interesting things to do and say in my life," "Lots of people want to be around me because I am stimulating, warm, and fun."

Affirmations

Affirmations are a form of positive self-talk. The rule on affirmations is to start your self-affirming statement with "I am" (not "Other people say I am…"). Don't start with a negative, such as "I am not fat, sloppy, or boring." When the word "not" is attached to a statement, the mind conjures up the negative images (of fat, sloppy, and boring) anyway. It's like being told, "Don't think about a pink elephant." What's the first thing that comes to mind? A pink elephant, of course. Resist putting thoughts in your head that you don't want your mind to latch on to. Instead, put only those thoughts in your head you want your mind to remember.

Be Your Own Public Relations Agent

What happens when you constantly criticize yourself? People will eventually believe you. After all, who knows you better than you? Often we say negative things about ourselves as a kind of protection, to minimize other people's expectations, or to deflect their jealousy. Avoid this trap. Instead, tell others all the terrific things about yourself, what you do, what you know, and what you can do for them.

Tip

Avoid saying negative things about yourself in the hope that the other person will say it's not true to bolster your self-esteem. The other person may not bite, leaving you in a lurch.

Express Yourself

Do this self-expression exercise. Look into a mirror and think of an encounter with someone. Speak your mind—do this without any fear of judgment, criticism, or disapproval. Watch your face and your expressions, and picture being another person looking into your face. Adjust your face to please you, and practice different looks that make you appear commanding or sexy.

Center Yourself

A lot of self-consciousness, nervousness, and fear comes from a feeling of being "outside" yourself, as you worry about being judged, rejected, or acting foolish. Do the following technique to regain your "center." Take a deep breath and follow your breath into your body, down into your solar plexus (a network of nerves below your rib cage and behind your stomach). Press there with your hand to help guide the breath. Focus on your feet, and feel their connection to the floor. Then press on your "third eye" (the spot on your forehead right between your eyes), concentrating your mind and breathe toward that point to focus on your spiritual energy, giving you strength.

Be Your Best

Dress and act your best at all times. As one hairdresser once told me, "Every day is show time!" Instead of saving your best clothes for special occasions, take them out and wear them! When you look good, you'll feel good, too.

Appreciate what you are, what you have, and what you do. In Japanese Naikan therapy, you say "Thank you" to all the objects and people in your life. Say "Thank you" to your toothbrush every morning for keeping your teeth clean, "Thank you" to the movie seat for supporting you while you are being entertained, and "Thank you" to your mother for all the times she calls to ask how you are. Showing such appreciation makes you realize how many people and things support you in your life.

Forgive Yourself

Emily says, "When I was younger, I constantly went out with guys who cheated on me and treated me badly. Now I try to date men who care about me, but I feel bad and embarrassed about my past, and don't want to share the details with anyone." Progress and change takes time. You may find yourself taking two steps forward and one step back. Appreciate your forward motion. Talk to yourself and accept that you did what you did for a reason. Keep up your affirmations: "I am worthy of love." Acknowledge your progress.

Make Yourself Over

Try new things and take risks. It's fun! Do those things that you always said you'd do if you had the guts, time, or opportunity. This can be as simple as trying a new hairstyle, a new style of clothing, or a new tone of voice. You'll feel empowered by being assertive.

Developing Body Confidence

Most of us have at least one body part we obsess about, a part of us that makes us feel unattractive. The irony is that other people may hardly notice the part that we're so focused on! It can be unnerving to think about someone seeing you in a bathing suit or naked for the first time, with no slimming black dress or dazzling fuchsia sweater to distract their eye. Fears that you won't measure up can put a real damper on dating. Read on for tips on how to conquer your fears.

Posture

How you stand affects the message you send out to the world. There is scientific evidence that posture affects mood—slouching produces a down mood, while standing tall lifts your mood. Try it. This theory seems to validate the old song lyric, "Whenever I feel afraid, I hold my head erect, and whistle a happy tune, so no one will suspect I'm afraid." It also validates the result: "When I fool the people I fear, I fool myself as well."

Here's another exercise to try. Take a deep breath and stand tall. Imagine a root running from your feet into the floor (grounding you, making you feel secure). Now imagine a string running from the top of your head into the ceiling, lifting you up. Picture your spinal column giving you a solid base, where no rejection can blow you over.

Turn Scars into Stars

Everyone has a body part they hate. What's yours? Bobby hates his big nose. Joni gets disgusted with her narrow eyes. Learn to love what you hate. If that part of your body could talk, what would it say? Love me. Ultimately, you can find someone who will love you if not for it, in spite of it. Consider how supermodel Cindy Crawford turned her mole into a million-dollar trademark, or how Barbra Streisand and Meryl Streep have made their unusual noses a part of their distinctive look.

Warning
Most of us have mild dissatisfaction with our bodies ("My nose is too wide" or "My shoulders are too narrow"). But if you experience severe body disgust, what therapists call body dysmorphia, I urge you to seek therapy.

Body Consciousness Exercises

It's hard to relax on a date if you've got the "What-if-she-doesn't-like-my body" blues. These exercises will help you learn to love yourself—so that other people will!

The Look/Touch Exercise

Examine yourself in the mirror. Look at all your body parts with curiosity, without criticism. Ban all negative thoughts, and focus on tactile things: silkiness, softness. As the old song line goes, "Accentuate the positive, eliminate the negative, and don't mess with Mr. In-Between." What are your best features? Play them up. If you have a tiny waist, wear big tight belts to show it off. If you have beautiful eyes, pull your hair away from your face to showcase them.

Now focus on your sexual body parts. I'm always surprised by how many women haven't looked at their genitalia, or how many don't love what they see. After a bath, put a leg over the tub, or lay on the bed and put a mirror between your legs and take a look. It's okay to touch.

The Talking Body Part Exercise

A popular technique in Gestalt therapy involves treating each body part as if it were a separate being communicating to you about how it feels. In this exercise, you "speak" from the body part as if it were a person. In this way, you find out what it has to tell you about its own condition.

For example, say you have frequent backaches. Sit quietly on a chair and close your eyes and put your consciousness into that body part—in this case, your back. Ask, "Back, what are you telling me?" Now imagine being your back and have a conversation with yourself. For example, your back might say, "I am tired of holding you up all day." Press for your back to talk on a deeper, more revealing level, like "I am hurting because I feel like you put a burden on me. I am buckling under the strain of all that anger you are holding in." This exercise can give you clues about what you are really feeling.

This is a great exercise when you have a sexual inhibition or problem. Speak to your penis and vagina and ask it what it feels and needs.

The Moving Body Exercise

Our physical actions both reflect and affect our inner being. For example, a frown reflects the body's inner sense of sadness and also "freezes" the emotional state into that state of sadness. Merely by taking another body position, the physical state can be changed. For example, research in NLP (neuro-linguistic programming) has shown that looking upward lifts the mood. The upward look of the eyes connects, or triggers, the brain to lift the spirits or emotions.

71

Imagine Your Ideal

Imagine yourself just the way you would like to be. The brain doesn't know the difference between a real image and one you fashion, so it will operate on whatever you picture. Visualize relating to someone in a charming, energetic way. Since your brain doesn't know if the image is true or false, your muscles will behave accordingly—your face will look as if you feel charming and energized.

Athletes have long understood this process of imagery, and will imagine a goal or an action before then performing it. You can do the same thing with your love life. Visualize how you want to look, how you want to come across, and how you want your love life to be. Now try to experience how you would feel if all of these things were true.

I also recommend the "repeat performance" technique. Remember a time when you were at your best, your most successful, your most seductive. Picture how you looked, sounded, and acted. Anchor this picture in your muscles and visceral body system by doing something physical (such as pressing two fingers together or snapping your fingers). Eventually, the physical act alone will trigger your nervous system to "remember" the outcome, and fire the appropriate mental and physical state associated with it, making it more likely that you will repeat this similarly successful behavior and positive mental state in the present.

Overcome Your Dependence on Others

In an episode of one of my favorite TV shows, "Silk Stalkings," Detective Rita Lance, one of the show's main characters, mused, "I had a college professor once who compared the world to a sculpture garden. Men were like statues, striking a pose, rough-edged, hard and cool; and women like ivy, softer, more dependent, forever attempting to embrace the stones...(fortunately) I know some women who prefer standing."

This perfectly captures the way in which so many women try to wrap themselves around men, as if their life has no meaning without this attachment. When they do this to unavailable, unattainable men, it's like trying to squeeze blood from a stone. What these women really need to do is focus on themselves—be their own tree, with solid roots, rather than clinging vines.

For example, Josie was going out with a charismatic TV reporter. Every time they were out together, people listened with rapt attention to his stories and opinions. He was constantly being invited places, and Josie loved living in his glow. When he dumped her, she was devastated. She had been living her life *through* him. Josie wasn't able to achieve true satisfaction, so she sought it through other people. When she lost her boyfriend, she felt as if she'd lost herself.

If you feel that you are overly dependent, follow this bit of advice: "Become the person you're looking to marry." Don't look for a partner to fulfill your dreams. You won't become rich, great-looking, fun, or fulfilled by clinging to someone who is. Rather than seeking a mate to fill your "holes," become whole yourself.

The Dream Scheme Exercise

We all have dreams of how we would like our life to be. Realizing your dream brings you closer to realizing your potential and increasing your self-esteem. Make a list of everything you desire in life, following these rules:

➤ *Use the present tense.* Say "My body is looking more like the way I like" instead of "I want to lose weight."

➤ *Be positive.* Concentrate on being cool and collected instead of not wanting to lose your temper. Negatives only reinforce that negative behavior.

➤ *Be specific so you can make it real.* Think "I will sing more and enjoy free time to take long walks" instead of "I want to be happier."

➤ *Make an action plan.* Translate "I want a rich guy" into "I want to be rich." Then design a plan of action on how you can make money. Brainstorm possibilities: Ask for more money from your current job, change jobs, or work a second job.

Keep repledging these plans until you start believing you are worthy of happiness and love in life. Obstacles you once thought were impenetrable will melt away—and the love of yourself will draw to you the love you want to share.

Go through all your fantasies and dreams and write them down. Make a plan to realize each dream. Break each dream into seven manageable steps (one for each day of the week). Put the steps in your daily planner or calendar, either written out or in code.

As Nike advertises, "Just do it." Japanese Morita therapy advises the same: Stop obsessing over feelings and just "do what has to be done."

Free Yourself From the Desperate Need for Approval

Almost everyone has mild fears of rejection and a need for approval, whether about dating ("What if he doesn't like me?"), shopping ("If I return this, what will the salesperson think of me?"), or work ("If I speak up at this meeting, will they think I'm foolish?"). The desire to please others can be charming and promise to enhance your self-esteem, but the need for approval becomes a serious problem when you lose your sense of self, your self-respect, and your self-control.

Let's look at a couple of examples. Barbara was so desperate for Kent's approval that she couldn't get dressed for a date without trying on everything in her closet. She would then ask him ten times if he liked her outfit—turning him off with her insecurity.

Larry was so afraid he'd say the wrong thing to a date that he'd barely speak at all—and women found him either dull or snotty. Ironically, people who desperately need approval sabotage themselves, either suffocating others with demands or driving them away.

How can you break free from seeking approval? Deliberately change your thoughts or beliefs that you need someone else's approval to get by. Realize that the worst that can happen is temporary or tolerable pain. Change your behavior to do what pleases you first. Try to get to the root of your insecurity (perhaps your father constantly told you that you were worthless). Rehearse behaviors that risk disapproval—practice saying no and disagreeing with a date. Decide what you need and either fulfill the need yourself, or ask someone else for help. This can be a simple request ("Please get me a glass of water"), or a more emotional request ("Please give me a hug").

Take Yourself Out on a Date

I am very serious when I say you need to take yourself out on a date. Go out to dinner, a play, or the movies. Treat yourself to the very best. It will raise your self-esteem and give you untold independence. You will never again be devastated if you're alone on a Saturday night, or if someone turns you down (despite the great tickets you got especially for the evening).

Think of something you'd really love to do. Ask yourself out to do it. Make plans, just as if you were trying to impress the most exciting date. Imagine yourself saying yes and getting excited. Mark the date on your calendar. When the day comes, get dressed up as you would for someone special.

I'm not suggesting that you delude yourself into thinking you're going out on an imaginary date with an imaginary friend. What I do mean is that you should imagine another "you" going with you. Have an imaginary conversation about what fun you're having and how great it is to be with you. Say all the things you would to a special date.

This should be a fun, thrilling exercise—one that will help shore up your confidence. Think of it as an inoculation against rejection, a character builder, a self-esteem booster. You'll also gain independence that will serve you through any date.

Discover the Real You

True self-esteem means finding out who you really are. According to a certain psychological theory, the self is made up of different components: the *real self* (the inner you), the *ideal self* (what you'd like to be), and the *social self* (how others perceive you based on the face you show to the world). Think about all those components, and how they operate in the dating world. Describe each:

MY *REAL SELF* (how I really feel):

MY *IDEAL SELF* (the way I'd like to be):

MY *SOCIAL SELF* (how others see me):

Getting Feedback

As you must know by now, I am very much in favor of open communication. If you wonder what someone's thinking or what they'll say, ask. If your lover doesn't call, ask why. If you can't figure out what your date meant by that remark, ask. Don't waste time wondering. A date is like a research project—it gives you the opportunity to learn about your own (and others') motivations, fears, and needs. And just like any other research project or experiment, you must collect data to make progress.

Do your dating research. If someone seems interested in you, ask for feedback. If they decide to break up, ask for an explanation (reassure them that you're not trying to control or change them, but just want to learn something for next time). Ask questions like "What did you mean when you said…?" or "How did you feel when I…?"

Be prepared that some people may be unwilling (or incapable) of responding honestly. They may be afraid, inexperienced, or insecure. If you like playing the open talk game, it's best to associate with people who also like open talk, or you may wind up frustrated and unfulfilled.

Beware of Suitors With Unsuited Confidence

The best, longest-lasting relationships are between two people who both have a solid sense of self and who don't try to hide who they really are. But some people may be good at hiding their true self. This section gives you some tips on spotting people with confidence problems.

The Braggarts

Bob loves to wine and dine women, but can't figure out why he never gets a second date. I asked him how he acts on his dates. Bob explained, "I told them they'd never find a guy who would treat them better. I have a fancy car, know all the best wines, and have been places they have only dreamed about." Exuding self-confidence can be positive, but don't overdo it. Bob's excessive self-promotion portrays a desperate need to impress and reveals his deep-seated insecurity that ultimately drives people away.

The Apologizers

Pointing out your weaknesses can be just as off-putting as excessive bragging about your excesses. Sally was willing to admit to me that she's pretty, but if a man compliments her, she quickly tells him how homely she was as a child, or that it is only makeup, or that it's just the outfit she's wearing. Her secret hope is that the man will heap on more compliments to counter her self-criticisms. Instead, men tend to take her at her word and back away. This is self-sabotage at its saddest.

The Manipulators

Peter's girlfriends are always the jealous type, wildly possessive of him. At first, Peter is flattered by their behavior, but he always ends up cheating on them and being mean. Deep down, Peter is projecting his own jealousy and possessiveness onto the girls he dates as a way of denying his own insecurities. Their behavior acts as a mirror of his own, and when he senses this (unconsciously), he gets angry and punishes them for it by pushing them away.

Alcohol and Drugs: False Self-Esteem Boosters

These two stories have a common theme:

➤ "I went to an office party where I had too much to drink. My co-worker told me that I really came on to my boss. I don't remember a thing."

➤ "My boyfriend wanted me to have sex with one of my girlfriends. I was shy about it, but after a couple of drinks I did it anyway. Now I can't even look at the girl when I see her, and I'm afraid that she's after my boyfriend."

Research has shown that alcohol does lower inhibitions. One drink over dinner, in a responsible dating situation, can give you the necessary boost to feel more relaxed and comfortable.

But beware, because excess alcohol leads to impaired judgment, which can get you into trouble. Everyone has a different tolerance level, but the danger level appears to be roughly three drinks. Overindulging leaves you prey to anyone else's desires, and you are apt to do things you wouldn't consider if you weren't drunk. I hear too many sad stories about unwanted pregnancies, betrayals, and contracted diseases because someone drank too much and then claimed that "It just happened."

The Loser Magnet

Janice complained, "I constantly fall for losers, guys who can't hold a job, or who are always down on their luck. Why do I do this?" She does it because it boosts her own flimsy self-esteem. But it's a false sense of power. Janice was finally able to see what she was doing: "If I can help them, I feel better about myself, but maybe the only real way to feel better about myself is to do it for me, not for them." Right on, Janice.

The Least You Need to Know

➤ A healthy self-esteem is the ultimate sex appeal.

➤ What you visualize is what most likely will happen, so visualize dating success.

➤ Consider yourself your own best date.

➤ Replace self-dumping with self-pumping.

➤ Enjoy your own company and you'll attract the company of others.

Chapter 7

Overcoming Shyness

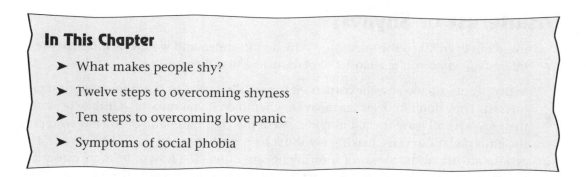

In This Chapter

➤ What makes people shy?

➤ Twelve steps to overcoming shyness

➤ Ten steps to overcoming love panic

➤ Symptoms of social phobia

Nearly everyone has suffered from it at some point in their lives. Even politicians, seemingly extroverted comics, and celebrities (from Michael Jackson to Barbara Walters) admit to it. Men suffer from it as much as women do. But to win in the dating world, you have to get over it. That is, get over being shy.

What is shyness? At best, it's being reserved; at worst, it's feeling so insecure or fearful of being judged that you don't act like yourself or you withdraw completely. Shyness can be caused by a history of rejection, by rules and behavioral patterns instilled in us as children, and even by chemical imbalances in our brains. No matter what the source, shyness is not something you have to suffer with.

Why Am I Shy?

Shyness may be a result of past experiences of not being accepted or loved. Sufferers may have been bullied or criticized by their peers or by adults when they were children. They may also be copying their parents' own shyness. Or they may have been taught not to be assertive, being told "Don't try that" or "Don't speak until you're spoken to."

Essentials
Studies have shown that men often suffer more from shyness than women because they are expected to be more assertive in dating, careers, and life in general.

Shyness can also be inherited. For instance, ten percent of the population is born with "stranger anxiety," which is partly caused by the balance of certain chemicals (monomaine oxidase, serotonin, and cortisol) in the brain. Researchers at Harvard University also found that shyness may be governed by the amygdala, an almond-shaped "switching center" in the brain responsible for stimulating reactions like fear and withdrawal. But even if the genes fit, you don't have to wear them. You can change by increasing your confidence.

Disinterest or Shyness?

I've often been asked the question: "Why do some men and women act like they're not interested, when you're almost 100 percent sure that they are?"

Many people are too shy, inexperienced, or socially scared to be up front about their interest. They don't know what to say or what to do if you respond. Or they're afraid their friends will tease them! I'm reminded of the classic scenario of the boy who pulls the girl's pigtails in class, making her think he hates her, when really he likes her. His actions are his awkward way of showing her attention. The lesson: Be more direct if you like someone. Don't play games or act indifferent to cover up your feelings.

Shyness can be charming, disarming (making others less fearful or threatened), and engaging (inspiring others to make you more relaxed and comfortable). But it can also give the wrong impression, and intimidate or frighten others away.

Shyness may also bore others because of the lack of assertiveness it implies. For example, Kelly complained, "Men always break up with me because they say I'm too nice," when she is really just too laid back. Whenever someone asks, "Where do you want to go?" or "What do you want to do?" she says, "Whatever." Her ambiguity leaves others with the burden of being in control, and also leaves them feeling confused about who she really is and how they should behave. Kelly should instead speak up and be clear about her preferences: "I'd like to eat Italian food" or "I'm in the mood for a funny movie."

12 Steps to Overcoming Shyness

Overcoming shyness may seem overwhelming or impossible. Not so! It takes effort, just like changing any behavior, but it is very possible—and well worth the effort. Remember, your fears are inevitably much worse than the reality of a situation. Here are some helpful steps to overcome your shyness.

➤ Work on improving your self-confidence (refer to Chapter 6, "Building Confidence and Self-Esteem").

➤ Understand why you are shy. What are you afraid of? Judd was afraid girls would think he's a loser. "I'm losing my hair and I'm shaped like a pear," he bemoaned. Judd is his own worst critic. People don't see our flaws as we do.

➤ Play-act. In the privacy of your home, act out the way you would like to be—taken to the extreme. For instance, walk around the room puffing out your chest and raising your voice. By going to the extreme, you slough off hidden anxieties, embarrassment, and shame, and come back to your center refreshed and reenergized.

➤ Mimic someone you admire who is not shy. Imitation is a key to learning. Other people's actions can be a guide on how to act the way you would like to be.

➤ Do something in life that makes you feel good about yourself. Start a project, clean out clutter, master a musical instrument. Becoming a success is a potent aphrodisiac to turning you—and others—on.

➤ Curtains up! Many people don't bother to look their best some days, either out of laziness or thinking that it won't matter. I'll always remember one hairdresser who chastised me for letting my hair get uneven and unruly. When I offered excuses—that I was too busy and had other priorities—he threw his hands up dramatically, proclaiming, "Oh my dear, but every day is show time!" Mothers used to say it in another way: "Always wear clean underwear because you never know when you might get in an accident." So, always be prepared to be seen or discovered whenever, wherever.

➤ Forget the "I'm not worthy" routine. Keep your mind on a power track with affirmations. Repeat to yourself, "I am a worthwhile person." No matter what happens, you are. You deserve to have and be what you want.

➤ Redefine shyness (not as fear, but as enjoying observing situations).

> **Tip**
> A saying from a "LovePhones" listener, Marianna, that helped her get over her shyness: "Everything in life has an end, so take risks, because you have nothing to lose."

➤ Combat your fear of rejection. Expect and accept that everyone at one time or another gets rejected. Rather than taking rejection personally, decide that you and that person just don't "fit" or the timing is off, and move on to something or someone else to distract and engage you. Read Chapter 20 for more on this.

➤ Take risks. Nothing ventured, nothing gained. Or, as my friend Rick McCarty says, "If you don't take a chance, you don't have a chance."

➤ Use self-disclosure. Confess to people that you're shy, so they won't misread you. The confession in itself can be endearing and an ice-breaker to a conversation. If it scares someone away, that person isn't right for you anyway.

➤ "Practice" dating. Nothing feeds success like success. As you gain more pleasurable dating experiences, you can feel more confident and your anxieties ease. In one program based on the book *The Shy Man Syndrome* by Japanese author Nobuko Awaya, shy men are assigned to a woman trainer for 12 two-hour practice dates. These practice dates are combined with group discussions before and after the dates that include role-playing and visualizations (imagining how he will behave and how the date will go). The therapist monitors realistic and unrealistic expectations. Men are taught to accentuate the positive (her smile, the way she leaned on my shoulder) and play down the negative (she didn't squeeze my hand back).

Do Looks Matter?

Feeling good about yourself is a key to overcoming shyness. One way to do this is to look your best. You must believe that you are attractive and worth getting to know better. Don't underestimate the possibility of overcoming any limitations you have in the looks department by making up for it with your energy, excitement, interests, and personality. But do make the most of your looks. Play up your good features with a hairstyle that shows off your pretty eyes, or form-fitting shirts that show off your muscular build, and hide less desirable features. Good grooming always pays off with attention to cleanliness and good style.

Also consider dressing up once in awhile; you don't always have to wait for special occasions. Are you one of those people who buy nice clothes and save them for special days—then rarely end up wearing them? Put away those raggedy old things—unless you can make them stylish, you'd do better to give them up.

Do the "closet-clean-out." A good rule of thumb is to get rid of clothes clutter by clearing out items that you haven't worn in a year—chances are you won't ever wear them. Instead, make room for things you *do* need and keep your best outfits in good shape. Remember this rule: When in doubt, throw it out.

Let's Talk

How you talk and what you talk about can say a lot about your personality—whether you're timid and shy or outgoing and spontaneous. Learn to speak up and say what's on your mind. Also, listen to your figures of speech. Do you repeat phrases such as "like" (which, by the way, drives me crazy), and "uh"? I once knew a woman who ended every sentence with "that is." Valley girls get made fun of by making every sentence into a question. If your voice inflection goes up at the end of every sentence, concentrate on deliberately dropping your voice at the end of a sentence.

Practice your most inviting, soothing, or comfortable voice. Like a sweet smell, a voice can emanate sex appeal. Speak deliberately, in a low tone, at a medium pace and volume. Then ask the other person, "What's the most interesting thing you did today?"

Also, engage in word-play. My father always emphasized the value of a broad vocabulary (he'd often open the dictionary and test me). Not only will you be able to understand some people better, you'll also impress others with your knowledge.

To broaden your vocabulary, consider purchasing study guides for GREs (Graduate Record Exams). These review books are available in university bookstores, and contain lists of vocabulary words students need to be familiar with in order to do well on the test. Or every day, just open up your dictionary and jot down a few words you'd like to learn, and study them while on the train or in your car.

Tip
Like everything else, learning to speak up and speak well takes practice. Make it a point to speak to three new people each day, whether at the supermarket, in a movie line, in the elevator, and so on.

Practice describing things in interesting ways, with vivid imagery. In radio—called "theater of the mind"—you learn to paint pictures with words. Instead of simply saying she has pretty eyes, say her eyes were "glowing" or "piercing."

Love Panic

Francine stood in front of Rick's door, ready to knock, when suddenly she was flooded with a rush throughout her body. The hallway felt warm, but her hands were cold. Her heart started pounding, and her knees went so weak she feared she would collapse. Adam called "LovePhones" to say, "I want to ask this woman out, but every time I look at her I end up sweating like a pig." And when Jocelyn was out with Tom, a guy she felt was "perfect" for her, she couldn't stop shivering.

Francine's flushes, Adam's sweats, and Jocelyn's shivers are symptoms of love panic—frightened feelings you experience when faced with someone you're attracted to. It's like the alarm you'd feel if you were standing on the edge of a thirty-story building with no handrail, or if a car was coming at you head-on at 65 miles an hour. People experience these things in situations ranging from giving a speech to having sex.

Warning
Symptoms of love panic are intense terror, trembling, sweating, chest pain, heart palpitations, shortness of breath, choking or smothering sensations, hot flashes or chills, nausea, faintness, numbness, and feelings of unreality.

But what's the difference between love panic and just having a case of the jitters? Jitters can be helpful—to prepare you to deal with a stressful situation or motivate you to solve a problem. Love panic, however, can flood you with so much anxiety that it interferes with your ability to do what you want and to be your charming self.

You're having a serious bout of love panic if your symptoms prevent you from taking your desired action(s), are persistent and frequent, or make you send out the wrong signals. For instance, Francine knew she had a real problem after she vowed never to return to Rick's house again for fear she would pass out at his door.

The Ten Steps to Controlling Love Panic

So how do you handle love panic? Both drug and non-drug therapies have been developed in the past decade to treat panic attacks. What works best depends on the person, but often a combination of therapy and medication is effective. The three types of medications used are benzodiazepine tranquilizers (Xanax, Atavan), antidepressants (Prozac, tricyclics like Tofranil), and monoamine oxidase inhibitors (Nardil). Patients usually take the medication for about six months to a year.

Besides medication, try following the ten steps outlined below, which are designed to help change your behavioral thinking and overall actions:

➤ *Step 1.* Understand the experience. Examine your symptoms, whether you're experiencing a racing heartbeat or weak knees. Why do you think your body is acting the way it is? For instance, Jocelyn realized that although she thought Tom was perfect, she also knew she wasn't ready to have sex with him like he wanted. As a result, her body was fighting her emotions.

➤ *Step 2.* Instead of interpreting your racing heartbeat as an impending heart attack, your breathlessness as a sign of suffocation, and your crazy thoughts that you're going mad, label your feelings as signs of fear. Reassure yourself that you feel cold or shaky, because you're nervous, and that it's okay to feel nervous.

Try one of my favorite techniques: paradoxical intention. Here you reframe the experience as the opposite of how you would normally see it. For example, instead of identifying nervousness as being a negative, purposefully see it as a good sign—that you are excited for action and that you are turned on.

➤ *Step 3.* Instead of trying to get rid of your feelings, become mobilized by them; embrace them to propel you into action. My famous rule to follow is: Turn Anxiety into Action. Purposefully slow yourself down by breathing more evenly and letting your energy pour out (energy sparks excitement). The former will make you more sensual and the latter more exciting. Instead of Francine holding back her hand from knocking on the door, she should knock more vigorously.

➤ *Step 4.* Admit nervousness instead of hiding it. Pretending to be calm and collected often escalates fear and self-consciousness. Instead, confidently announce that you are *excited*, not *scared*. When Rick opens the door, Francine should admit: "I'd love to appear calm and collected, but my heart is actually beating a mile a minute, from rushing here and from being excited."

➤ *Step 5.* Brainwash yourself with positive affirmations. Instead of worrying, "Do I look okay? Does he like me?" fill your mind with self-loving thoughts: "I'm a great person and I'm fun to be with."

➤ *Step 6.* Rationalize your responses. Instead of worrying about how you responded, reassure yourself that you can always have another chance at another time (to explain your reactions to the person or to behave differently).

➤ *Step 7.* Distract yourself from your nervousness by focusing on something else. Think about the food you're eating or the music you're listening to, since the brain can only think one thought at a time. These thoughts will replace your anxious thoughts about how you're coming across, how you look, and whether your date likes you.

➤ *Step 8.* Breathe to calm down. Anxiety causes your throat and chest muscles to tighten, which constricts your breathing—all of which make it difficult to talk. Inhale deeply through the nose and exhale through the mouth. Repeat this three times before you speak.

➤ *Step 9.* Give yourself an "out"—one that is actual or imaginary—from the anxiety-provoking situation. If you're at a get-together and you see a woman you'd like to speak to but realize that you're becoming noticeably nervous, make a graceful retreat if you have to, and go to the restroom or another spot for an "emotional break."

Essentials
Physical activity burns off nervous energy and increases blood flow to the brain—all of which make you more relaxed.

➤ *Step 10.* Move and do some activity. Even making gestures can help you to relax and clear your mind.

Social Phobia

Shyness and love panic can become so extreme that it is termed "social phobia." You are suffering from social phobia when:

➤ You avoid people altogether. You won't eat, write, or speak in front of people, won't use public bathrooms, and won't answer the phone. You may even refuse to leave your house.

➤ You experience an unprovoked episode of at least four of the above symptoms within a month, or one attack followed by the fear of having another.

Tip

If you think you're experiencing social phobia, contact the following associations for help:

The Anxiety Disorders Association of America, 6000 Executive Blvd., Rockville, MD 20852, (301) 231-9350. Send $5 for postage and handling for a list of therapists in your area.

The New York State Psychiatric Hospital. Anxiety Disorders Clinic, 722 West 168th Street, New York, NY 10032, (212) 960-2357.

Besides medication, the three types of therapy used to treat people with social phobia are behavioral therapy, exposure therapy, and panic control treatment.

Behavioral therapy usually involves breathing and relaxing exercises. These are the prelude to the process of desensitization, which helps people become less sensitive to their situation by reintroducing them in small steps to the sources of their fear while feeling calm.

Exposure therapy involves "in-vivo desensitization," whereby a therapist or guide accompanies a person in the real world to face their fears on the spot, with support.

Under panic control treatment (PCT), the physical sensations of fear that the person usually experiences are aroused in the safety of a therapist's office. For example, if a person feels dizzy when dating, he is spun around in a chair until he is dizzy to make the point that dizziness is survivable—and does not cause heart attacks or death.

Other, more probing therapy includes examining sources of deep emotional conflict that may stem from childhood. During this kind of therapy, some questions I ask my patients are:

➤ What important person in your life have you lost? Losing a parent, close friend, or love—through death, divorce, or other circumstances—can cause you to become afraid of investing emotions in anyone else because the pain of loss is too great.

➤ Were you ever afraid to leave home? Dating fears can sometimes be traced to a time when you were scared to go to school for fear that Mommy would not come back to pick you up, or be there for you when you came home.

➤ What are you afraid of losing if you win the date you want? I know this sounds crazy at first, but some people are really afraid to succeed because deep down there are things they will lose if they win. This is actually called the "secondary gains" of a problem—goodies you get from suffering. For instance, you may complain that you're lonely from having no dates, but you may secretly enjoy the benefits you get from complaining about it: feeling sorry for yourself, getting sympathy from others, or covering up a fear of dating. Some people don't want to give these things up.

➤ Who are you really saving yourself for? Some people hold themselves back from dating because they feel attached to someone already—a past partner (who may have rejected them or died), or even a parent.

It's reassuring to know that even the most extreme forms of shyness can be overcome. You absolutely deserve the joy of feeling confident in expressing the real you.

The Least You Need to Know

➤ Shyness can be caused by past experiences, behavior copied from or taught by parents, inborn traits or predispositions, and certain chemical balances in the brain.

➤ You can overcome shyness by increasing your self-confidence.

➤ An extreme form of shyness is social phobia. If you think you suffer from this, get professional help.

➤ Believe that whatever you do and whoever you are is worthwhile and desirable.

Part 2
Getting to Know You

Let me let you in on the biggest secret of all in dating: sex appeal comes from self-appeal. You are most likely to meet someone when you are at your most attractive and exuding good feelings and a sense of self-confidence. If you enjoy your own company, others will want to join you. So don't worry about not having a date. You already have your best date—you!

Some meetings feel like fate. "I never go into that hardware store," Carol told me, "so it was really a stroke of luck that Martin was in there at the same time, looking for light switches. I innocently asked him which one I should buy, but as he began to answer, I looked at him and thought, 'Wow.' And what do you know, he offered to come over and install the switch for me, and let's just say the lights went on in my life!"

Carol was ready and open to the possibilities. There are so many things to pay attention to in life, we are in control of what we look at and think about. At that moment, it was circumstance that Martin and Carol were in the same place at the same time. But then, she had to be open to the possibility that he could be someone for her.

Chapter 8

Asking For the Date

In This Chapter

➤ How to increase your chances of getting a "yes"

➤ What to say when making your move

➤ How to turn someone down

➤ What to do when you get no response

So you think you've met the person of your dreams. Now it's time to take that dreaded next step—making the connection. What's the best way to ask someone out on a date? Is there a right way? Traditionally, asking someone on a date may have involved a formal invitation that was extended in advance. Many times, couples make dinner plans that end up feeling awkward and tense, as they sit across the table not knowing what to say.

A date, however, doesn't have to be a formal outing. A better bet is to make the date a casual time together doing something that's enjoyable. "Hang out" and get to know one another's likes and dislikes. By understanding that conceptual approach to a date, you won't build all kinds of anxiety in your mind about asking someone out.

Dating 101: Preliminary Steps to Take

Before asking someone out, brief yourself on the following dating tips to increase your chance of getting a "yes":

➤ Your conversation with someone should lead naturally into an invitation. Popping the question should not come out of nowhere. Ideally, you have both just finished discussing something in which you're both interested and something you would like to do together.

➤ Your invitation should not build anxiety—either for you or the other person. Wait for a moment when you feel relaxed.

➤ When asking someone on a date, consider what you enjoy doing. Participating in something you are good at or comfortable with will increase your overall confidence (if you like basketball, take her to a game).

➤ Ask, "What's in it for my date?" Just as John F. Kennedy said, "Ask not what your country can do for you, ask what you can do for your country," the same basic rule can be applied to dating: Always offer something to others, before expecting or asking that something be done for you.

Think of a date not as "getting" but "giving." When asking someone to a party, say, "There'll be some people there I know you'll enjoy." Or combat resistance by pointing out advantages, like "Come play golf with me. Even if you don't love the sport, you'll be outdoors getting sunshine and exercise, and seeing beautiful sights."

If a prospective date sees what he can get out of the evening, he will be more receptive. What does she like to do? How will the date benefit him? For example, if he is thinking of buying a new car, offer to spend a day visiting car showrooms.

➤ Remember the basic point: Be yourself, instead of feeling the pressure of others' expectations.

Who Makes the First Move?

The first move has traditionally been left up to the man. However, as the role of women in the workplace continues to expand, so is their role in the dating world. People often ask me, "Is it okay for a woman to ask a man out?" "Do men like women who make the first move?" The answer to both questions is a resounding "Yes!" More men have grown tired of always being the ones to make the first step. In fact, they appreciate women who take the initiative, and are relieved to know when a woman is interested in them. In addition, many men (as long as they're not intimidated) find women attractive when they are assertive, confident, and in control of their lives.

Tip

The telephone is a tremendous aid in dating—unfortunately, one that men have traditionally been shy about. Get over your phone fears by taking a deep breath, identifying yourself to the person you're calling, and providing some information that connects the two of you ("Remember when we met at Bob's party?"). Talk a short time and then end with a compliment: "It was great talking to you."

Closing the Deal

Asking someone on a date is like trying to make a sale—that is, you are trying to sell *yourself*. When making the proposition, follow the "Rule of Three Yes's"—ask three questions that will all lead to favorable responses. You never want to ask a question that will lead to a "no." That stops the conversation and injects negativity.

You also want to ease the person into agreement, without him feeling he's risking too much, and by giving him an "out" at each stage—so as not to embarrass either of you. Of course, you have to do some research first and learn something about the person so that you can figure out how to set up your questions. You may have to use your creativity to find out what those questions might be. Then you close the deal by asking three "yes" questions.

Consider this scenario. Bill wants to ask Kate out. He does a little research first and discovers that she likes Kung Fu movies. His conversation opener, therefore, can be something like: "I heard you like Kung Fu movies." He then does more fact-finding by asking open-ended questions like "What's the latest Kung Fu movie you've seen?" or "What's your favorite Kung Fu movie?"

Or, after a conversation about something else, Bill can close the deal on his date by asking three "yes" questions:

➤ "So, you really love going to the movies?"

➤ "I heard you love Kung Fu movies. Is that true?"

➤ "Wouldn't it be neat to see the latest Kung Fu movie that's playing?"

Warning
Men who are threatened by a woman's assertiveness may prove troublesome in relationships, as they tend to resist her requests and insist on proving their own superiority or control.

Tip
When asking someone on a date, offer alternate times. If they can't make it one night, they may be able to make it another. But if that person declines all suggestions, you're better off letting the whole thing drop.

Then Bill can add, "I'm thinking about going to see (that movie) sometime this weekend. If you're free, maybe you could go with me. What do you think?" (Of course, this won't always get you a definite "yes," but you gave it a good shot.)

Notice these characteristics of Bill's dating request:

➤ Pose the question as if you're already going and she can join you. This takes the pressure off you to take her out formally and off her feeling guilty about hurting your feelings if she says "no." You also avoid sounding desperate. (No one wants to board a sinking ship—they *do* want to board a ship in full sail!)

➤ Be casual about your invitation. This is my favorite suggestion. I've encouraged you to take risks, but don't jump into water that's too deep before you've tested it.

➤ Point out all the benefits of the deal. Folgers sells coffee not by quoting the price but by showing how warm and cozy consumers will feel sharing coffee with their mate early in the morning.

When selling a car, two of the biggest tricks to close the deal are to say something like, "So which color do you want?" and then, "How do you want to pay for it—in a three-year plan or a four-year plan?" The first question makes the assumption that you are interested, which encourages your interest further because the dealer is acting as if the hypothetical were a reality. The second question is a clincher because it continues to promote the hypothetical as reality. The question gets you to focus on choices and avoids offering you a chance to say "no."

Now apply this method to dating. Ask, "Which day should we meet, Friday or Saturday?" and then "Would you prefer going to the movies, or out to eat, or both?"

➤ In case of a lukewarm reception, use another rule of selling: Always leave the door open. You can say, "Okay, I'll call you in a week and maybe we can go then," or "I'm sure we can find something that would be great to do together another time." This keeps your ego from being totally deflated.

> **Tip**
> My friend Donovan, lead singer of the band Nancy Boy (and ex-Calvin Klein jeans model) heartily endorses telling your target's best friend about your interest, so she'll tell her friend, who'll be more prepared for—and hopefully receptive to—your invitation. It's how he won over his current love.

> **Tip**
> Think of a date as a TBC ("To be continued") television movie. Be positive and complimentary at the end of the date. Tell the person, "I enjoyed talking with you. You're so interesting. Let's do it again."

Tip

When finalizing the date, consider giving out your business card. I learned the advantages of trading business cards from spending a lot of time in Japan, where it's *de rigeur* to exchange "name cards" when you first meet someone. By having someone's business card, you won't have to worry about forgetting the person's name, what she does for a living, and how to contact him.

Having business cards drawn up isn't a big deal. Visit your local print or card shop, or even use your own computer—many are able to print out business cards. You can also order personalized business cards through some catalogs.

Keeping Your Emotions in Check

When dating, it's important not to have any expectations. Enjoy the process and not the outcome, the journey and not the destination—or you'll be headed for disappointment. The best actions are the ones that come from the heart, that have good intentions and no concern for a response. Have fun flirting, without worrying whether it'll lead to a ride home, a date, a roll in the hay, or a marriage proposal. Expectations inhibit spontaneity. Your expectations may also make your date feel obligated, guilty, and resistant. People need to feel free to say "yes" or "no" instead of giving in out of guilt, fear of hurting you, fear of retaliation, or fear of anything else—that can doom any relationship.

Just Say No—Gently

Some men and women feel guilty about saying "no," like Heather: "I hate going to parties because I usually get stuck with some creep, and I can't get away. Sometimes my girl-friend and I give 'rescue signals' to each other, but if she's occupied with someone else, my whole evening is ruined." So how do you make a graceful exit?

I'm really impressed when people ask me how to let a casual encounter down easy—it shows that they care about other people's feelings. When letting someone down, one rule to remember is to always be kind. It could happen to you, and what goes around comes around. So I was pleased when Billy called "LovePhones" and said, "I'm a pretty good-looking guy, and lots of girls do ask me out. I don't want to blow them off because I've been hurt myself and I know what it feels like. What can I do?"

Kudos to Billy for being considerate. People who have been rejected know what it feels like and are more sensitive to not hurting someone else. Similar rules apply to exiting casual encounters as to ending a relationship (as described in Chapter 20). Let someone down easy by reassuring them that they're nice, and by giving a neutral but firm excuse (so they get the picture, instead of trying even harder). Here's a suggestion:

> "You're interesting/that's fascinating/ nice talking to you, and it'd be nice to talk to you more, but I need to make a phone call/talk to my friend/get something to drink, but it was a real pleasure to meet you."

If the person persists, talk kindly but drop something into the conversation about another relationship or say something like, "Please don't take this personally, but I don't feel like talking right now."

It's one thing to be nice; it's another to sacrifice yourself. If you're wasting your time, you're wasting the pursuer's time too, and are only being misleading. Disengage yourself nicely, and consider that you're doing both of you a favor.

Psychologically, people who can't break away are usually oversensitive to rejection themselves. Deep down they may have merged with the other person, so that the rejection is also a blow to themselves. These people have to learn to set boundaries and stop fearing that they will be punished for rejecting someone else. For instance, Jackie's mother always warned her, "What goes around, comes around." As a result, she feared that if she turned a guy down, some guy would turn her down, too.

Getting No Response

Remember, dating, like selling, is a numbers game: you have to go through a lot of "no's" before you get a "yes." Learn to welcome the "no's," because they just mean you're getting closer to a "yes." Even the best hitters in baseball get on base only about once every three times at bat, and also strike out occasionally!

Tip
Track your progress. Keep a journal of your goals, plans, reminders, and successes. Review these to boost your morale. You can even leave sticky notes on mirrors or doors to remind you to be assertive.

If you get a "no" from a person, don't obsess about it. Instead, pick up your marbles and go to another playground where you might be welcome. Immediately turn your attention to others who might be interested.

A common question I'm asked is: "Why is it that a girl seems interested, but when you ask her out on a date, or begin to show you are interested, she doesn't want to speak to you again?"

Unfortunately, when people feel awkward or embarrassed, they may avoid talking to you, making you feel bad. You may have jumped the gun—interpreting friendliness as an interest in dating. If you approach someone and she does not respond the way you want her to, accept that she was just being nice and did not mean anything more or to lead you on.

If you want to be big about it, you can be the one to use the "Let's just be friends" line, so you don't feel totally rejected. Come right out and say, "It's okay that it's not going to work out between us. I don't expect anything from you, so we can just be friends. That'll work much better for both of us."

Don't Blow Up if You're Blown Off

John couldn't accept women who turned him down. If he approached them and they turned away or said something rude, his temper flared out of control. He was like Jekyll and Hyde—one minute an innocent flirt, the next a raging bull. John and other rejected suitors need to:

➤ Realize that everyone has a right to say no. Don't take rejection personally.

➤ Realize that your hair-trigger temper over rejection is related to your need for instant gratification (getting what you want when you want it). Instead, consider patience a virtue.

➤ Trace your reactions to childhood experiences. Were you spoiled? Did you always get what you wanted? Remember, the world will not indulge you like your mother did.

Tip
If you are easily upset by rejection, interrupt the eruption by stopping and taking a deep breath. Then smile and turn your attention to something else.

➤ Identify past events that are currently fueling your present anger. Separate the past from the present so that you can react effectively now. When one woman rejected John, he was flooded with memories of all the other women who had slighted him.

Essentials

Research has shown that getting past hurts off your chest is helpful to your physical as well as mental health. A group of people who wrote about their past traumatic experiences for 20 minutes a day for four days had fewer visits to the doctor than those who wrote about trivial topics. In addition, those who wrote about their feelings were happier, less anxious, and seemingly healthier than those who described events nonemotionally.

The Least You Need to Know

➤ Don't think of a date as a formal outing. Think of it as a casual time to get to know each other.

➤ Consider dating like selling—always ask questions that lead to a "yes," and even consider a "no" as leading you closer to an eventual "yes" from someone else.

➤ Don't take rejection personally. Consider that one road not taken leads you down another (better) one.

➤ Keep your spirits up. Never give up hope. Keep trying, and you're bound to find someone special!

Chapter 9

The First Date... and Beyond

In This Chapter

➤ What to do and where to go

➤ Dating do's and don'ts

➤ How to tell if it's going anywhere

➤ What men and women need to know—from each other's point of view

"Cup your hand over your mouth and check your breath."
—First-date rule (John, guitarist from the Dopes)

So you leapt over the first dating hurdle by asking to get together. Now get ready to jump again, because here's another one—your first date. If your mind instantly fills with images of tripping over your own feet, wrestling with your linguine, or worse, appearing mute by having nothing to say, relax. A first date is bound to be fraught with some anxieties. Remember to treat it as simply getting to know a person better. Remind yourself that your date already likes something about you, or she probably wouldn't have agreed to go out in the first place!

So what do you do and where do you go on a first date? The key is to go to a place you'll both enjoy and where you will both feel comfortable. The more confident you both feel, the better you will come across.

Where to Go

Most people think of going out for dinner or drinks on a first date. Such a setting is certainly a good way to talk and find out about one another. Make sure to pick a restaurant in which both of you will feel comfortable. Do you prefer quiet and romantic, or noisy and trendy? What about your date? Also, imagine the mood you'd like to set. Do you want a place that is calm and intimate or a place with distractions that can help take the pressure off?

Tip
If you're driving yourself crazy drumming up first-date ideas, consider simply asking your date, "Where would you like to go?" or "What do you enjoy doing most?" Better yet, plan something together.

Sometimes the idea of staring at each other across a dinner table is anxiety-provoking—some people can't stand the pressure. For this reason, I favor doing something other than just eating on the first date. Consider going to a movie, for instance. Although you don't get a chance to talk much in the theater, you'll be able to get used to each other and share an experience that you can talk about together later.

Tip
To make the first date as casual, nonthreatening, and non-anxiety-provoking as possible, think of going somewhere public. Other people make for an easy distraction. Also, consider limiting the time you spend together on your first date (you might say you have to get home early because you have a meeting early the next morning). This gives you a preset, easy out if you're not having a good time. It also gives you a good excuse to make another date if it turns out you do want to get together again.

Some creative dating outings include horseback riding; shooting pool; bowling; going to the theater, ballet, or zoo; barbecuing in your backyard; or watching videos. (Refer to Chapter 2 on hunting grounds for more suggestions.) Also, when deciding where to go, consider the person's dating style. For example, an adventurous person may love to go hiking or hang gliding as opposed to going to a movie.

What to Wear

How you dress can say a lot about you. Think about what your clothes say about your personality as you decide what to wear on your first date. What impression do you want to make? Do you want to look professional and conservative, casual yet savvy, or cool and hip? Also keep in mind your date's own clothing style and interests. Of course, you want to be yourself, but you can also decide to dress to please your date. For instance, when Paula planned her first date with Rich, she remembered how much he liked motorcycles, so she wore her black leather jacket and high black buckle boots and was a hit. When Sarah met Stephen, he was wearing gray slacks and a blue blazer. So for their first date, she dressed in an equally conservative outfit of a white blouse, black skirt, blue jacket, and black pumps.

Dating Do's

Finally! It's time for your date. Here are some tips to help things run smoothly:

➤ DO feel confident.

➤ DO look your best.

➤ DO smile.

➤ DO address your date by name frequently.

➤ DO compliment your date.

➤ DO listen attentively and repeat things your date says.

➤ DO be honest about whether you're interested in seeing the person again. If you're not, the more painful the aftermath will be; and if you are, the more pleasurable the positive feedback.

Dating Don'ts

Some tips to help avoid disastrous dates include:

➤ DON'T put yourself in uncomfortable situations (like ordering messy food—unless you're into the "9 1/2 Weeks" erotic feeding scene).

➤ DON'T suggest overly-expensive places or events for a first date unless you clarify who's paying.

➤ DON'T look at other women/men.

➤ DON'T monopolize the conversation.

➤ DON'T lie about anything (for example, your marital status or your financial situation).

➤ DON'T talk about your ex-relationships.

➤ DON'T become too intoxicated (unless it's with each other).

➤ DON'T make sexual approaches too quickly or insistently—send out vibes and wait for a welcome response.

After the Big Date

Okay, you cleared the first big hurdle. The first date is over. You can breathe easier now. So how did it go? Do you think you've met the person of your dreams, or someone

Tip
Start your relationship on an honest foot by playing it straight—act and say exactly how you feel. Remember, honesty is a key ingredient to long-lasting relationships.

you'd rather just keep as a friend, or worse, a dud or jerk you never want to see again? No matter how a date goes, I'm a big believer in grace after dates. That is, after the date, always call and thank the person for going, whether it worked out or not. Emily received a call from her blind date who said, "I had a nice time with you but I don't think it's going to work out between us." As much as it hurt her to hear this, Emily knew herself that it wasn't going anywhere, and appreciated the acknowledgment and the closure his phone call gave her.

Essentials
A woman usually expects to hear from a man the day after a date. Men, on the other hand, usually make contact days or even a few weeks later. I recommend calling the day after the date, or at least within three days, whether it's to just say "thank you" or to indicate further interest. If she cares, she'll be happy to hear from him soon (knowing she's on his mind), and if she doesn't care, there's nothing lost.

Subsequent Dates

Hopefully, the first date worked out and you're planning another get-together. Consistent with the principle of going up a stepladder, take each of your subsequent dates up a notch by spending more time, and doing more things, together (for instance, do dinner *and* a movie). Also, make an effort to get more creative as your contacts increase. Think of more varied situations to be in together so that you can get a sense of each other and how both of you approach life. For example, be alone as well as with people, do something in the daytime as well as in the evening, be indoors at a museum and outdoors at the beach, spend a quiet evening at home and an active one at a club or bowling alley. It's true: Variety *is* the spice of life.

Tip

If you're planning to cook for your date at home, make dinner a sensuous experience. For example, choose suggestive textures, smells, colors, and tastes: crunchy string beans; tangy sauces; red tomatoes. Consider food-shopping or cooking together. Also, find out if your date is health-conscious or vegetarian, so you don't turn her off with greasy burgers and french fries, too-salty appetizers, or heavy cream sauces. And tidy up more rooms than just the kitchen.

Is This Going Anywhere?

So you've been out with the person a few times, but you're still not sure if the person is really interested in you. You may ask yourself, "Is this going anywhere?" Chances are, if you have to ask—be cautious. However, to help determine your date's interest, answer the following questions:

➤ Are you the one who makes all the approaches or issues all the invitations?

➤ Are there things your date says that don't ring true?

➤ Do you find yourself thinking, "Does he say that to all the women he sees?" (If so, ask him and see how he reacts!)

➤ Does she seem unresponsive or distant at times? Is her attention toward you inconsistent?

➤ Does he rarely return your compliments?

➤ Has he turned down two or more of your invitations?

The more "yes" answers you have, the less likely it is that the other person is really interested in you. Of course, it's possible other things are getting in the way, but generally, if you answered "yes" to all of these questions, it's best to turn your attention elsewhere.

You can usually gauge someone's interest by how he acts. But if you're unsure about someone's intentions, get feedback. It's a good idea to set things straight early in a relationship. Say something casual, like "I had a great time. We should do it again sometime." Things are probably not going so well if you're tempted to ask more pointed questions, such as, "Is this going anywhere?" or "Are we both wasting our time?" Trust your instincts—your doubts are likely valid.

Playing Games

People play games to protect themselves from being hurt. Some self-help books and articles suggest that people play games to create mystery and keep a partner guessing. You're beginning to know by now why I don't subscribe to this theory. If you play games, then a game-player is what you'll attract, and neither person will be open about their intentions. Eventually the game *will* break down and your true self will emerge.

When Is Someone Your Boyfriend or Girlfriend?

How you refer to the person you're dating both reflects and affects your level of intimacy. I don't approve of people who use the terms "boyfriend" and "girlfriend" too casually. All too often people will call "LovePhones" and say, "I saw my girlfriend talking to another man" or "My boyfriend didn't call me," and when I ask, "How long have you been going out?" they say, "Two weeks" or even "Three days." It seems a bit premature to use the term "boyfriend" or "girlfriend" so early in a relationship. By not exaggerating the importance of the person you are dating so early in the game, you won't feel as bad if the relationship does not work out. And when it does, the word will have more meaning.

What Did You Call Me?

What does your date call you? How do you define your dating status? Here are some terms and phrases you can use:

➤ *"This man/woman I'm going out with."* Use for first dates and casual acquaintances.

➤ *"This man/woman I'm dating."* Use to suggest you may have been out on a few dates, but may not be exclusive or committed.

➤ *"This man/woman I'm seeing."* Reference to show you have been dating for at least a few weeks and plan to move on to a more serious level.

➤ *"My girlfriend/boyfriend."* Reserved for when you have been dating for a few months, and have some level of commitment to spend time together, share experiences, and see each other regularly (but perhaps not exclusively).

➤ *"My lover."* Reveals an open admission of sexual intimacy that usually implies exclusivity.

➤ *"My significant other."* This term was created by the Census Bureau to imply that a couple was sharing living quarters and, therefore, aspects of their daily lives. Usually, this term implies a stable or longer-term arrangement. It is also often used in same-sex relationships when someone doesn't want to be specific about the sexual nature of his relationship.

Tip

How many people should you date at the same time? You can date as many people as you like, as long as you don't deceive anyone. And you *must* be practicing safe sex. There's absolutely nothing wrong with playing the field—you get to meet many interesting people while learning a lot about yourself. However, you might prefer to concentrate on one person at a time. Remember, the more people you see at the same time, the less time you have to devote to one person and the less opportunity you have to see whether you can satisfy each other's needs.

Men, Women, and Dating

Men and women definitely approach the dating scene differently (as you'll see in Chapter 13). The following are a few guidelines for both men and women to consider at this stage of the game.

What Men Need to Know: The Woman's Point of View

➤ Be romantic and sensitive in your words and actions. Send cards. Bring small gifts (flowers, thoughtful trinkets).

➤ Listen attentively. (Eye contact is critical here, or if on the phone, ignore your call waiting.)

➤ Agree to do things with her family and friends.

➤ Build her trust by being faithful, truthful, and always "being there."

➤ Spend time cuddling.

➤ Don't expect or demand sex.

➤ Learn about her body and erogenous zones. Enjoy afterplay. Take time.

➤ Don't expect her to date you exclusively and then play around yourself.

What Women Need to Know: The Man's Point of View

➤ Don't expect him to profess his love for you so soon. (See "When to Say 'I Love You'" in Chapter 15.)

➤ Don't push him into a commitment or an exclusive relationship.

➤ Don't snoop.

➤ Don't nag him into talking about his feelings.

➤ Take the initiative, instead of expecting him to always be the aggressor.

➤ Don't take everything personally.

➤ Loosen up your inhibitions.

➤ Don't compare him to other lovers (unless it's to tell him he's the best).

➤ Don't badmouth him to your girlfriends.

➤ Think of dating as fun without weighing it down with overly-heavy emotional complications.

➤ Let him withdraw once in awhile—understand his need to be alone or to take things slowly.

➤ Accept him without judgment.

The Least You Need to Know

➤ Women as well as men should take the initiative in dating.

➤ Go somewhere on your date where you will both feel comfortable and enjoy yourselves.

➤ Be open about your interest in pursuing the relationship.

➤ Always thank the other person for the date.

➤ Be sensitive to what men and women need.

➤ The initial phases of dating may take some time and effort and cause anxiety, but hang in there. Your efforts will eventually pay off!

Chapter 10

Matching Your Dating Styles

In This Chapter

➤ Getting to know yourself and your date

➤ A quiz to test your dating personality style

➤ Understanding the four basic personality types

➤ Dating game questions

➤ The Noah's Ark test

➤ Matching that makes "sense"

➤ Matching by the stars

This chapter is about making a love connection. It's about finding a mate whose lifestyle, personality, and dating expectations are compatible with your own. While no mate will ever be perfect, there are certain types of people who make better matches. When two people are running on the same track, the connection can be blissful. But when love trains collide head on, or when their tracks diverge, the pain and disappointment can be over-whelming.

From psychology to astrology, theories abound as to why certain people get along and others clash. While no theory tells the whole story, many offer useful clues about human behavior and compatibility. I've adapted certain personality theories to come up with the quizzes in this chapter. Keep in mind that these are simplifications of some very complex theories and assessments. Use them as fun guides in your search for a lifelong love, or at least a pleasant dinner date!

Basic Dating Rule: Know Your Love Target!

Janet is a former patient who came to me to help her figure out why all her relationships turned sour. Janet is the spontaneous type. An artist, she loves to wear colorful, sequined dresses, and she tends to move around a room like a jackrabbit. At a business party at the art gallery that represents her work, she met the gallery's accountant, Albert. Stunningly handsome, he was wearing a starched shirt and a dark suit, and he spoke slowly and deliberately—unlike Janet, whose sentences tumbled out a mile a minute. Drawn to Janet's energy, Albert followed her around all evening and then offered to drive her home. He lingered at her door as they said goodnight, and Janet, sensing his passion, grabbed him wildly. Standing in her foyer, they embraced passionately.

Janet thought about Albert all week until she finally saw him again at another business function. Sidling up to him, she whispered in his ear, "I'm mad for you." To her shock, he pushed her away and muttered, "I don't want you to do that," making a leveling motion with his hand as he walked away.

Devastated, Janet tried to make sense of his behavior. How could he be so hot one minute, so cold the next? I explained to her that while Albert was so attracted to her "wildness," it probably frightened him—as did his own loss of control. If there was ever to be anything more between them, Janet would have to tone down her behavior and proceed more slowly. She agreed, but decided that Albert was not worth the effort.

My point is not to suggest that you adapt yourself, chameleon-like, just to get a date. But if you are attracted to someone whose outward style is radically different from your own, you may have to be a bit more calculating in your approach. Sometimes it's easier to win over a person if you approach them in *their* style—even if it's a little against your nature. Albert, the starched-shirt accountant, was probably mortified that Janet came on to him during a business meeting, thus his rude rebuff. If her come-on had been less aggressive (if she'd been more sensitive to his nature), the results might have been different. They may not have walked off into the sunset, but she probably wouldn't have walked away wounded, either.

The Personality Style Quiz

The following quiz will help you assess your own style and that of your love interest. Take the quiz with a partner or with someone you've been dating. If you aren't sure about asking your current love interest to join you in this quiz, take an educated guess at his or her answers.

Essentials

Over 30 years of research have shown that most people fall into one of four main personality categories (see "The Four Basic Personality Types" later in this chapter). This reflects the dominance of one of the four quadrants of the brain. Brain dominance determines how we think, relate to others, choose jobs, and fall in love. Once you determine which type you are, you'll have a better chance of determining who you like and don't like—and why. And once you know another person's basic type, you have an advantage in influencing or pleasing that person.

I've adapted this quiz from an extensive computerized questionnaire developed by the Ned Herrmann Group in Lake Lure, North Carolina. I've used it for many, many years and know that it works! Answer the questions as they apply to you, choosing the answer that applies most of the time. Remember, most of us are a mixture of personality types, but the results of the quiz may offer you some useful guidelines on compatibility. Be honest!

1. Dates usually like me because I am

   a) spontaneous and full of fun

   b) romantic and a good talker

   c) reliable and punctual

   d) intelligent and rational

2. Dates who don't like me think I am

   a) too wild, unpredictable, and off-the-wall

   b) overemotional, hypersensitive, and needy

   c) stubborn, boring, and unemotional

   d) controlling, opinionated, and argumentative

3. My feeling about love is

   a) it's magical and inspires me to explore, create, and take risks

   b) I'm happiest when I'm in love; I don't like being alone for too long

   c) romantic love is transient, so make practical choices

   d) it alters your perceptions, making you overlook limitations, and requires you to suspend more rational assessments you would make in other situations

4. When it comes to spending money on a date, I believe in

   a) splurging for something special

   b) spending on friends

   c) sticking to a strict budget

   d) spending when there may be a payoff

5. If I disagree with a date, I like to

   a) consider possible solutions that make both of us happy

   b) immediately say how I feel and insist on talking the situation through

   c) try to forget it and move on

   d) figure out the right thing to do before saying anything

6. It would turn me on to hear a date say

   a) "Let's take off on an adventure next week and do whatever strikes our fancy"

   b) "I love the way you talk to me and how you make me feel"

   c) "You make me feel secure; it's like I've known you all my life"

   d) "I've been thinking it over and I think we are right for each other"

7. My idea of a perfect evening together consists of

   a) doing something new or going somewhere different or exotic

   b) a romantic dinner and intimate talk

   c) clear plans of what to do, such as something we enjoyed in the past

   d) stimulating conversation or a debate over a new movie or current events

8. When it comes to sex, I like

   a) fantasies and being playful

   b) feeling close or like soulmates

   c) to stick to proper times and places

   d) when I feel in control and perform well

---

9. When it comes to sexual fantasies

    a) the wilder the story, the better

    b) I like fantasizing, especially about romance, being adored, or giving in

    c) I don't believe in fantasizing when I have the real thing

    d) I have some fantasies, but I don't think it's wise to share all of them

10. When I consider a future together, I need to

    a) picture lots of exciting things, some of which I can't yet imagine

    b) feel warm and wonderful

    c) feel secure that things will go as planned

    d) know I have made the right decision

To find out your score, total the number of a's, b's, c's, and d's you selected. Multiply each total by 10, and record them in the table below.

	Your Score	Your Date's Score
a		
b		
c		
d		

Now plot your numbers on the matrix on the following page. Use one pen color for your score, and a different color for your date's score. Match the number of your score for each of the four dimensions (a, b, c, d) along the line in each corresponding quadrant of the circle. Start from the center of the circle, "0," and move out to the outer line marked "100." Connect the dots (to make a figure) so you can more clearly see your preferences.

The further your plots are from the inner circles, the more you prefer a particular style; the closer they are to the center and inner circle, the less you prefer that style.

Notice where your plot and that of your date overlap, and where they diverge. The plots intersect in areas where you have the greatest mutual preferences or concerns. For example, if you both land on the same spot on the relaters dimension, it means you probably have a fairly equal desire to express emotions. If your score is high on the creative

111

scale while your partner's is higher on the conservative scale, the two of you may be out of synch much of the time. If you are aware of your differences, you will be in a better position to understand your partner and work through the difficulties that are apt to arise.

© *Ned Herrmann Group*

The Four Basic Personality Types

No one personality type is inherently good or bad, desirable or undesirable. The challenge is to understand your own tendencies and those of your partner. If you are not in a relationship, you can use this information in your search. For instance, if you are basically conservative but would love a more spontaneous mate, you may have to adapt your style to attract this type of person.

Use your quiz answers to assess where you and your date fit into these four broad personality types:

➤ *Creatives* (mostly "a" answers): Imaginative, free-spirited, impulsive people who thrive on experimentation and taking risks. They are often artists, CEOs, or entrepreneurs.

➤ *Relaters* (mostly "b" answers): Emotional, expressive, sensitive people who value personal relationships and communication of feelings over facts. Psychologists and teachers frequently fall into this category.

➤ *Conservatives* (mostly "c" answers): Practical, organized, detail-oriented people who go by the book and value predictability. They are often administrators, planners, or computer operators.

➤ *Thinkers* (mostly "d" answers): Analytical, rational, logical people who love to win arguments and solve problems. They often choose professions such as banking, law, or engineering.

Creatives often seem a bit off-the-wall, but they are great innovators and often have terrific ideas. If you are attracted to this type, encourage the person to let his or her imagination run free. Don't expect them to focus on details or take "It can't be done" for an answer. Enjoy their fantasies and have fun!

Relaters cherish feelings and relationships. If you are interested in a person of this type, talk a lot and emphasize your feelings and willingness to get along. Ask, "What are you feeling?" instead of "What are you thinking?" Give lots of hugs and attention.

Conservatives often seem picky and unimaginative, which may be frustrating for Creatives, who like taking risks. But appreciate their caution, discipline, and punctuality. If you are looking for security, a Conservative is a safe bet. Be cautious in your approach; don't surprise a Conservative by being overly emotional. Initially, at least, be predictable and punctual to make them feel safe.

Thinkers like to be right and need to know the facts. So, with these people, you wouldn't be wise to come on with a barrage of emotions. Instead of saying, "This will be fun" (a typical Creative response), or "I feel good about this" (a Relater's response), you might ask, "What do you think?" Thinkers can be controlling, which is something to watch out for.

Essentials
Personality type is just one factor in the great mate equation. Compatibility is another. The key to compatibility lies with the three A's: *acceptance*, *appreciation*, and *adjustment*.

While the cliché is that opposites attract, in fact it is common that "like" initially attracts "like." For instance, creative types who are into fantasy and adventure are more likely to pick partners who share their interests. But what happens in the long run when neither is willing to buckle down and balance the checkbook or attend to household details? All this similarity in temperament may create friction; a creative man may wish he'd ended up with a conservative woman, or vice versa!

Warning
Opposites may at first attract, and then repel. For instance, a thinker may be attracted to a relater for her warmth and outgoingness. But as the relationship progresses, he may accuse her of being overly emotional. The thing to keep in mind is that the very traits that are endearing in the beginning of a relationship may be the same ones that drive you apart (if you let them).

The Quick Assessment: An On-the-Spot Quiz

The quiz you just took is most useful when you know someone well or have the time to ponder the various facets of his personality. But what if you've just met someone? Are there clues to help you figure out where he fits into the four basic categories? The answer is yes, and the following questions should help.

1. *The Sheet Test.* The sheets on her bed are

   a) wildly patterned

   b) flowered

   c) plain white

   d) striped

2. *The TV Clicker Test.* On TV, he would rather watch

   a) "Beyond 2000"

   b) "Oprah"

   c) The Learning Channel

   d) "L.A. Law" reruns

3. *The Restaurant Test.* She would rather eat in a

   a) gazebo or hot-air balloon

   b) romantic spot

   c) quaint, old-fashioned place

   d) highly recommended restaurant

4. *The Video Rental Test.* If we rent a movie, he would most likely pick

   a) "The Rocky Horror Picture Show"

   b) "Sleepless in Seattle"

   c) "Of Mice and Men"

   d) "Presumed Innocent"

5. *His Bedclothes Test.* Which of the following would he be more likely to wear to bed (other than "nothing")?

   a) "Betty Boop" boxers

   b) silk boxers/robe

   c) plain pajamas

   d) blue cotton pajamas

6. *Her Bedclothes Test.* Which of the following would she be more likely to wear to bed (other than "nothing")?

   a) satin teddy with fur trim

   b) silk nightie from "Victoria's Secret"

   c) long flannel nightgown

   d) cotton pajamas

7. *His Date Attire Test.* Which of the following would he be more likely to wear on a date to go out to dinner?

   a) leather jacket with black jeans

   b) black shirt and slacks

   c) gray wool suit

   d) navy blazer and khaki slacks

8. *Her Date Attire Test.* Which of the following would she be more likely to wear on a date to go out to dinner?

   a) sequined jacket and satin pants

   b) flowered dress

   c) blue suit and black pumps

   d) navy blazer and beige slacks

To score, match the a, b, c, and d answers to the personality types described earlier.

Tip

By all means be yourself, but also be sensitive to your date's reactions. For example, you may be the spontaneous type, likely to exclaim enthusiastically on a date, "Wow, I have a great idea about what we can do." But if your date is a more formal, conservative type, who could be unsettled (even if attracted) to such forthrightness, you might temper yourself a little and present an idea more calmly, to let him get used to it.

Coming to Your Senses

Our senses play a large part in why we choose dates and partners. Just as some of us are more creative and some of us more emotive, some of us are more focused on scent and others on touch. This section helps you determine which sense dominates your daily experience, and how you can figure out which sense is dominant in another person. Once you know which sense is dominant in your love interest, you can use that knowledge in your seduction.

Essentials
Neuro-linguistic programming is the scientific term used to describe the various ways in which we process information.

Think back over your recent relationships. What is it that you first recall about your partners: the touch of their skin; their particular scent; the sound of their voice; their eyes; the feeling of closeness?

If your dominant sense is visual, you'll probably create a picture of a person in your mind. If your dominant sense is aural, you are more likely to recall a voice or the songs you listened to when you were together. Kinesthetic types focus on how things feel—his strong arm muscles, her soft, silky hair. Some of us are most sensitive to aroma, with a particular scent producing an instant flood of memories.

How can you tell which sense dominates in people you know well or barely know at all? Pay close attention to the words they use. Visual people use words to create pictures: "I see…" "Let's look at…" "I imagine…" and so forth. In a restaurant, they may reach for a pen to sketch on the tablecloth.

Aural types might use phrases like "I hear that…" "I say…" "That sounds like a good idea…" "Something tells me…" and so forth. They may touch their ears when you're talking, or close their eyes so they can hear you better.

Kinesthetic types are touch-oriented; they literally take a hands-on approach and concentrate on how things feel. They frequently use words that describe touching ("I can't put my finger on… "I'm touched that…") or textures ("This feels like…"). They shake hands readily and hold on longer, and find opportunities to touch you whenever they can. They may rub their chin or stroke their hair as they talk to you. They may also have a difficult time sitting still and move around a lot.

Scent-focused types pay attention to how things smell. They'll sniff the food, your perfume—and probably you!

Putting Your Knowledge to Work

If your love interest is visually oriented, choose eye-catching clothes and try gazing lovingly into her eyes.

If your lover is more attuned to sound, try seducing the person over the phone. Before you make the call, rehearse detailed descriptions of what you're doing and feeling. Have music playing when he comes over.

If the person is a touchy-feely type, wear clothes that beg to be touched, such as silk or fur. Occasionally offer a gentle touch on the hand or shoulder.

Perfume, flowers, incense, and scented candles are obvious devices for attracting someone whose dominant sense is the sense of smell. But since the wrong choice can be a turn-off, ask about favorites.

The Noah's Ark Test

There are countless tests for determining compatibility. Some are scientifically based, such as the Personality Style Quiz, based on personality styles, earlier in this chapter. Others are more playful, based more on common sense than on scientific research. These fun tests are a useful way to encourage openness between you and a date. For example, consider the following hypothetical situation:

Imagine the world has come to an end. There is one boat: Noah's Ark. You can take just one animal as your companion. Which of these animals would you choose: a horse, tiger, sheep, or peacock?

The horse symbolizes a career, the tiger symbolizes power, the sheep symbolizes love, and the peacock symbolizes pride. Following this, a person who chooses the horse might be most focused on their work, and might tend to put relationships on a back burner. Someone who chooses the tiger might need to exert a lot of control over your relationship. Be prepared to give the person who chooses the peacock a lot of attention, compliments, and flattery; and the one who chooses the sheep a lot of affection.

The Dating Game Quiz

TV shows such as "Love Connection," "The Dating Game," and MTV's "Singled Out" use simple questions and hypothetical situations to help couples find out whether they are well matched. Here are some questions like the ones from these shows to help you assess your styles and preferences, as well as your date's. If you're not sure about asking your current love interest to answer these questions, take an educated guess at his or her answers.

For each of these aspects, underline the one that you prefer and put a check mark over the one your current love interest prefers:

Characteristics:

➤ Brains: Einstein or beer stein?

➤ Body: slim and trim or muscle-bound?

➤ Height: delicate mouse or giant elephant?

➤ Facial hair: baby face or scratchy face?

➤ Sleep style: wrap-around or "Move over, baby"?

➤ Lifestyle: fireside chats or disco inferno?

➤ Dating style: one and only one or play the field?

➤ Hair color: dark fantasy or light and bright?

➤ Underwear: silk boxers or cotton briefs?

➤ Eating: raw veggies or raw meat?

➤ Experience: "Presumed Innocent" or "Basic Instinct"?

➤ Career goals: Wall Street or Easy Street?

➤ Commitment: stay free or landing pad?

Questions:

➤ Which is more important to you: looks or attitude?

➤ Vampires: romantic or blood-sucking freaks?

➤ Do you like Snoop Doggy Dogg or Snoopy the dog?

➤ Where would you prefer to go: Venice or Vegas?

➤ In the morning, sleep in or "rise and shine"?

➤ Do you consider the Internet a superhighway or superdrag?

➤ Do you find strip clubs sleazy or sexy?

➤ Magazines: save 'em or toss 'em out?

➤ Dress up every day or only on special occasions?

➤ Bungee-jumpers: daring or deranged?

➤ Wonder Bra: boon or bust?

➤ Socks with holes: wear 'em or throw 'em out?

➤ Lie to break a date or go out anyway?

➤ On a guy, ponytail or earring?

For these situations, write in what you or your date would say.

Situations:	You	Your Date

➤ I caught you with another guy, and now your head is in a guillotine. What would you say to get out of it?

➤ If you were a dessert, what would you be? (The guy who won the date on this one said "chocolate mousse.")

➤ You're on the "Oprah" show. What's the topic?

➤ I keep a secret diary. What would the entry read on the night I met you?

➤ What was your high school nickname and why?

➤ If you could be a famous cartoon character, who would you be and why?

➤ If you met me at a crowded club, what would you do to get my attention?

➤ It's Valentine's Day and you wrote me a love poem. Recite it.

➤ If you were an ad campaign, what would the slogan be?

Feel free to come up with your own questions to help stimulate conversation and display your creativity, as well as cue for specifics you want to know about your date.

What's Your Sign?

It's become humorous to ask someone the old 1970s line, "What's your sign?" But humor aside, there may be something to be learned from the 12 astrological types. Your star sign can give you specific tips on what appeals to you and your mate. Learning that there may be reasons why you and your date act in certain ways should enlighten you and in turn make you feel more in control. That sense of control heightens self-esteem. Keep in mind, however, that this method, like the Personality Style Quiz and the Dating Game Quiz, should be used only as a general guide to understanding each other and as a way to spark communication between you and your date, and not as the last word. The following descriptions were developed with the expert help of New York-based parapsychologist Gerri Leigh.

➤ *Aries (March 21-April 20).* These people are strong and always like to get their way. They have few sexual inhibitions, and like to dream up and play out their wildest fantasies. Because they love to be worshipped, tell them that they're great and show excitement during intimate encounters. They love self-expression, so talk things out to your heart's delight (good news for women who want a talking man). But be careful if you need attention, too, because Aries men and women can be selfish.

➤ *Taurus (April 21- May 21).* These people are similar to what Freud called "oral" characters—they like to be fed (either with real food or with love). Superficial dating doesn't cut it; they like the deep stuff. However, bulls tend to be possessive and want to "own" their mate, which can lead to jealousy and smothering. If they're controlling, intrusive, or jealous, try not to get angry; it's just their style. Sensualists at heart, win them with languorous kisses and by wining and dining. Nature lovers, they can be seduced with a walk in the woods or a fur bedspread.

➤ *Gemini (May 22-June 21).* These childlike, changeable folks may make you feel like you're in bed with two or even four people at the same time. So be fresh and youthful and play along with their fun. Try to role-play and plan lots of surprises. However, beware of love turning into a brother-sister relationship. Since they also tend to change their minds often, be sure to pick the right time to approach the subject of commitment.

➤ *Cancer (June 22-July 22).* These homebody romantics will eat out of your hand if you serve them homemade apple pie, and cuddle by the fire looking at old photographs. But beware—you'll have to be the one to light a fire under them if you want to party. Reminisce with them about how you loved them at first sight. Mother them and they'll never leave you for another partner. But since they tend to parent you one minute and want to be babied the next, be sure to set aside time to be lovers. Make those times cozy, with candlelit dinners and bubble baths.

➤ *Leo (July 23-August 23).* Like the lion in the "Wizard of Oz," Leos search for companions with heart and a lot of courage. Once smitten, they'll pursue you with a strong will and, if you allow them, rule over your life. Whimper, and Leos will roar loudly (crybabies turn them off). Pamper them and they'll purr like pussycats. Treat them like kings and you'll preside as the queen in return.

➤ *Virgo (August 24-September 23).* Since these people chronically analyze things, you're likely to accuse your Virgo of being too critical. But they can just as easily put you on a pedestal. Be confident that they'll care enough to please you and bring you to the peak of pleasure. Virgos are wholesome health enthusiasts. They like to be right and are very organized, planning every detail, so emphasize compromise and challenge them with the following question: "Is it really important to you that we do it your way?"

➤ *Libra (September 24-October 23).* The scales of justice symbolize the Librans' balancing act: they'll be inclined to do anything to keep the peace, including giving in. Their challenge is to stop vacillating and take the bull by the horns when it comes to love. They tend to express what they really feel, and are die-hard romanticists who appreciate beauty and dressing up. Make sure to spoil them as they would spoil you. Take them to the opera or serve them juice in a silver goblet, and watch love blossom.

➤ *Scorpio (October 24-November 22).* Wild, even kinky desire abounds in these passionate partners, who brandish sex as they do power and money. You won't hear "Sorry, no sex, I've got a headache" from them, and encounters could last all night. Try body-painting or washing each other's hair. Make homemade videos of your love. Tell them you have a "hunka hunka burning love" for them and watch them swoon.

➤ *Sagittarius (November 23-December 21).* Adventurers by nature, better take your Sagittarian on a weekend fling to some faraway place before he goes off alone. But you make the bookings (even for a hotel in town), since they're hard to pin down. Once they commit, though, they'll struggle to be loyal and settle down. How do you seduce a snob? With Dom Perignon champagne and eelskin attaches. Sags get turned on by high-priced tickets. Don't expect homestead living; their house can be in disarray, but they don't care because freedom and being on the go matter more.

➤ *Capricorn (December 22-January 20).* Like a goat holding steadfast on a mountain slope, Capricorn lovers stick to routine. They like simple and traditional styles, like a black dress with pearls. As partners they can seem boring, but don't nag or they'll become defensive and depressed. Let them learn on their own to be more spontaneous, and that love and sex do not just serve a practical purpose. Staunch idealists, they covet the "perfect" partner, but will soon settle for Clark Kent rather than endlessly seeking Superman.

➤ *Aquarius (January 21-February 19)*. These humanitarian folks are very sensitive to feelings. They can satisfy your desires, but expect you to do the same for them. If you don't call the next morning, or tell them how wonderful they are, they'll be hurt. Verbal intercourse is the way to their hearts. Turn their minds on and their bodies will follow. But as much as they thrive on intimacy, they're essentially gypsies or loners—friends to all, but owned by none. So don't expect a long-lasting commitment except on the deepest spiritual level, since these eccentric and enlightened souls will likely be off pursuing a million interests and saving the world.

➤ *Pisces (February 20-March 20)*. These slippery fishes are hard to catch. Blinded by Hollywood love scenes and idealism, they paint illusions over real lovers, and load them down with high expectations. They pursue until their love objects give in or until they find imperfections. You'll hear them say, "There's chemistry between us" or despair over "The mystery is gone," but they'll be drawn to you if you're the life of the party and boost their confidence.

I've met some people who uncannily fit these descriptions. But of course, even astrological profiles require consideration of much more extensive aspects (rising signs, moon signs, and many others). So treat these very simple sketches as fun, and if you're intrigued, explore the subject further with astrology books and consultations.

The Least You Need to Know

➤ Learning about your own (and your date's) love style can increase your chances of finding a compatible match.

➤ No personality type is inherently good or bad, desirable or undesirable. The challenge is to understand your own and your date's inclinations.

➤ Sometimes it's easier to win over a person if you approach them first in their love style.

➤ Even though quizzes or tests of your love style are not definitive, they can be a fun and informative way to learn about each other and to get you talking.

➤ Many tests and quizzes about personality and behavior—no matter how cursory— can give you valuable clues about you and your dates.

Chapter 11

Dating Disasters and Dilemmas

In This Chapter

➤ What to do when he doesn't call

➤ Breaking out of the dating daisy chain

➤ Dangerous liasons to look out for

➤ The ugly trio of feeling used, abused, and foolish

➤ Hit-and-run lover alert

➤ What to do with cheating

➤ Breaking out of abuse

It would be wonderful if all of dating was a smooth, happy road. Unfortunately, there are bound to be some bumps and possible painful collisions.

Through every dating horror, painful moment, and disappointment, always remember to maintain your self-esteem. Never do anything to compromise it or hurt yourself. Think of your most precious

Tip
Think of dating like the stock market; when the stock drops too far, it's time to bail out and cut your losses.

possessions: your car, your childhood teddy bear, your best suit. You wouldn't want these items to be stained, smashed, and least of all dragged through the mud. Now think of your heart. Handle it gently, even if others don't. If your dating disasters seem repetitive, strive towards less pain, quicker exits, and wiser choices.

Unmet Expectations

When dating, people inevitably make assumptions about what the other person feels or needs. These assumptions can lead to misunderstandings, resentment, guilt, and disappointment. You can prevent these feelings by keeping track of your realistic and *un*realistic expectations.

When Laura invited Dave to her best friend's wedding weekend activities, she was hoping to be with someone she could feel close to on such an intimate occasion. Overcome by the feeling of love in the air, Laura wanted Dave to hold her hand and look at her admiringly. Instead, Dave was chilly towards her. Dave later admitted that he had fallen for another girl the week before and assumed that Laura just needed an escort.

Laura's experience teaches us a few lessons:

Warning
Demands for loads of affection can become overbearing for your partner. Back off and give him or her a chance to willingly initiate love and tenderness.

Warning
It's dangerous to hook up with someone to try to change him. People can change, but only if they want to.

➤ Know the person better before you get into a situation that stimulates your expectations.

➤ Have no expectations, since whatever happens between two people is unpredictable, and since some people react poorly to demands. You get more if you're in "non-demand" mode.

➤ Be clear about the "deal"—what you both want out of the time together. Does he just want to have a good time? Is she looking for romance?

➤ Be honest about other relationships you each have. Ask "Have you met someone else?" If his or her mind, heart, and sexual energy are elsewhere, the relationship becomes confusing and possibly emotionally devastating.

➤ Be aware of your "love script"—the role you want the other person to play. Sometimes the person is either not aware or not interested in your plans, making the outcome upsetting for both of you.

The "Why Doesn't He Call?" Dilemma

It's a common and painful experience: "We had great sex and then I didn't hear from him." You end up feeling used and foolish. You also begin questioning yourself ("What's wrong with me?"), blaming yourself ("I should have been more loving or less demanding"), or resolving never to love again.

Instead of focusing on yourself as the problem, you should consider many other possible explanations. For example, she may be preoccupied with matters that have nothing to do with you. She could be a relationship-dysfunctional person: a user (who uses people for sex or otherwise and then discards them easily), a loner (who really doesn't relate to others or fails to follow through on plans), an immature person (who doesn't know common courtesy), or a non-committer (who can't keep up a relationship beyond a one-night stand). Or she may not view sex the same way you do (for you it might be connected to love, for her it's just sex).

Whatever the reason, you shouldn't obsess about it. Learn from the experience. If you feel used, then you gave much more than you received, and you need to make sure that you get your needs met, too.

The Dating Daisy Chain

Groucho Marx once joked, "I wouldn't want to belong to any club that wants me as a member." It's a common scenario: every girl James wants doesn't want him. But every girl who does want him, he doesn't want. I call this the "dating daisy chain." This scenario involves low self-esteem: thinking if someone wants you, he can't really have good taste, because deep down you know you're not worthy. It may also involve self-sabotage: you ensure that you never get what you say you want. Or a twisted love antennae: you're attracted to the wrong ones, the ones who don't want you. Face the truth—no matter what you say, you really don't want to find someone, because no one ever works out!

It's not uncommon to go through many relationships, repeating a pattern, until you finally realize what you're doing. Think of love as a tabula rasa—an empty canvas—where we choose the colors and make the shapes. Remember, you're the producer, director, and all the actors in your own love drama. What leading lady/man are you going to cast? What is the script? Are you in the dangerous "Fatal Attraction" or the more tender "An Affair to Remember"?

Tip
Look at every relationship as a mirror. If you're trying to change someone, you're really trying to change yourself through that person.

Always Going for the Unavailable and Unattainable

Kimberly: "I'm only attracted to men who have girlfriends or who are married. If they're single, I think there's something wrong with them."

This reveals a need for a challenge to prove you are desirable and attractive, competitiveness, low self-esteem, and a fear of true commitment. Both men and women get caught in this trap, going for someone who is clearly unavailable and unattainable.

Examine your fears of getting involved, your need to compete (perhaps traced back to childhood sibling rivalry or Freudian dynamics to win one parent from another), and your need to test your attractiveness by stealing someone else's partner. Take up more constructive challenges, like race car driving or rock-climbing.

Also, remember that people are on different wavelengths and have different needs. Peter, for example, thought his last girlfriend was "the one." But she told him she wanted to work on her career and didn't have time for him. If you find yourself in this same situation, it doesn't mean that you're wrong for that person—only that you're wrong for that person *at that time*. Remember, love (as unromantic as it sounds) has a lot to do with convergent needs—the two of you being in the same mental place at the same time.

Attracts Only When Already Taken

Heinz wants to know why women always seem to like him when he has a girlfriend, and avoid him when he's free. The answer is simple—some men and women act more confident and carefree when they're involved, so naturally they become more attractive. In contrast, when they're not dating someone, they feel insecure and desperate, exuding unpleasant vibes that repel others.

Living With Ghosts of the Past

We carry with us ghosts of past loves that infringe on current relationships. If you've been hurt before, you might anticipate being hurt again, or protect yourself against it by hurting someone else. April, for example, has stayed away from dating because three past relationships have failed and she doesn't want to get hurt again. Tom got hurt in the past, so now he acts badly toward women first, before they get a chance to hurt him. Healthy love requires entering each relationship fresh, without acting out past love scripts.

Nothing Ever Works Out

So many women and men feel they are losers in the dating game. They blame themselves for the fact that nothing works out. Even though I don't want you to be too hard on yourself, it can be helpful to take some responsibility.

Leslie: "I'm really bad at relationships. Guys always break up with me after one month. I'm tall and attractive and I have a strong personality, so maybe they get intimidated. What could be wrong?"

What you resist persists, and what you embrace evaporates. It's entirely possible that an attractive, strong person like Leslie intimidates others. If so, *play* with changing your behavior to see how it affects people drawn to you. Or stay the way you are and *enjoy* the dating scenarios you create.

Warning
Be cautious if an old lover calls to relive the past. Directly ask what her intentions are. She may simply be using you to fill an empty need.

Les Liaisons Dangereuses

Although the thought of having a dangerous liaison may seem adventurous and exciting, it may also be exactly that—dangerous. You and others may end up devastated and hurt. Watch out for these potential disasters:

➤ Flirts who try to catch you in their web and use and manipulate you for their own ego.

John: "I work with a woman who says she dreams about me kissing her. But she has a boyfriend. What should I do?"

Teases like her can be dangerous. She's playing a deadly game and John is the bait. Don't get caught up in this spiderweb. If you're drawn in, take note of your own vulnerability to getting attention.

Warning

Some people put their lovers through unreasonable tests and traps that end up backfiring on them. For example, Rosa put a note on her boyfriend's car as though it was from another woman (it said, "I look forward to seeing you"). When her boyfriend didn't mention it, Rosa decided he was untrustworthy—when in fact he assumed it was a mistake and didn't want to upset her. Rosa's test led to an unnecessary and unfair test of his devotion.

➤ Flirtations with associates, friends' partners, and boyfriends' or girlfriends' parents can be deadly.

Trish: "My friend's husband followed me into the bathroom at a party and we had a quick one. I have a hard time facing her now."

Examine your own apparent need to mix into a relationship or family (what went on in your childhood?). Learn to control your urges and to think of others and the consequences of your actions before seeking immediate gratification.

➤ Messy relationships in circles of friends should be avoided. Like Tom, who is attracted to his ex-girlfriend's sister, who is dating a friend of his. But Tom's ex wants to get back together with him. It's best to step out of the whole mess, since it's loaded with land mines of jealousies and competition.

➤ Dating several friends is playing with fire.

Theresa: "I'm dating three guys who are all friends. Is there anything wrong with this?"

Dating friends gives you a sense of power—that you can control others so much they'll sacrifice friendships for your attentions. Recognize your need for "ego food," and don't be surprised if one day *you're* the one left out in the cold.

➤ Dating several people at the same time can be stressful. Like for Rosanda: "I'm seeing two guys at the same time, but it's really complicated. How do I choose between the two?" Sometimes it's best *not* to choose. Enjoy your popularity. Give yourself permission! Say, "Look how desirable I am!" Appreciate the opportunity to see many suitors, to be able to sample many types of people and ultimately to decide who you really like being with more exclusively. Just don't lie or break agreements.

➤ An obsessive attachment to bad boys/bad girls can be deadly. Bridget can't get no-good guys out of her mind, even though she feels used by guys who have girlfriends and call her for late-night sex, or expect her to have sex with their friends. Dawn's ex-boyfriend had been verbally abusive, calling her names. He cheated on her and she cheated in return. Eventually she had to get a restraining order against him, and he was put in jail. "But I still love him," she cried, "and I want him back." Like moths attracted to a flame, Bridget and Dawn are in danger. If you fall into this category, you must examine how allowing yourself to be mistreated reflects your low self-esteem.

➤ The moth attracted to the flame is a dangerous scenario.

Roger: "My ex-wife made me feel worshipped, like I was the best, and then dumped me—several times. Then, this new woman did the same thing. I met her last weekend and I had that chemistry for her and fell in love. But she's a real party girl, always drunk and high on cocaine. I left her several messages to meet me somewhere, but she never called." Roger saw a pattern, but wasn't willing to stop it.

➤ Powerful people are dangerous. Many people may feel the urge to become rude and mean when hurt, and try to hurt others back. Mark was on that verge. "I was seeing this woman and brought her flowers and perfume, and then heard rumors that she's been cheating on me. What can I do to get her back?" Don't spread bad energy, punish others for the ill will of one person, or defend yourself by becoming belligerent and rude to all partners. Tune your love antennae better to draw nicer people to you.

➤ Michael dated a woman a few times. On one date he thought they were having a ball "car dancing" (dancing in the car at a stoplight). When he dropped her off, he started telling her how great he thought she was and what a great time he had, but he could see her eyes glazing over. Being an amateur cartoonist, he sent her a cartoon to ask her out for Valentine's Day, but she never called. "How can she blow me off like that?" he wondered.

People can have a good time, but that doesn't necessarily mean they're really into you. It seems outrageous, but even though you can laugh and talk and even be physically close, it doesn't imply a next time. Obviously, that person was enjoying him- or herself but was just not into you. It's sad, but something you have to realize and accept.

The Ugly Trio: Feeling Used, Abused, and Foolish

When you give your heart innocently and unselfishly, but then feel used, abused, or foolish, it's devastating—but a learning experience.

Brad was dating Nanette for nine months, and had just asked her to move in with him. When his phone bill came, he noticed calls to another state. Since the phone company claimed they were legitimately made from his phone, Brad called the number. A man answered, but when Brad asked for his girlfriend, she was there—with another live-in boyfriend.

Maria had been seeing Peter for six months. Since he was a struggling photographer and she was making good money as a TV producer, Maria paid for everything, including fancy restaurants, Broadway shows, and movie tickets. One night, at a party, Peter seemed to spend a great amount of time with a magazine publisher who came from a wealthy family. Maria dismissed it until months later, when Peter claimed that he was spending weekends with his sister (whom Maria didn't know he had), who was stricken with cancer. Later, a friend told her that she ran into him one weekend on the publisher's yacht.

Brad, Maria, and hundreds of others want to know, "How could this happen to me?" "How could I have been so blind?" Double-crossers do their dirty deeds to be in control, to have their cake and eat it too, and to have the security and freedom to find the best "deal." The double-crossed are lulled into false security; they deny the evidence and are temporarily blinded. It happens to the smartest of men and women when they have their guard down. Learn

Tip
Men and women can pack on the pounds easily when they're frustrated about dating. Food becomes a substitute for love. Instead of eating, do something else to make yourself feel better. Call up friends, start a hobby, get active.

to interview your partners more carefully and be sensitive to troublesome clues early on. Trust your instincts (Maria was puzzled to suddenly learn that Peter had a sister), and tune your love antennae for someone with more honesty and integrity.

Dumped for No Reason: The Hit-and-Run Lover

Tip

Singles often find holidays such as New Year's Eve and Valentine's Day stressful and depressing. To prevent any unhappiness, make plans with friends—it's better to be with those who care about you than to be alone or to take a risk on someone you're unsure about.

It's another common woe: "I was dating a guy for eight months. Things were going well, I thought, when all of a sudden he dumped me for no reason. Why did he do this?"

It is very painful to be pursued wildly but then summarily discarded, leaving you confused and frustrated. If this happens to you, you have a right to ask why. Your former love's answer will help you learn more about dating, people, and yourself. Something may have been missing for the other person. An imbalance in feelings while dating is all too common—and painful. It feels great when you are both in the same place, at the same level of interest. But it feels awful when one person cares more than the other. Learn a lesson from a date's quick exits. Obviously, he wasn't playing straight with you, or he would have given you more clues about wanting out. Be more alert to subtle cues that someone isn't committed.

Tip
Conscious Singles Connection has prepared a 40-minute audiotape to help singles lower their stress level and find positive ways to enjoy the holidays. They can be reached at (212) 873-7187 or (800) 337-4796.

Play fair and kind in the dating game by not being a hit-and-run lover, who, like a hit-and-run driver, leaves blood behind. Why have someone else's bleeding heart on your conscience? And remember, what goes around comes around. Keep your dating karma clean.

Skeletons in the Closet

Keeping secrets can be destructive for a relationship, but sharing them at the wrong time or when trust is not established can be even more devastating.

Tip

Most people keep memories of past loves: gifts, letters, cards, photos. People who save them have a need to remember their history or to be reassured of their past attractiveness. This is fine as long as these keepsakes aren't excuses or escapes from moving on.

Some people "freak out" when they discover a partner's keepsakes. Keep in mind that everyone is entitled to their personal belongings. If your partner's keepsakes upset you, examine your own insecurities: Are you jealous that you don't have similar memories or important past relationships? Is your current relationship fragile?

Secrets You Should Tell

Most of us have secrets we'd be afraid to tell others. Yet intimate sharing can be one of the strongest bonds between two people. For this reason, you must think carefully about sharing very private matters, to decide what impact it will have on your relationship.

Example 1:

Sandy: "I'm 28 and still a virgin. I don't want this man I'm dating to know. I'm embarrassed and I don't want him to think he's conquering me."

Some men *love* to know that they're someone's "first." Face your feelings (embarrassment, fear, worries about how you'll perform), and get over them. Instead of being embarrassed, you should be proud. Keep in mind that sex is not about power, or about a guy owning you. Sex is about two people sharing their bodies and souls with each other, but maintaining their own integrity of self.

Example 2:

Heather: "My boyfriend thinks I'm a hairstylist, but he doesn't know I'm also an escort. I've been saving money for a new car. Should I tell him the truth?"

Yes. If he finds out on his own he'll be furious that you kept such a big secret from him and will likely not trust you again. He may be titillated or threatened by your secret job, but he has a right to know in the interests of safe sex and overall honesty.

Secrets You Should Not Tell

Here are some secrets that men and women have been unsure whether they should tell.

Chrissie: "I live with a guy, but we haven't had sex in ages. So two or three times a week I sneak out of bed in the middle of the night while he's sleeping and go to his best friend's house. Should I tell him what's going on?"

131

Chad: "I got drunk at a party and ended up spending a lot of time with two girls. I love my girlfriend, but should I tell her?"

Brian: "My girlfriend gets me right to the edge of sex but then stops. She admitted to me that she's gone all the way with other guys, so why doesn't she with me?"

Before you would ever reveal a potentially harmful secret, consider the following:

➤ Examine your intentions. What do you want the other person to give you? If you want absolution from your guilt, work that out in church. If you want to hurt your date, examine why you are so bitter. Sometimes you want to be found out. Often when a mate is unaware, or denies, that you cheat, you end up resenting him for living in denial or not caring enough. For example, it's unlikely that Chrissie's boyfriend doesn't suspect that something's going on.

➤ Consider other ways to get what you want. If you need more love, attention, or sex, ask for it directly. For example, Brian might get his girlfriend to have sex with him if he stops pestering and criticizing her, and if he helps her discuss her fears about love, sex, and any past bad experiences.

➤ Anticipate the impact such a confession will have on the other person. Be considerate. Sharing some sensitive past sexual experiences may make your present partner obsess endlessly about it. When Jake told Alice about his exciting past with an uninhibited woman, Alice couldn't stop counting her orgasms with him and feeling she came up short.

Confronted With Cheaters—Changing Them or Changing Yourself

I get heartsick from hearing so many stories like "My boyfriend cheats on me and lies, but I still love him." How can you love someone who treats you so poorly? *That* is a sure sign of low self-esteem and a lack of understanding of what love is. And when you do discover that a lover has cheated, anger, depression, and distrust will run rampant. Accept these feelings as normal, clarify your relationship, and decide whether you can come to a new agreement about fidelity or whether you should break up. Avoid cheating and guilt by not making agreements about fidelity that you can't keep. Allow yourself to rebuild trust without wallowing in disappointment or generalizing that all men or women are rotten and deceitful.

Tip

One way to get over the desire for continually new partners when you're in a committed relationship is to always treat each other like new lovers. Often, couples start out dating by putting their best foot forward, trying to impress one another, and then fall into a rut, taking each other for granted. Keep asking each other questions that you would on a new date: What did you do today? Have you seen any good movies lately? What's your favorite food?

Eve and the Apple of Temptation

Think before you act. Consider the consequences of any sexual encounter. Angela had been seeing Frank for two years when he proposed. They had become best friends, but the sex was not there anymore. Meanwhile, Angela's old boyfriend has come back on the scene. With him, the sex was hot and Angela wants to taste it one more time before she marries. But it would be far wiser for her to take that passion and re-ignite what she has with Frank.

Early Promises

Greg's story is typical. "I'm going away to college and I told my girlfriend I would be true to her, but I know I'm going to get there and there will be lots of other women. What should I do?"

Some people pledge fidelity even when they know it will be difficult because they don't want to lose their "steady," even if they want to be free to date others. In other words, they want to have their cake and eat it too.

Rather than break an agreement, it is wiser to be honest. Your partner may be relieved and might also want some freedom. If not, it's better to deal with disappointment up front, and clarify your relationship, rather than cheat and face betrayal and hurt. If your relationship is genuine, you won't need to *act* faithful, whether you're two states or two streets apart. Forcing someone to promise faithfulness doesn't make them genuinely feel it. And making an "exclusivity contract" before you're ready can make you feel resentful, frustrated, and suffocated. Agree to see others without telling about your other liaisons, unless one becomes significant enough to change your relationship. You could be so upset by the thought of your lover seeing other people that you genuinely want to make more of a commitment to each other.

Snooping

It's understandable to want to confirm your suspicions of a partner's infidelity. Snooping can be irresistible. Amanda dug around in her boyfriend's closet and found a book of letters, including one from a girl that said, "I don't care about Amanda's feelings, what happened between us was great and we can't fight it." Steve read his girlfriend's diary and found entries about her fantasies about other guys he knows. MaryBeth's boyfriend said he was going away on a business trip, but when she listened to his answering machine she heard his ex's voice saying, "All is okay. I'll see you at the appointed place."

Short of hiring a private detective, you can use your own ingenuity to get at the truth, from checking phone bills to credit card receipts. When Lauren spied on her boyfriend, Jack, she found him kissing one of her friends. She then started carrying around a camera, and the next time she saw them together, she snapped a picture of them and had it enlarged. She confronted Jack, and after he lied about the incident, she whipped out the telling photo.

Indeed, Lauren expended an awful lot of energy being sneaky rather than just confronting Jack with what she saw. In general, when you suspect or discover infidelity, don't be afraid to confront your partner directly—however you choose to. But be ready for denials and even lies. In that case, you may have to be a little more creative, as Lauren was. Gathering evidence and direct confrontations can help restore the badly damaged self-esteem that results from feeling fooled.

Long-Distance Love

"Out of sight, out of mind"—is it true? Or does absence make the heart grow fonder and distance lend enchantment? Many men and women ask me if long-distance romances can

Tip
If your long-distance love doesn't want to give you the freedom you want, you may have to give it to yourself. If you lose your long-distance love in the process, the relationship wasn't solid enough to last.

work. They can, if you keep sharing (by phone, fax, letters, cards), plan reunions in enough time to satisfy both your needs for closeness, and keep clarifying your commitment status. But "out of sight" can lead to "out of mind" if the time intervals are longer than your tolerance and need for closeness, if you neglect reassuring each other, and if you develop too-separate lives, interests, and relationships. When Ricky had to move to another state for work and asked his girlfriend to come with him, she refused—not wanting to leave her job and family—and the relationship was doomed. Clearly, being with him was not as important to her as the other anchors in her life. Ricky needed to give her an ultimatum to join him, or to let her go.

Abuse—Stop It Before It Begins

When dating someone, it's important to pay close attention to how you're being treated. If you're being treated poorly in the dating stage, it won't get better—and will likely get *worse* if you continue the relationship. Don't stand for any abuse, whether it's physical, sexual, or psychological. Also, note how past abusive experiences (date rape, harassment, incest) affect your current relationship in terms of being hesitant to trust and to commit.

Essentials

Surveys show that one in four women, and up to one in seven men, have been abused at some point in their past. A research study on my radio show "LovePhones" revealed that over a third of my callers admitted to some kind of abuse while dating.

Tip

Here are some general guidelines to bear in mind to keep you from being trapped in an abusive relationship:

➤ No one deserves to be abused.

➤ No one has the right to touch you or demand sex from you.

➤ You're not to blame for being abused.

➤ Men as well as women can be abused.

➤ Protect yourself from abuse by being assertive, avoiding dangerous situations, and avoiding alcohol and drug use.

➤ If you have been abused in the past, share that experience with a mate who has proven to be trustworthy.

➤ Report any abuse to authorities.

How Do You Know if You're in an Abusive Relationship?

Many times when you are abused, you really do care for the person, especially when they act kindly or lovingly in spells. You might even tend to deny that you are in an abusive relationship. The following can help you recognize the signs of a destructive union:

➤ If you are being put down/criticized/controlled

➤ If you are ever shoved, pushed, or slapped

135

➤ If you are ever forced to do anything despite saying "no"

➤ If your partner apologizes for treating you poorly but does it again

➤ If you wish you could get out of the relationship but feel trapped

➤ If you have a history of similar relationships

Tip

Avoid destructive and dangerous power relationships involving sexual favors. If you are threatened with sexual harassment, tell the person his approaches and demands are unacceptable—and illegal. Contact the Human Resources department where you work, school officials, or the National Association of Working Women, 614 Superior Ave. NW, Cleveland, Ohio 44113 (216) 566-9308.

Essentials

Most rapes occur by people who are known to the victim rather than by strangers. A 1991 study prepared by the National Victims Center reports that more than 12 million women have been raped, with 57 percent of the younger women victimized on a date. Prevent date rape by avoiding situations that could lead to danger (like drinking too much at wild parties), dispelling harmful sex-role stereotypes (that girls owe boys sex, or that sexually active girls ask for or deserve date rape), and communicating clear sexual intentions.

Why People Stay in Abusive Relationships

Despite the pain of abuse, some women and men choose to stay in abusive relationships, clinging to excuses such as the following:

➤ *"He was my first."* People often get addicted to their first love or to the first person they had sex with. They want desperately to believe in the fantasy of a beautiful first love, and are unwilling to face the reality that it has turned ugly.

➤ *"We've been together so many years already."* Granted, it's hard to turn your back on years with someone, but think of it as an investment. When you've sunk money into a stock that keeps going down, there comes a time when you have to cut your losses and sell, instead of hoping and praying that some miracle will happen.

➤ *"I know it can change."* People addicted to bad relationships (called "co-dependents") have a problem themselves if they are willing to sacrifice their own happiness and life in order to save an abusive or addicted partner. If you suffer from this sad syndrome, you need to concentrate on saving *yourself*.

➤ *"I'm afraid to lose him."* Think about losing your self-esteem instead and convince yourself there will be someone else who will love you in a healthier way.

➤ *"If I leave, he'll kill me."* When your safety is threatened, you had better get out. True love does not mean being controlled by another person or living in a prison of fear.

Warning

More people are aware of abuse when it involves physical blows or forced sexual acts, but not when it erodes self-confidence and self-esteem. But psychological abuse can be just as damaging and even more difficult to recognize, because it can be subtle at first. For instance, Pam was dating Patrick for seven months. In the beginning he would just butt in whenever she spoke, and criticize and contradict her. But over time, his behavior became nastier—telling her to shut up in front of people and calling her stupid when she voiced an opinion. Eventually he began calling her derogatory names. As Pam learned, even though psychological abuse evolves slowly and subtly, it does evolve and is just as damaging as physical abuse.

Getting Out of an Abusive Relationship

Ending abuse is a sign of self-esteem. It requires self-esteem to say "I will not put up with this" and "I deserve better." But it can be very difficult to get out of an abusive relationship when you have limited financial, social, or emotional resources, or really care about the person. You can help yourself break free of an abusive relationship by doing the following:

➤ Recognize that the abuser has a serious problem, requiring professional help.

➤ Realize that you have a choice.

➤ Do not believe threats that you are undesirable or unworthy.

➤ Face the ghosts from your past and separate these from your present.

137

➤ Repair your self-esteem. Practice affirmations: "I will only be spoken to in loving terms," "I deserve to be treated well."

➤ Take responsibility for your choices. Ask yourself "Why do I allow this person in my life script?" "What do I need to teach myself?" Remember, the people we are attracted to reflect something about ourselves.

➤ Tune your love antennae only for those who will treat you well. Take inspiration from Grammy-winning singer/songwriter Alanis Morrisette, who told me that after years of being treated poorly by a man, she can now tell within 15 seconds of meeting someone whether that person will treat her well or not. While it is not always possible to spot an abuser right away, since most people are on their best behavior at the start of a relationship and others become abusive when they drink, you do have to learn to develop the skill of observing people as much as possible to determine their potential for abuse.

➤ Stop making excuses for the person who is treating you badly and for yourself for staying in the relationship. Sympathy is sweet, but self-destruction is stupid.

➤ Realize you help the other person by refusing to be abused. Only when you stop putting up with the abuse does the abuser have a chance to get help.

➤ Get support from family and friends and professional help to turn powerlessness into empowerment, and to turn being a victim into being a survivor.

➤ Consider legal action to bring the abuser to justice and to further restore a sense of personal power.

The Least You Need to Know

➤ Resist making assumptions about other people's feelings or needs.

➤ Always maintain your self-esteem, no matter how bad the date was, or how badly you feel.

➤ Examine your dating patterns carefully—they may reveal a great deal about your own personality.

➤ Think twice before having a dangerous liaison. It may be disastrous to both you and others.

➤ Before you tell a secret, evaluate your intentions.

➤ If you were cheated on, allow yourself to rebuild trust in someone else.

➤ Stop any kind of abuse—remember, it won't get better!

Part 3
Making a Match

The search for love should be fun and bring you happiness. If you are suffering in your search, there may be something wrong with your approach. In this section, you learn about communication, commitment, and the differences between the ways that men and women approach love.

Remember my advice: don't play games. Contrary to what others may say about keeping the "mystery" alive, I advise you to be yourself. Putting up a mysterious front is a temporary ruse and a waste of time and energy. If you want someone who is going to appreciate you over the long haul, give them the opportunity to know the real you right from the start.

My ultimate goal is to help you to love yourself and be yourself. Be who you are, do what you like, and people will flock to you!

Chapter 12

Essential Communication

In This Chapter

➤ A quiz to determine your communication type

➤ Is your mate a good communicator?

➤ What to do if he won't talk

➤ What to share and what *not* to share

➤ Communication do's and don'ts

➤ How to read his mind

In a roomful of potential mates, who's the one you'd feel most comfortable with? Likely it's the one who seems "on your wavelength"—someone you can talk to. Good communication is the key to a good relationship. Whether you're the silent type or a talker, you have to feel that you can relate to and are understood by your partner—that you "speak the same language."

However, people do have different styles of communication. If you date someone whose style is different from yours, it is possible to adapt—as long as you know your own style, and what you're adapting to!

Communication Quiz

What kind of communicator are you? Find out your communication type by taking the following short quiz:

---

1. You've just had a big fight with your friend when your mate calls. He tells you that he has just lost his job. You:

   a) Tell him all the details about the argument you had with your friend first.

   b) Warn him that you're upset, but then drop it to listen to him.

   c) Listen and pretend nothing happened to you.

2. You've been dating for a while and have a minor disagreement that you feel could erupt into your first big fight. You:

   a) Need to blow your stack and say everything that's on your mind.

   b) Don't want to talk about it until you both cool down.

   c) Want to forget about the disagreement completely because you feel there's no point in talking about it.

If you selected answer a) to both situations, you have the need to spill out your feelings—no matter what. I label these kinds of people as *Niagara Falls* communicators—people who need to pour out their emotions in order to relieve their tension.

Niagara Fallers clash with *Boulder Dam* communicators—those who answered both situations with choice c). These people don't like facing and revealing their emotions, either because they're too frightened of their feelings or because they feel it's a waste of time. They usually have problems being intimate because they don't want anyone or any feelings to get the better of them.

Though they are opposites, Niagara Falls and Boulder Dam communicators may be drawn to each other. Boulder Dammers look to Niagara Fallers to unleash or vicariously express their feelings, and Niagara Fallers look to Boulder Dammers to help them control their troublesome outbursts. But ultimately, a match between these two types can lead to unhappiness, as the Dammers get too uncomfortable and the Niagara Fallers get too frustrated.

Steamship communicators, those who answered b), are sturdy communicators who aim to be reasonable. They hold a steady course so that they are never running the rapids of uncontrolled Niagara Fallers, but are also never stagnated like the Boulder Dammers. Because they have a little of the two extremes, they can get along with either type of communicator.

Two Boulder Dammers and two Steamships usually get along easier with each other than two Niagara Fallers. This is because Niagara Fallers often blow up easily, leading to fights with no one there to referee.

Talkers Versus Silent Types—Which Is Better?

"When my boyfriend and I fight, is it better to talk it out right away, or talk about it later when we both cool down?"

The answer to this question depends on your communication styles and how you both deal with anxiety. A person's communication style is determined partly by anxiety management. Some people need to get their feelings out and have an argument resolved right away, or their tension grows. As soon as these types of people have let off some steam, they feel relieved and more connected, and their anxiety is reduced. For others, talking about something right away is what makes their tension grow, so they need a cooling-off period before they can communicate. Neither style is right or wrong, it's just a matter of understanding what works for you and your partner. Then you can adjust and accept each other's way.

When He Doesn't Talk

It's the biggest complaint women have about men: they don't talk about their feelings. The good news is that men are making progress in this category. The bad news is that men still have a long way to go. Women tend to interpret a man's silence as deadly. Often they ask, "What are you thinking?" when they really want reassurance: "I'm thinking of you." Rather than saying, "You never talk to me," it's better to say to your male partner, "I'd really like to talk about (something specific)" because men respond better to specifics.

Essentials

Women and men are conditioned at a very young age on how they should communicate. From childhood, tradition still reigns, where girls are taught to openly express their feelings while boys are taught to hold in their emotions. Girls tend to spend hours on the phone talking to their girlfriends about their problems while boys are taught to solve their problems on their own. And, unfortunately, some people today still perceive emotional men as being "weak."

143

"My boyfriend is afraid to express his feelings and has a hard time admitting them. What should I do?"

Be gentle, kind, patient, and reassuring. Some people are scared to reveal their feelings. It makes them feel vulnerable, exposed, and out of control. Reward your mate when he does make an effort to express himself by saying "Thank you. I love when you say how you feel." Or, "I know that was difficult for you to say, but thank you for doing it." Or ask him about his experience in a reassuring way: "Now that you've said that, how do you feel about it? You may have expected some disaster or that you would be hurt. But, see, nothing like that happened."

"My boyfriend has a hard time expressing his feelings. But he did admit that he's scared to because he was hurt once before. What can I do to make him less frightened?"

First of all, appreciate the effort it took for him to tell you he's scared, and that he was hurt before. Those are two huge confessions and show a tremendous effort to open up.

Reassure him that everyone has been hurt and that being with you will not mean a repeat of the past. Tell him that he can recover slowly by building up his trust again. You can even agree on a label for his feeling—for example, call it the "fear factor." Make it humorous. Every time he feels it, have him alert you. Then both of you can turn it into something funny: "Oh, the fear factor is rearing its ugly head again."

"My boyfriend sends out mixed signals about whether he really wants to be with me. When I've confronted him, he's withdrawn. I'm afraid if I confront him again, he'll get tired of me and really break it off."

It's one thing to be a different kind of communicator from your mate, it's another if you feel threatened by trying to communicate. Don't suffer from anxiety. If you need an answer to a question—get the answer! If you push and he ends your relationship, what kind of future would you really have with that type of communicator anyway?

Keep in mind that these communication issues don't apply just to men. Interestingly enough, I hear more men these days complaining about the same issues in their relationships with women. One reason is that as women become more independent in their financial, social, and sexual roles, some have taken on more of the traditionally male ways of communicating.

Is Your Mate a Good Communicator?

Take the following quiz to discover how well your mate communicates with you.

Picture the following scenarios:

1. You tell the man you're dating that you're scared to get involved because you once had a bad experience where you got really hurt. He:

   a) Changes the subject, figuring it's too hurtful for you to talk about and he's really not interested anyway.

   b) Turns the table around and talks about his dating experiences.

   c) Asks you what happened.

   If he changes the subject, a), you should find out why. Is it because such openness makes him uncomfortable or because he isn't interested (both are bad signs)? Is he afraid you'll be too hurt to discuss the subject (a better reason but still an avoidance of your feelings)? If he always turns the conversation to his experiences, b), he's too self-centered to care about you. The best answer is c), because your mate shows that he has *empathy*. The mates who ask questions and say, "Tell me more," care about finding out about the real you and are able to show it.

2. You tell the man you're dating that a friend of yours is miserable because she was dumped by her boyfriend a few weeks ago and you're still upset for her. You then mention her name a few times in the next conversation you have with him. He:

   a) Says he doesn't remember what you said about her before.

   b) Asks you who she is.

   c) Asks you whether you want to ask her to join you the next time you go out.

   Remembering what someone told you and doing something about it is a sign of a good communicator and shows the person really cares about you, as in choice c). However, choices a) and b) may show that the person either doesn't concentrate on what you say, or isn't interested enough.

3. You call your girlfriend on the phone and she's on the other line with another friend. She:

   a) Asks you to call her back later.

   b) Puts you on hold and comes back much later to your line.

   c) Gets off the other line to talk to you.

Placing priority on the relationship and making the other person feel important is a sure sign of good communication and caring. There's nothing more exciting than thinking that you come first, no matter what. Answers a) and b) are not unacceptable, but a c) answer raises your self-esteem and strengthens your bond together.

4. You tell the woman you're dating that you were hurt by something she did. She:

   a) Tells you that you're too sensitive.

   b) Denies that she did anything wrong.

   c) Apologizes and asks what she did to hurt you.

   Defensiveness, as in answer a), and denial, as in answer b), shut down communication and sabotage closeness and openness. Someone who can accept your feelings and examine their own behavior, as in answer c), is the best choice.

Tip

Paying attention and noticing details are also parts of good communication skills. It's a tremendous high to feel "heard" by someone. For example, while Andy and Alissa were riding in the car, Alissa noted her favorite song playing on the radio. The next day, Andy surprised her with the CD containing that song.

5. You tell your partner that you would like to spend more time with him. He says:

   a) "We already spend a lot of time together."

   b) "Just like all women—it's never enough."

   c) "Okay, but why? Do you feel like we're not close enough?"

   Pointing out whether someone is right or wrong, as in answer a), doesn't get to the heart of the matter. Generalizing, as in b), further negates the person's feelings. Choice c) shows that the person is not being defensive, but rather is truly open to what is really troubling you.

Tip

One way to show a person that you've been listening carefully is to repeat what the other person said. For example, if your mate just said "I'd like us to be closer," you say, "So you want to be closer." Then follow it up with a question like "Tell me more about what you mean by that."

---

6. You're trying to tell your boyfriend how you feel about something he said. He:

   a) Gets impatient because you're not spitting it out fast enough.

   b) Asks you what you mean.

   c) Finishes your thought for you.

Intuition, as in c), is another high state of communication. People really in synch with each other can anticipate each other's thoughts and can finish each other's statements. It's an exciting and affirming experience—but not one you should expect. Nor should you think that if someone cannot do that with you, he doesn't love you. Answer b) shows that the person is patient and is trying to understand you—a good sign, and certainly better than answer a), which shuts you up and shuts you out.

Mind-Reading

When two people are in sync, they can often tell what the other is thinking and feeling. But reading each other's mind is not always possible, nor does it mean you're not right for each other.

"What are you supposed to do when a woman wants you to automatically know everything she's thinking, and then gets angry when you don't?"

You tell her that if she cares about you, she should share her feelings with you and not play mind games. She needs to be more open and assertive when expressing her thoughts and feelings, without expecting you to always know her needs.

If you are the silent one, why are you afraid to say what's on your mind? Are you afraid that you'll be judged, sound silly, or be misunderstood? Are there feelings or memories you don't want to face? Or are you afraid of getting hurt if you open up?

On a piece of paper, write down some thoughts or experiences you'd love to—but fear to—share. Writing them down is an important step to clarifying the experience, feeling the fear, and possibly sharing the feeling.

Some people were indulged by their parents when they were children. Their parents anticipated their every need and made sure to meet each of them. Consequently, as adults, they expect their lover to do the same. Unfortunately, they are quick to lose patience with their mates who are not intuitive to their feelings. These people need to learn to be patient, accept that their lovers are not their parents, and learn how to communicate directly without resentment to others.

Although you may think you're terrible at "reading" people, you're probably better at it than you think. I use an exercise in my classes to prove that everyone is capable of being intuitive.

Find two other people to do this exercise with you. Person A thinks of a situation and assumes a body position consistent with the experience. Person B mimics the body position of Person A and concentrates on what that feels like, and reports on what Person A must be thinking. Person C monitors and adjusts Person B's position to match Person A's position as closely as possible. It's uncanny how often Person B is right in reporting what Person A is thinking.

The exercise proves that concentrating on the other person's emotions and getting into his or her mental as well as physical "space" can help you tune in to others (since a large proportion of the messages of what someone means is communicated through body language).

How Much Should You Share?

Some books tell readers to "hold back" on some of their feelings and not to give away everything. As you've probably noted from my advice throughout this book, I don't agree with this type of game-playing. If you feel that you have to resist being yourself, the relationship is not right for you. A good relationship is one where you feel you can ask your partner anything, and one where you can say or do almost anything.

But there *are* certain limits to what you should share:

➤ Don't talk about past loves unless you are perfectly sure that your date won't feel jealous or threatened. Evaluate why you are discussing the past (are you trying to foster jealousy or boost your own ego?).

➤ Don't confess to something in order to selfishly get over your own guilt. For instance, suppose you want to tell your date that you weren't really busy at work, but instead had a date with someone else. Always assess what the impact of such confessions would be on the person you're seeing. Of course, you should have thought about the betrayal before you did it. But once the damage is done, why throw salt on an open wound? Put the shoe on the other foot. How would you like to know someone lied to you? You'd be distrustful of him and others. Learn to forgive yourself. If you want to have a clear conscience, go to church. Don't expect a hurt person to absolve you and make you feel better.

Handling Some Touchy Situations

Even the touchiest situations can be dealt with if you know how to communicate effectively. Here are two examples:

"How do I tell my boyfriend that he's cheap?"

Have a general discussion about money and what it means to both of you. Consider using an ice-breaker so that he's not put on the defensive. Ask him to explain his fears about money. What did he learn in childhood about handling money (he could be copying his father)? Money can also be symbolic of a person's security, so discuss those deeper feelings.

"How do I tell my girlfriend, who has been under a lot of stress lately, that she's put on weight as a result of using food as a stress-reliever?"

Losing weight involves changing your lifestyle, exploring your emotional needs, and adopting an eating and exercise plan. You may suggest to your girlfriend that she's using food as a way to relax or to comfort herself, and that you'd like to help her find other solutions. Offer support and reassure her that you love her for who she is, not for what she looks like. Suggest that you exercise and eat more healthily together. Never drop hints about how heavy she looks; it will only damage her self-esteem.

Tip

When pointing out something you don't like about a date, it's important to say what you *do* like first. Be careful not to criticize your date; criticisms only make people defensive and deflated. When the brain creates a positive image, positive behavior can follow.

Guidelines for Good Communication

There is no one right or wrong way to talk and express yourself. Learn to trust yourself and your style first. Any attempt at communicating will be appreciated and is a step in the right direction. Here are a few points to keep in mind:

➤ Talking is an ongoing process. You can't always cover a topic all in one conversation. If that's the case, end the conversation with: "We can continue this at another time."

➤ When expressing yourself, be as honest and straightforward as you can without beating around the bush. Get to the point and be clear about what you want to say or ask.

Tip

When asking a question or putting in a request, your best chance of getting what you want is to ask without expectations or demands (called "nondemand" requests). Simply state what you'd like without implying punishment or guilt-inducing feelings. This way the other person is free to give willingly or refuse without being defensive.

➤ Be open to questions. Give permission to your date to ask you anything.

➤ Be a good listener. Learn to listen without interpreting.

➤ It's okay to be embarrassed. Some topics are scary to discuss. Admit that you feel this way.

➤ Say up front what you think your boyfriend or girlfriend might fear when trying to discuss a topic. Preface the discussion by saying something like, "I don't want you to be hurt" or "I don't want this to scare you."

➤ Practice talking about difficult things: "I'm hurt by what you did."

➤ Not knowing what to say is okay, but you can always come up with some explanation or answer. Nothing is more frustrating in a conversation than to hear a person say "I don't know," or worse, say nothing at all. You can say "I'm not sure why this happened, but it could be because…" Or you can ask what the other person thinks or feels.

➤ Don't run away from a conversation. Talking is not always easy. Don't let your anxiety get the best of you. If you have something to say, say it.

➤ Know what's motivating and affecting you. Getting to the bottom of an issue is like peeling the layers of an onion. Talk is often a smokescreen for something else. What is your real need (to be loved, to be listened to, to be reassured)?

Communicating Do's and Don'ts

Words can be reassuring by easing your mate's fears, and can be alluring by promising pleasures to come. In order to get to these benefits, keep in mind the following helpful guidelines:

➤ DO relax. Anxiety ruins your concentration and confidence. Take deep breaths every time you feel like ending a conversation out of fear.

➤ DO listen to your mate.

➤ DO be prepared for repetition. If the issue comes up again and again, it hasn't been resolved. Instead of complaining that your date is nagging, ask "What is really going on here? Why is the subject still bothering you?"

➤ DO be patient. Give the person time to express himself.

➤ DO admit that both of you have differences, which are okay.

➤ DO expect to feel uncomfortable. It's not always easy to confront issues.

➤ DON'T think you have to solve everything at one time.

➤ DON'T put your date down with vulgar terms and expressions. It's disrespectful and cheapens not only your date but yourself as well.

➤ DON'T criticize, judge, or make fun of what your date has to say. You both have to feel comfortable sharing.

The key to having good and open communication with someone is to make him or her feel secure, loved, and respected. Speaking your mind and sharing feelings creates a bond that's sure to deepen your relationship. Doing this in a mutually respectful way also raises your self-esteem—and your partner's.

The Least You Need to Know

➤ Good communication is the key to a good relationship. It requires attention, acceptance, and appreciation.

➤ Understand and appreciate other people's communication styles.

➤ You can get non-talkers to communicate more by offering a lot of encouragement and appreciation for when they do open up.

➤ Always be respectful, open, and honest, and give sharing your best effort.

Chapter 13

Men and Women: What's the Difference?

In This Chapter

➤ Sex role stereotypes

➤ Why men and women talk and love differently

➤ Left-brain versus right-brain approaches to life

➤ The new gender war

➤ Exercises for breaking sex stereotypes

Best-selling author and psychologist John Gray has summed up the differences between the sexes with this catchy metaphor: Men are from Mars and women from Venus.

Eastern philosophy has always acknowledged those differences between the sexes. The Chinese "yin-yang" symbol shown below depicts the masculine (active, positive) and feminine (passive, negative) aspects of nature as two contrasting, but complementary, parts of a circle. Their interaction is essential to maintaining harmony and balance in the universe.

So if interaction is essential to harmony, why do men and women seem to clash and miscommunicate so frequently? In this chapter, you'll see why men and women express themselves so differently, and what you can do to help prevent or ease the friction that sometimes arises in your own relationship.

Left-Brain Versus Right-Brain Approaches to Life

Essentials

The Virginia Slims Opinion Polls taken over the past quarter century indicate that certain sex role stereotypes persist. Women comment that men would rather get lost than stop and ask for directions; are bad cooks; monopolize the remote control; and can't find things around the house without a woman's help. Marlo Thomas once joked that hubby Phil Donahue always asks her where his shoes are, "as if my womb had sonar for his shoes and socks."

It's easy to make gender generalizations: men are stubborn, women clingy. Men love violent movies, women prefer romantic comedies. But are there any facts to back up these contentions, or do most of us simply fall back on cultural clichés? In fact, there *is* a lot of scientific information to help us understand what most of us sense already—that men and women communicate differently!

Research at the Ned Herrmann Group, with whom I've been associated for many years, suggests that most men are more predominantly left-brained, with their cognitive style being more logical (they tend to focus on problems and solutions). Women, on the other hand, tend to be more right-brained, with more of an emphasis on communication and emotion. This left- or right-brain dominance affects all kinds of everyday interactions and exchanges. The following table describes many of the ways in which right- or left-brain characteristics can show up in everyday life.

How Differences in Brain Dominance Affect Behavior

Left Brain	Right Brain
Values power, being in control	Values love and communication
Is motivated by being right	Is motivated by togetherness and harmony
Needs approval and acceptance	Needs appreciation and attention
Fulfilled by achieving goals	Fulfilled by expression and relating

Left Brain	Right Brain
Hates being told what to do	Accepts direction
More interested in news and sports	More interested in romance novels and self-help
Relates well to objects and things	Relates well to people
Likes to prove things	Likes to improve things
Comfortable with gadgets and hi-tech	Comfortable with gab groups

Brain differences help explain why many men won't ask for directions (he needs to be right), and why many women get upset when men want them to get off the phone too quickly (she needs to gab). Women like to improve things, and will offer to help their mates without being asked (as a sign of love). But men need to prove themselves, so they may interpret a woman's offer of help as an implied criticism (he's just not good enough). It's easy to see how differences in brain dominance can lead to breakdowns in communication!

Communication Styles

Men and women also have different *styles* of communicating. I've summarized the differences in the following table, based on my own experience as well as on the research of psychologist John Gray and linguist Deborah Tannen, author of the best-selling book *You Just Don't Understand*. Keep in mind that these are generalizations. In the past 20 years or so, many men and women have come to see that it is important to "own" both "masculine" and "feminine" parts of themselves. Many men have tried to become more sensitive, while women have made strides in becoming more assertive and independent. Yet certain differences persist, and it's helpful to see how these differences play a part in the dating and mating world. Use these observations as guidelines to expand your possibilities: if one column describes you, consider the usefulness of the other.

Essentials

What do most women list as their top complaint about men? According to my own and numerous other surveys, one of women's biggest complaints about men is that they are unable to talk about their feelings!

How Men and Women Communicate Differently

What He Does...	What She Does...
Speaks to make a point	Speaks to share feelings
Says "I"	Says "we"
Interrupts	Invites others to speak
Takes credit when things go right and blames others when things go wrong	Gives others credit and takes blame on self
Talks about facts	Talks about feelings

Differences in communication styles between the sexes are perhaps most apparent when it comes to problem-solving. When a problem comes up, there are three basic factors or steps in discussing it: the problem, the feelings about it, and the solution. Men tend to skip step two, while women tend to dwell on step two.

For instance, let's say a couple is having a conflict with punctuality—he's kept his date waiting enough times that the subject has become an "issue." She says, "It really hurts me when you keep me waiting. It makes me feel that my time doesn't mean anything to you. And when you don't call, I feel even worse." He responds with, "You've got to understand that my boss is forever dumping last-minute projects on my desk that I can't ignore." To which she responds, "How hard is it to pick up the phone? You never even bother to call." And his response, "Look at my cellular phone bill. You'll see otherwise!"

In this instance, the man is using the fact of his workload as a legitimate excuse for his tardiness. The woman, on the other hand, may accept the fact that he is overworked, but still puts an emotional spin on it. In her view, if he cared enough about her, he'd get there on time. The fact that he doesn't means that he doesn't care.

It would be easy for the discussion to stalemate right here. His next response might go something like this: "You're being ridiculous. I was swamped, and the time got away from me. Don't cast me as the bad one just because I want to get ahead." You can imagine the downward spiral from here.

Both parties need to step back and follow my three A's: acceptance, appreciation, and adjustment. He needs to acknowledge her hurt and disappointment, and get to the bottom of what she really means, emotionally. In return, she needs to understand and speak *his* language by sticking to the facts, being specific, and avoiding being overly emotional—at least at first, so they don't turn off and stop talking.

Assertiveness and Power

Assertiveness and power are no longer considered exclusively male traits, with more and more men choosing to express their "feminine" sides, and more and more women realizing that aggressiveness is not necessarily a negative attribute.

Assertiveness

In many cultures, men have traditionally been more assertive than women, and have set out to grab what they want. Women, on the other hand, have tended to be more passive, waiting for things to be given to them. The women's movement has helped changed this dynamic somewhat. In the past, an assertive woman was labeled aggressive, or even a nastier term. While times have changed, I still find that women need encouragement to be assertive, and need to take more initiative to ask for what they want.

Power

Traditionally, it is believed that men hold the power in life and in relationships. But feminist and male movement leader Warren Farrell, the first male President of the National Organization for Women, takes a controversial stance. In his book, *The Myth of Male Power,* Farrell points out that men have only the *illusion* of power. He goes on to say that men are historically the ones who sacrifice their lives in war, suffer more physical illness from work, feel more pressure to perform sexually, get trapped in frustrations that make them abusive, and die younger.

ACE-ing It

How do assertiveness and power factor into the dating game? Well, it's useful to recognize the different ways in which men and women approach life. This recognition can help both men and women achieve the three A's (acceptance, appreciation, and adjustment); the three C's (confidence, compliments, and compromise); and the three E's (encouragement, energy, and empowerment). All these put together—ACE—is your key to self-fulfillment and satisfying relationships.

Coping With Problems and Stress

Traditionally, men and women react differently to problems and handle stress differently, as described in the table on the following page, according to the "six F's" of possible problem-solving behaviors (that elaborate on John Gray's "four F's").

Men	Women
"Fight": Take the offense, blame, judge, justify themselves to feel they've won	"Fold": Give in and assume blame
"Flight": Withdraw (going into their cave)	"Fake": Put on a happy face
"Focus": Focus on what to do	"Flood": Overwhelmed by emotion

Women like talking about problems; it makes them feel better to express their feelings about things even if they don't reach a solution. Men, on the other hand, feel frustrated until they *do* something to solve the problem.

For example, Paul was stressed out at work, but couldn't figure out how to relieve the pressure. As a result, he neglected his girlfriend, Patty. Hurt that she hadn't heard from him in a few days, she finally called him but he brushed her off, saying he couldn't talk because he was too stressed out. Patty said, "Please, talk to me about it, I'd like to help make you feel better," to which he responded, "I'll call you next week when this project is finished." Patty was hurt, and suspected he was seeing someone else, because if the situation were reversed, her first impulse would be to call Paul so that he could help make her feel better.

Suppose Patty complained, "I'm furious at you." Paul might say, "Leave me alone," or "You're always so demanding. Let's break up." His response only makes the problem worse, because what she really wants is for him to talk to her more, reassure her, and let her help him.

If your discussions tend to reach this kind of stalemate, what can you do? The healthiest approach is for both of you to face the problem *and* your feelings. Then work through the situation without blame and with each taking equal responsibility for what you do and how you make the other person feel.

On Commitment

Both men and women can certainly be possessive, jealous, or obsessive in love. But traditionally, it has been men who are more skittish about commitment. However, lately I have heard more and more stories from men complaining about the women they love. Either they complain that their love interest is cheating, or that she's ambivalent about commitment. A typical complaint: "I met this perfect woman last week and fell madly in love. Now all I do is think of her and I can't stand thinking of her with anyone else, but she says she wants us to keep seeing other people." This is a trend (explored further in Chapter 15) that certainly shows the tables are turning.

Both sexes can certainly be tortured by the desperate need for attachment, but more often men are possessive in the service of their ego ("owning their property"), while women are trying to satisfy their needs for merging (feeling together).

It has been said that men love like yo-yos: they want to run to the end of the rope to express their independence, with the confidence that the rope will snap back to the secure base of the woman's love, that is more like a favorite blanket or teddy bear—always there to offer warmth and comfort.

Women's love, on the other hand, is usually more stable. Women are usually more ready for commitment at a younger age, partly because they have been prepared for commitment by their upbringing, conditioned through life to share, sacrifice, and compromise.

As society's traditional caregivers, women are expansive and tend to subjugate their own needs to the needs of others. In contrast, men are more inward and focus on their own needs (thus appearing inconsiderate without even realizing it).

Thus, when a woman is despondent about a guy breaking up with her, I encourage her to assess the situation. Does she still think she has to have a man to be happy? Was he really ready to love? Does he have the emotional and intellectual capacity to give, devote, share, listen, care?

Essentials

National surveys conducted by the Virginia Slims Opinion Poll over the past 25 years reveal that four out of ten women find men selfish and self-centered. The most recent survey further reported that almost half of the women polled think men are still more interested in their own sexual satisfaction than that of their partner, only slightly improved from five years ago.

Sex Stereotypes

Monica called my "LovePhones" radio show to ask whether it was okay to have phone sex. She described how she talked to her boyfriends on the phone, repeating hot graphic fantasies, such as, "You grab me and take your hard throbbing member in my mouth." I asked her, "That's getting right to the heart of the matter fast. Is that what you really want to say?" "No," she answered, "I'd really like to say something more romantic, like

'Lower me gently onto the bed and we'll embrace longingly, our lips lingering lovingly over flesh afire with desire,' but I know guys wouldn't go for that. They prefer the raw stuff!"

Monica's experience was certainly helping to reinforce sexual stereotypes. But many of these ideas about men's and women's sexuality today are myths, based on outdated ways of thinking. Here are some typical examples:

➤ *Stereotype:* Men's sexuality is rated "NC-17," while women's is rated "R."

    Fact: Many women enjoy raunchy sex, and many men enjoy romanticism.

Tip

Women: To help him be more romantic, reassure and appreciate him every time he says or does something sensuous. Alternate telling him "hot" things with sensitive things. Read novels or watch videos together with romantic story lines to give him ideas. Trade off by enjoying a hot fantasy of his.

Men: Encourage your woman to be more comfortable talking about hot sex scenes. Recite them for her as you'd like to hear her say them. Accept her embarrassment. Trade off by enjoying a more romantic fantasy of hers.

➤ *Stereotype:* Men get more satisfaction from sex than women.

    Fact: There is no question that men have an easier time having orgasms. They tend to climax more quickly than women, and are comfortable with more types of partners, and under more varied circumstances (in a car, a stairwell, or just while making out). Most women need longer, more direct stimulation (from both a physiological and emotional point of view). Part of the reason is that a man's genitals are more exposed, allowing easier access.

In addition, women tend to be less comfortable with their bodies—less than 50 percent of all woman admit to masturbation, compared to 96 percent of men. Only a third of all woman surveyed experience regular orgasm during intercourse; most report that they can only achieve orgasm in certain ways. But once a woman learns to be more comfortable with her body, she can have as much satisfaction, if not more, than a man—in part because of her emotional investment.

➤ *Stereotype:* Men always want sex.

Fact: Survey results indicate that it is a myth that men are always clamoring for sex. I've talked to some men who don't want it as much as their female partner. Or they feel that their lack of constant desire means that something is wrong with them. Men are brought up thinking that an unquenchable desire is manly—and mourn the passing of their teenagehood, when raging hormones seemed to create incessant desire.

Essentials
Survey results show that men are just as interested in romance as women, with their top three romantic fantasies being candlelight dinners, sunset walks on the beach, and bubble baths.

Additionally, it's easier for men to get sex than it is for women—there are more outlets, legitimate and illegitimate. For many men, sex and emotion can be separate entities, so they can fulfill the need for sex with very little emotional investment. As a result, they may be less choosy about who, where, and when!

➤ *Stereotype:* A man who sleeps around is a stud; a woman who sleeps around is a slut.

Fact: Social mores are responsible for cheering the man who sleeps around, but jeering the woman. Fortunately, this stereotype is dying out, as society, and women themselves, accept the notion of sexual freedom and experimentation. I'm hearing from an increasing number of women who want more sex and wilder sex (outdoors, with several partners, trying different positions or actions) than their male partners, as well as from more men who are confused because *she's* the one who's pushing *him*!

➤ *Stereotype:* Women are monogamous, but men can't be.

Fact: Surveys have suggested that women can have the same problems with monogamy as men! By this decade, despite the fear of AIDS, it was estimated that up to eight out of ten married men, and half of all married women, have had affairs. In some animal species, the females are the infidels—they like to upgrade their mates to find the most fertile males and those that are most capable of caring for her young.

➤ *Stereotype:* Women can easily have multiple orgasms, but men can have only one per session.

Fact: While the stages of the male and female sexual response are the same (excitement, plateau, orgasm, resolution), the timing is a little different. Women can linger longer in the excitement and orgasm phases, leading to multiple orgasms.

Fortunately, men can train themselves in this approach by controlling their timing instead of always ending in a quick release.

➤ *Stereotype:* After sex, men like to just roll over and fall asleep.

Fact: The physical exertion and orgasmic release during sex can certainly produce relaxation conducive to rolling over and falling asleep, but there is no reflex that *makes* a man do that. Better explanations include fatigue, force of habit (guys learn as adolescents to have a quick release at bedtime), stress relief, and even escape from post-orgasmic intimacy.

Chemicals released in the brain during sex may have a sedative effect (for women too)—but consider that increased blood flow and heart rate have stimulating effects. Women often want *more* sex even though their partner is finished, often because they did not have orgasm (which can cause discomfort, restlessness, or unquenched desire), but also to enjoy more closeness or the afterglow.

➤ *Stereotype:* Men are more capable of having sex without love.

Fact: Here is one that still has some residue of truth, since I still hear from and treat lots of women who have sex just to get or keep a man. Men, on the other hand, are much more capable of having pure sexual relationships, saying: "It was nothing, it was just sex." This attitude produces a kind of sexual bribery, with women feeling that they have to give in if they want anything back. These days, more women are allowing themselves the freedom of sex without commitment, but still, deep down, expect and desire more emotional involvement than men do.

➤ *Stereotype:* Between the ages of 20 and 30, men just want sex, while women are looking for love. By age 40 or so, the opposite is true.

Fact: As men age, they are not as ruled by their hormones, and their lifestyle is not as conducive to casual sex, so they do become more interested in relationships. Studies at Florida State University and the University of Kansas suggest that men's sexual motives vary with age. For men under 25, physical release is the key; for men over 30, love takes precedence over pure pleasure.

Physical changes account for some of this shift (it takes an older man longer to get an erection and more time to "rebuild" between erections); but in recent years, men have started reevaluating traditional sexual attitudes and have become more attuned to sensuality and romance. Conversely, as women become more confident, they become more willing to express themselves sexually, and are more open to sexual experimentation—including sex for sex's sake, without deep emotional attachment.

➤ *Stereotype:* Guys rush through foreplay, and head right into intercourse.

Fact: Too often, men do what comes naturally—the quick build-up and release. And too often, they don't understand how women in general, and their partner in particular, like sex. If your partner is insensitive to your needs and desires, educate him! Show him what you like, and express your appreciation when he gets it right.

➤ *Stereotype:* Men love watching two women go at it, while women are completely turned off by the idea of watching two people together sexually.

Fact: Men have traditionally been more open to unusual sexual practices. Also, society has revered the beauty and sensuality of two women together. In addition, men get turned on thinking that the two women are really putting on a show and warming up for them. However, surveys indicate that an increasing number of women *do* entertain fantasies about watching a couple (men, women, or a man and a woman) have sex. This is probably the result of women in general becoming more experimental and open about their sexual desires. But keep in mind that *thinking* it does not mean you have to *do* it, and remember that scenes in your mind are not the same as in real life, when people's feelings become complicated.

While differences exist, there are still some trends and efforts toward bringing the male and female sex drives more in synch. This *is* possible. Women do take longer than men to get sexually aroused to the same point (because of differences in the male and female sex response cycle), with the result that women tend to need more time, and respond to slower, more sensuous touches (remember the popular song line, "I want a man with a slow hand"). Yet women today allow themselves a wider variety of love-making, with more active, vigorous activity. Similarly, though men have shorter response cycle times, making quicker, faster stimulation more common, an increasing number of men are learning the pleasures of more leisurely love-making.

The Gender War and the Movement Toward Peace

The "war" between the sexes has raged in the past few decades as women have vied for equality in all areas of life. While "war" sounds harsh, some aspects of this combativeness still exist, but fortunately cooperation is becoming more desired of late.

I still hear so many complaints from women about men, and from men about women. As I've suggested, women frequently complain that they'd like men to listen more attentively; be more communicative and honest; be less selfish, pushy, and obsessed with sex; and help out more around the house. Men want women to be less emotional, and to stick to the facts at hand during an argument.

According to surveys, women's complaints about men have changed very little in the past 25 years! Only half the women in the 1995 Virginia Slims Opinion Poll report being satisfied with the man in their life—a slight improvement from 1990. When women were asked to list the things in life that please them, men rated fourth—after children, friends, and motherhood.

Interestingly, men think they are doing better than women think they are. Three-quarters of the men surveyed in the Virginia Slims Opinion Poll think they are better able to express their feelings and are more understanding of women's needs than they were five years ago, but fewer women think so. Additionally, men think they've questioned the need to act "macho"; yet over half of the women think the "macho man" lives on. Over half of the women surveyed also think that men are self-centered and commitment-shy. Not surprisingly, few men believe this to be true.

The tensions between what women think about men, and what men think about themselves, have created a new male backlash—many men say they will give less if this is all the appreciation they get. But all is not lost (if all the steps that follow are taken).

Sex roles have blurred, and seven out of ten men and women surveyed admit to being confused. Some women admit to wanting to be a woman of the 1990s when it comes to their career (with equal job opportunities, pay, and power), but a woman of the 1950s when it comes to love (being taken care of and being provided for).

Reaching Détente in the Gender War

Men and women can learn to understand each other better and come to a compromise. It's important to:

➤ Accept your differences and communicate your needs. Your partner is not a mind-reader. You've got to express your desires, your frustrations, and your pleasures.

➤ Accommodate your partner's needs and requests. Within reason, adjust to each other's ways.

➤ Acknowledge that men have made progress. Despite the many complaints that women have about men, I must note that overall men *have* changed. My professional experience, as well as many survey results, suggest that there is a new man, more like what women have been demanding. He's more able to express his feelings, even with other men. He's more involved with children. And he agrees that he shouldn't make all the decisions.

As callers to my "LovePhones" radio call-in advice show have indicated, more men with those proverbial cold feet have warmed up. I get many calls from men bemoaning how they want to make a commitment and need help to do so. Or they can't find a woman who wants to settle down. Or they feel used for sex. On some phone calls, if I didn't hear a distinctly male voice, I wouldn't be able to tell if it was a man or woman complaining, "I'm shy, how do I meet someone?" or, "I got dumped and it hurts so bad." Just the other night a husband admitted that he criticizes his wife because "I guess I feel inadequate."

On my show and in my practice, I try to point out the *similarities* between men and women. Women need to understand that men have the same feelings, but just handle them differently. A little understanding will make both men and women feel less helpless and more empathic.

How can we eliminate sex role stereotypes? Try retraining your brain. As soon as the thought comes into your head, snap your fingers (to interrupt it) and change the thought to, "Men and women can *both* be…"

Role-Reversal Exercises

"I never heard of a couple breaking up because they understood each other." My long-time friend and men's movement leader, Warren Farrell, opened his seminar last summer about "Resolving the '90s Gender War" with that very line. Try to put yourself in your partner's moccasins—that's the surest way of reaching a true understanding.

Farrell's seminar (open to the public, drawing about 20 of us) was held at Esalen, the New Age center high in the mountains of Big Sur (where Indians had walked in *real* moccasins for centuries). It had been over 20 years since my last visit (I was a typical "flower child" from the East, curious about the West Coast "enlightenment" hype), but one step onto the property was enough to transport me back into the '70s feelings of innocence, openness, and trust—states I still believe are crucial to resolving misunderstandings between men and women.

At the seminar, we performed role-reversal exercises, which you may wish to try. The exercises were designed to promote understanding of the opposite sex's way of thinking and to help shake us from our traditional ways of behaving.

First, the *dance*. We picked partners, and each woman led her male partner, controlling his every move. He had to follow and look at her with awe (what Farrell calls "awe training"). One man said, "It feels wonderful to let someone else be in charge for a change." Another was more skeptical: "I didn't like following. I'm used to being the one in control." A few women enjoyed leading, but most preferred looking up to the man.

Then, we were asked to *reconstruct dating choices in adolescence*. We started by thinking about the person we would have loved to have asked to the prom. Most women thought of guys who were good-looking and successful (the jock or student government leader). The guys also chose good looks. But leadership? *Yawn.*

Next came the *male beauty contest*—a lesson about being a "sex object." The five biggest "studs," as judged by the women in the group, were herded into a large room. As they stood before us, the emcee, a woman, called each of their names. The women, clapping and hooting for the ones they liked best, whittled the group down to the top two "pieces of meat," who then competed on talent and brains. One women asked, "How do you feel about birth control?" Another asked, "What would you do if your girlfriend had to move for her job?" For the talent contest, one guy sang and the other stripped. The stripper won the contest, judged by the women's howls—perhaps proving that sexual seductions have more power than tamer talents.

Next came the *"success-object" contest.* The women lined up in rows according to income, with those earning over $55,000 in the front row and those making $5,000 or less in the back. The idea was for women to feel the sting (or satisfaction) of being judged by their bank account—as men often are. Money, instead of looks, have become the criteria for their being chosen, and the exercise gave women a sense of how men struggle in the dating selection process.

Then came the *role-reversal date.* The women had to ask a guy to lunch. The men were told to say yes or no, depending on the woman's ability to support him and children. The men in the group realized that the woman who would normally be their first choice based on looks was not necessarily the same one they'd pick as a provider.

We also played opposite roles on the "date." My date, Brian, asked me questions about my work, and listened with apparent rapture while puffing out his chest. Mimicking a guy, I chatted on, and paid the check. Back in the group, we shared our experiences. One woman nearly cried. "I sat in the last row because I make no money and the three guys I asked out all turned me down. Now I know how devastated guys feel." A guy confessed, "It was horrible, worrying if I was pretty enough."

Finally came the *tolerance lessons.* After we'd walked in the opposite sex's shoes, we were asked to close our eyes and think about what we'd learned. Had we learned tolerance and empathy? Could we put our lessons to work with our co-workers, family, and friends?

In typical Esalen style, we hugged each other and clapped for ourselves. And we were given a task for the future—to truly encourage equality, we must help train boys for caring and girls for financial independence; we must learn to communicate and cooperate rather than compete.

Farrell added his favorite message: "Women cannot hear what men do not say." Just as the women's movement empowered women to speak up and ask for what they want, men need the same encouragement. When both sexes learn to listen to each other, we can have the loving dialogue that will end the gender war.

The Least You Need to Know

➤ Men and women communicate differently.

➤ Brain differences account for some of the differences in communication.

➤ Men and women are raised with different expectations and communication styles.

➤ A good way to overcome a discussion or relationship stalemate is to accept, accommodate, and acknowledge your partner.

➤ The traditional gender war is far from over—but there have been many gains where men and women have understood and incorporated each other's behaviors.

➤ Role-reversal exercises can help you understand the other sex's dilemmas and give you new insights and behaviors that bring men and women closer together.

Chapter 14

What's Up With This Person?

In This Chapter

➤ Different personality types and how to recognize them

➤ When and why to end the relationship

➤ Dealing with addictive or unhealthy behaviors

We've all run into them—the over-emotional types, the egomaniacs, the obsessive types. Is there any way to do a "quick read" on a person before plunging into a possibly ill-fated romance? In this chapter, I describe some basic personality types you may date, and provide clues that will help you figure out what you might be in for. The more aware you are of what makes someone tick, the better prepared you'll be to either accommodate their flaws and eccentricities—or run!

As I've stated throughout the book, the key to success in dating lies in using the three A's: acceptance, appreciation, and adjustment. But sometimes, despite our best efforts, a person's problems might be far larger than we want to take on. If the person you are seeing has insight into their own problems and is willing to work toward change, then it might be worthwhile to hang on. But don't get into situations where you fool yourself into thinking that you can change a person—especially one who refuses to acknowledge a problem and has no desire to change.

Narcissistic Types

There's a long-standing joke that describes the typical narcissist: "Enough about me. Now tell me—what do *you* think about me?" Narcissists are so self-involved and self-centered that they see all lovers and friends simply as extensions of themselves. But they are also very seductive, and will use endless charm and flattery in pursuit of their own happiness. "God's Gift" comes in male and female varieties.

For example, Kathleen was mesmerized by Al, with his dashing looks, red Porsche, fancy suits, and impressive talk about his promising future as a famous movie star. An aspiring actress herself, Kathleen fell for his constant flattery and was seduced by his talk about how great she'd look by his side when he won his Oscar. Kathleen felt her Prince Charming had finally come.

But at an industry party, Al met another aspiring actress who fed his grandiosity even more than Kathleen. Taken with this new admirer, Al began to pick on Kathleen, pointing out how her dresses were getting tighter, and how bags were beginning to show under her eyes, until he finally dumped her for his new "arm charm."

Al is a self-centered exhibitionist, obsessed with flattery, demanding adoration and attention. He also exaggerated his own success, and as if to prove it, exaggerated the success and beauty of the people he dated. Narcissists are so taken with themselves that they are only attracted to others who flatter, embellish, or enhance their image in their own or others' eyes.

While they may seem self-confident, narcissists crave attention because their egos are so fragile. They (and their love interests) become victims of their own "hero-zero" mindset—vacillating between feeling like the "cock of the walk" or the biggest loser of the year.

Ask yourself these questions to help identify a narcissistic type:

➤ Does the conversation always revolve around him?

➤ Does she lose interest when she's not the center of attention?

➤ Is he grandiose, constantly referring to himself in the same breath as superstars?

➤ Does he make you feel like a million bucks with constant flattery?

➤ Does she have a pattern of supposedly "ideal" loves who end up disappointing her with some fatal flaw?

➤ Is he a show-off, courting compliments?

➤ Does she fall apart in the face of criticism—for example, if you mention that she looks tired or has made a mistake?

➤ Does he fly off the handle if he doesn't get special treatment (the best table at the restaurant, the best seat in the theater)?

➤ Does she use people to get what she wants, only to discard them when she doesn't need them anymore?

If your love interest displays five or more of these characteristics, be cautious—you may have a narcissist on your hands. Most psychologists say that true narcissists are among the most difficult patients to treat—so there is little reason for you to take on the challenge. If you are looking for attention, commitment, and devotion, you won't find it here.

Over-Emotional Types

Joanna was the life of the party, always attracting the coolest guys in the room. But inevitably, after a few get-togethers, her dates would begin to feel uncomfortable. Joanna liked to grab her date's arm—a little too tightly. She also liked to gaze longingly into her man's eyes, with a look that indicated she was expecting affection in return. Within a date or two, she would turn the talk to their fabulous future together—despite the fact that they barely knew one another.

Women like Joanna (and some men, too) love high drama. Their emotions spill out quickly, which makes their dates wonder about the genuineness of it all. On the upside, these people can be charming and engaging; but on the downside, because they're so driven by their need to be taken care of and loved, they can try to make others responsible for them, becoming helpless and dependent, clingy and suffocating.

Such histrionic women often seem "wild" in bed, yet ironically, many are unable to achieve orgasm because of their fears of really letting go.

There's no question that these emotional types are trapped by a desperate need for love. In psychological terms, they are looking for a lover to help them recapture the comfort of the early mother-child union.

Ask yourself these questions to help identify this personality type:

➤ Does she cry at the drop of a hat?

➤ Does she squeal with enthusiasm when meeting a casual acquaintance?

➤ Does he ask you often "Do you love me?"

Essentials
The ancient Greeks thought that histrionic females had exaggerated emotions because they were afflicted with a "wandering womb." Freud believed sexual trauma in childhood was a better explanation.

➤ Is she a chronic flirt?

➤ Does she fly off the handle (for example, if she caught you flirting with another woman, would she throw her glass at you)?

➤ Does she talk too soon or too often about how perfect you are for each other?

➤ Does she always ask other people's opinions of what she should do?

➤ Does she have a history of abusive relationships?

➤ Does she always seem to be helping or "saving" others?

➤ Does she seem overly sensitive about rejection?

If you are seeing someone who displays five or more of these characteristics, suggest that she seek treatment. Many people who crave love so intensely are suffering from what's called *hysteroid depression* (a mixture of over-emotionality and depression). With treatment, these people can develop a stronger sense of self and a greater ability to fulfill their own dreams and needs.

If this description fits you, learn to enjoy yourself and your life instead of looking for a lover's approval and admiration. Resist the temptation to seek approval. "Re-parent" yourself by picturing yourself being both the little child and the parent giving you the attention you need (thereby learning to rely on yourself instead of making others your "replacement" parents). Check your emotions before you let them loose, and purposefully *under*-react, so you will actually *feel* something. (When you exaggerate emotions, you are actually pushing away your true feelings.) If you break up, focus on simple facts of the situation ("He met someone else," "We went our separate ways") rather than exaggerating how you feel ("The world has come to an end," "I'll never find anyone else").

Passive-Aggressive Types

Pam had been dating Tim for four months when she complained to me, "I can't figure him out. On one hand, he says he's more relaxed with me than with any other woman, and I can ask him anything, but then when I do, he complains that I'm like every other demanding woman. When I try to talk to him about his mixed message, he says that nothing's wrong and walks away."

Pam's lover is a typical passive-aggressive (PA) type who gives double messages—come closer, move away. Such a person can leave you on an emotional seesaw between hope and frustration. The "aggressive" part of the person is seething with unexpressed anger, while the "passive" part expresses that anger in subtle ways, such as with "innocent" remarks and little digs that are really intended to hurt.

Passive-aggressives are big on using the "silent treatment" to thwart confrontation. They pretend to cooperate but then don't do what you ask, and shift blame to you, making you feel guilty for being demanding or angry. Because they are terribly conflicted about intimacy and aggression, dependency and competition, they can't express love and either sleep around or completely withdraw from relationships.

Ask yourself these questions to help identify a passive-aggressive type:

➤ If you complain that he's late, does he claim you're too demanding or that it's your fault?

➤ Does he refuse to say "I love you" because he says you should know how he feels?

➤ When you get angry, does he give you the silent treatment?

➤ If you walk ahead of him, does he complain you're rude, but if you hold his arm, does he protest you're crowding him?

➤ Does she pout unless she gets her way?

➤ Does he promise to make love to you when he's in the mood, but he never is?

➤ Does he agree to pick up dinner or make a phone call, and then forget?

➤ Does he forget your birthday, anniversary, and dates, but always come up with excuses?

➤ Is she always lagging behind, dawdling, running late?

If your love interest displays five or more of these characteristics, you may be involved with a passive-aggressive type. If you fall for this type, think about whether you also have a tendency to stifle anger. If you stay with this person, resist doubting your perceptions about situations, and resist the pressure to blame yourself. If your mate backstabs or twists the facts of a story, state your feelings and the facts clearly and unemotionally. Call your partner on his unexpressed anger, and insist that you not be subtly abused.

Essentials

In his book *Living With The Passive-Aggressive Male*, Scott Wetzler describes three types of women who fall for PA men: the Victim, who willingly suffers humiliation for scraps of attention, thereby losing his respect; the maternal Rescuer, whose cleaning up after him earns his resentment instead of the appreciation she seeks; and the Manager, whose need to control attracts his dependence but incites his rebellion against feeling trapped.

Obsessive Types

Whenever she's out on a date, Jackie is totally distracted with worries that she's forgotten to turn off her computer, which, she's convinced, will blow the machine's memory. And then there's Larry, who is so worried about germs that he can't even contemplate a goodnight kiss without going into a panic.

Both Jackie and Larry display degrees of obsessive behavior. Obsessions range from simple self-doubt to more serious distortions (such as about being contaminated). Many of us know what it's like to have rituals—we walk to the bus every day, following precisely the same route, or we put on our shoes and socks in a certain manner, or we're a bit compulsive about filing. But for certain people, rituals become overwhelming and interfere with normal functioning and relationships.

For example, Jack flies off the handle if his girlfriend moves anything on his desk, even something as simple as a memo pad. Kris wants to look so perfect on her dates that she irons her dress five or more times, causing her to be late. Jason can't get out of the house in the morning because he keeps rushing back to the kitchen to make certain that he's turned off the lights (sometimes checking ten times or more before he feels "safe" enough to leave).

Ask yourself these questions to help identify an obsessive type:

➤ She repeats phrases compulsively (such as "Don't you think...").

➤ He is a neat-freak (CDs all in line, books alphabetized).

➤ She constantly doubts herself.

➤ He has to repeat certain acts in a particular way (such as locking all the doors in sequence).

➤ She checks things (her car, keys, schedule) over and over.

➤ He counts things repeatedly.

➤ She repeats herself and goes over details endlessly.

If your love interest displays five or more of these characteristics, he may be an obsessive type. Obsessive or compulsive people are driven by a need to control—their lives, their emotions, and the lives of others. Some obsessive types can become extremely successful in positions of power (in politics, business, money dealings), that can be very attractive. On the downside, because they are controlling and are threatened by feelings, they can be rigid, stuffy, and detached.

The need, but inability, to control (oneself, one's emotions, one's life, or others) can lead to serious problems, like alcohol and drug abuse or eating disorders.

> **Warning**
>
> A good many dates begin with dinner, lunch, or some other event where food takes center stage. But for the thousands of people with eating disorders (either anorexia or bulimia), a simple meal can set the stage for all kinds of interpersonal dilemmas. Eating disorders are serious illnesses that involve the need to control one's feelings and life, and require intensive psychotherapy. If you're involved with someone with an eating disorder, urge the person to get treatment.

Mood-Swing Types

When Joe started dating Martha, he was taken with her passion. If she loved a film, she would describe it as "awesome," and would go on and on about how much she loved it. On the other hand, if she disliked a movie, she'd be totally unable to discuss it reasonably, calling it "repulsive," and commenting that anyone who'd like it must be a total idiot. While the strength of Martha's opinions at first intrigued Joe, the attraction began to wear very thin. He began to realize that with Martha, there were no shades of gray. She had a long, checkered career history, with jobs that started out with promise but ended in disappointment. And it was the same with the men in her life.

People like Martha often seem pretty normal at first. They seem to function on an acceptable level (or even at a high level), but on the inside they feel like lonely, terrified children. They cling to a partner one minute, but push him away when they become terrified of being "swallowed up." This dramatic inner battle becomes totally confusing to an unsuspecting partner, who doesn't seem to be able to find a happy medium in the relationship.

Ask yourself these questions to help identify this type:

➤ Does she cling to you as if her life depended on it, or at other times push you away angrily?

➤ Does he either love or hate people in extremes, calling them the best or the worst (or switching from one extreme to the other)?

➤ Does she seem to use people?

➤ Does he fly into a rage or withdraw if the slightest thing doesn't go his way?

➤ Does she have an addictive personality, relying on drugs, shopping, alcohol, food, or gambling?

Warning
It's a good idea to suggest that the person get a psychiatric consultation if any of his behavior becomes too extreme.

➤ Is he "accident-prone"?

➤ Is she endlessly confused about "who she is," or does she frequently say she doesn't know what she wants to do in life?

➤ Does he seem unable to spend an evening alone?

➤ Does she experience dramatic mood swings?

If your love interest displays five or more of these characteristics, he may be prone to extremes in his behavior. If you date a person of this type, expect a roller-coaster ride of emotions—you may be on a pedestal one minute and in the doghouse the next. If you have the stomach for it, strap in for a bumpy ride. Sometimes the disorder is a chemical imbalance that requires psychiatric attention and medication.

Attention Deficit Disorder (ADD)

Sarah called me to complain about her recent boyfriend. The relationship was going reasonably well, but she frequently felt hurt by his inattention. She told me that even when they were holding each other while watching TV, he'd suddenly jump up to make notes in his daily planner, or he'd decide it was time to reorganize his CD collection. "Am I so boring that he has to escape?" she asked.

I pointed out that it sounded as if her boyfriend was suffering from Attention Deficit Disorder (ADD). More often recognized and treated in children, ADD also afflicts millions of adults, but usually goes undiagnosed. Because they are creative, quick, unconventional, and spontaneous, people with ADD can excel at work, especially in structured jobs. However, they may fall apart in more unstructured situations such as dating, becoming easily distracted or unable to concentrate.

Essentials
ADD is a neuro-biological disability that tends to run in families. Researchers estimate that about 35 percent of siblings, 80 percent of identical twins, and 40 percent of children with an ADD parent have the trait. Symptoms can be triggered by fluctuations in hormone levels, as well as by increased stress levels and frustration. Medication and pyschological counseling can help.

If you date someone like this, don't take his distractions personally. Identifying and understanding a problem is half the battle to overcoming it.

Forgive your date and try to improve your communication. Talk about the problem and schedule private, intimate time that won't be interrupted by distracting tasks. Rather than referring to him as hyper or exasperating, tell him you appreciate him for being so energetic and stimulating.

Depression

Who hasn't felt depressed at some point in life? You know the symptoms—you're "down in the dumps," you may have trouble sleeping, you're eating too much or have lost interest in food. Such feelings usually pass. But depression that lasts more than a few days, or is accompanied by feelings of doom or despair, is a different matter.

For example, Paul called "LovePhones" to say, "I've been dating this woman for six months, and she's become increasingly depressed. At first she just seemed a little blue, but lately she's been sleeping for ten or more hours a day, and she has even said that she occasionally feels that life just isn't worth living. What should I do?"

Depression is a serious illness that requires medical attention. If you are seeing someone who seems depressed (not just "blue"), urge them to talk with a professional.

Don't blame yourself for a partner's depression, but if you find yourself chronically attracted to depressed people, look inward. Use my "Mirror Law of Attraction" and ask yourself if you're the one who is really also depressed. If so, face your own problem instead of picking lovers who protect you from facing your own feelings of desolation or hopelessness.

Insecure or Paranoid Types

Gordon called me to complain that his girlfriend was always accusing him of seeing other women, which was simply not true. He went on to say that when he came home, she examined his clothing for hairs and other indications that he'd been with someone else. While she'd always been a little insecure, he felt that she was getting completely carried away with her suspicions and accusations. Was it something he was doing?

I told Gordon to face her accusations honestly. If his girlfriend truly has no reason to doubt him, he must insist that she stop accusing him and work on her own self-esteem and inner security, lest she destroy the relationship once and for all.

Many of us throw around the term "paranoid," but chronic distrust can be a serious problem. Here are some clues for recognizing overly suspicious, paranoid types:

➤ False and frequent accusations that you are looking at someone else

➤ False accusations that you are trying to make your partner "feel bad"

➤ Distrust and over-generalization beyond reason ("All women are just after one thing: money")

➤ Excessive guardedness ("You can't be too careful about people these days")

➤ Frequently doubting others' loyalty

> ➤ Jumping to irrational conclusions ("I saw you talking to that man, which is proof that you're cheating on me!")

> ➤ Over-concern about hidden motives and meanings ("You and your friends seem to have a secret signal to quiet down when I walk into the room")

> ➤ Easily blames or takes offense ("You purposefully ruined my night")

If your date displays more than five of these clues, he or she may have a seriously distorted view of reality. Don't blame yourself, or constantly try to prove or defend yourself. You don't have to settle for a person whose problems are too large to take on.

Too-Smooth Dudes

Beware of fast-talking, smooth operators, with great lines and too-good-to-be-true promises—they just might be taking you for a ride. You read about such sociopaths all the time in the tabloids—from gigolos who con unsuspecting, naive, and lonely women out of their savings, to polygamists, who keep a string of wives and families.

Sociopaths are often delinquents, thieves, liars, and poseurs (one notorious guy performed surgeries, though he had never gone to medical school). But they are also often bright, charming, and exciting. They're good at seducing women, but inhumanely aggressive once their prey submits. A deep resentment and hatred for women, and inner weakness, may unleash a violent rage.

Catching on to these people (most of whom are men) is difficult because they're good cons. And changing them is near-impossible, since true sociopaths feel no reason to live by the rules that govern the rest of society and therefore, feel no guilt or pain for hurting other people.

Be suspicious of slick lines and of someone who sounds too good to be true (the handsome "high-roller" with no visible means of support but lots of slick schemes). Remember the adage: "Fool me once, shame on you; fool me twice, shame on me."

Addictive Behavior

If you find yourself falling in love with a drug addict, whether the drug of choice is alcohol or narcotics, keep this simple thought in mind: you cannot "save" an addict. The only addicts who clean themselves up are those who take steps to help themselves. If you are seriously involved with an alcoholic or drug addict, join a support program (like Al-Anon) and start living your life—for yourself.

Most rehab counselors recommend that recovering addicts refrain from new relationships for a year while they reestablish their life. There are no guarantees. Recovery is a "one-day-at-a-time" process. It can be done, but it takes willpower.

Smokers

Many people are adding "smoking" to their dating criteria list, rejecting those who do.

"I hate that ugly thing hanging out of his mouth," Charlene said. She added, "If he needs something to suck on all the time, why doesn't he stick a pacifier in his mouth?"

No doubt smokers are hooked on nicotine, but psychologically you could say they are stuck in the "oral" stage of Freudian development, where the child has to have something in his mouth to feel secure. The smoking habit is one of the hardest to kick, so if you fall for one who smokes, be prepared to lend tons of support while he tries to kick the habit, or accept it if he won't change.

Deciding Whether to Stick It Out

It's wonderful to be understanding and sympathetic when you fall for someone with a problem. But it's important to know when to cut your losses and cut yourself loose.

If you're in extreme pain, danger, or you are being abused, you need to get out. Also bail out if your partner's behavior is getting you in trouble.

Remember my "Mirror Law of Attraction"—we tend to attract people who reflect our own needs. Examine what your partner's behavior means to you or tells you about yourself. Are you living vicariously through your lover? Are you co-dependent, sacrificing your own well-being to save the other person? Are you hiding behind your partner?

The Least You Need to Know

➤ You can't change people; they have to want to change themselves.

➤ If the person you're dating acknowledges problems and is willing to change, it might be worth staying in the relationship.

➤ End the relationship if your partner is mentally, physically, or sexually abusive, or is putting you in danger.

➤ We attract people who reflect our own needs. What does your partner's behavior say about you?

Chapter 15

What Is This Thing Called Love?

> **In This Chapter**
>
> ➤ Three essential characteristics of love
>
> ➤ Some tests to tell whether it's love
>
> ➤ Can love at first sight work?
>
> ➤ The stages of love
>
> ➤ When and how to say "I love you"
>
> ➤ When you can't choose between two lovers

In my years of experience hearing people's stories about love, not surprisingly, I have come up with some thoughts on the subject! For starters, I have come to recognize three essential factors for determining whether someone is really in love:

> ➤ Do you have compatible needs for independence or togetherness? Some people need time alone or time on their own; other people want to be with their lover all the time, or feel a passionate need to "merge" with another in order to feel whole. In my view, the healthiest relationship is when neither party is overly dependent or independent—when two people are *inter*dependent.

➤ Do you both have a strong desire to make your relationship work? Not all love comes naturally. The daily grind, arguments, outside pressures, and various other factors can get in the way of love, and test your commitment to one another. But almost all barriers can be overcome if you both *want* to make it work.

➤ Do you experience the intermixing of physical love (sex) with emotional sharing and spiritual connection?

What Is Love?

Love—everyone craves it on some level. And we certainly date in an effort to "find" it. Without it, many people feel a gaping hole inside, their inner child crying out to be held, the adult longing to adore and be adored, cherish and be cherished.

But we use the word "love" to describe our feelings for so many things. You can love your friend, parents, pet, movies, even chocolate ice cream. We use it to describe the hormone-raging lust of teenagehood, but it also certainly applies to the comforting togetherness our grandparents experience in old age. In each case, we mean something a little different.

Who hasn't swooned after meeting someone and exclaimed, "I'm madly in love!" But this is a far different feeling from the deep connection we feel after being in a relationship with someone for years.

According to my definition, love entails the five C's: caring, communicating, compromising, commitment, and cheerleading. But true love also includes honesty, sacrifice, and sharing. In an effort to get at *your* definition of love, start with the following exercises.

Exercise #1. Describe what it feels like for you to be in love with someone.

_____

_____

_____

Exercise #2. List the top three things that come to mind when you think about love, along with any other thoughts you might have on the subject.

1.

2.

3.

Other thoughts:

> ### Essentials
>
> In a landmark study of 500 passionate lovers, Dr. Dorothy Tennov listed a dozen components of strong romantic love. These included constant thinking about the person you passionately desire, longing for reciprocation, inability to act in love with more than one person at a time, and an "aching" in the heart when uncertain about your relationship.

Putting into words (as in Exercise #1) how you feel when you are in love with someone makes it more real to you, and helps you focus on what's important to you. Once you list the qualities of love, as in Exercise #2, you can reflect on different relationships and see if these experiences were present. If they were missing, you can understand more about why the relationship did not work out. Also answer the questions as you think your dates would, to see if your definitions of love are similar.

> ### Essentials
>
> Loving touches not only feel good, but are good for you! Research has proven that touching strengthens your immune system by stimulating certain chemicals in your brain. Furthermore, the feelings of emotional security that are nurtured by loving strokes facilitate relaxation, which helps guard against stress.

Tests of Love

Is there a simple test to determine whether you are really in love? Of course not. But certainly there are questions you can ask yourself (and your mate) about your relationship. Here are some questions that may help you gauge your level of commitment:

➤ *The Mood Test.* Are you flowering in your relationship or dying on the vine (are you worried, threatened, criticized, etc.)?

➤ *The Sacrifice Test.* Remember the classic test: If the two of you were onboard a sinking ship with only one life vest, would you keep it for yourself or give it to your mate? A more true-to-life related question might be: If you had something important to do, but your mate requested you to do something important for him, which would you do?

➤ *The Thoughtfulness Test.* Do you know your date's favorite treats? Do you go out of your way to indulge him in special ways? Does he do the same for you?

➤ *The Unconditional Love Test.* Would you love him no matter what he did for a living, or if she lost her looks? Do you feel your date is capable of loving you for who you are?

➤ *The Security Test.* When the two of you are apart, do you feel a sense of trust and security, or do you fear betrayal or loss?

While even true lovers will occasionally stumble on the above (and be selfish, ill-tempered, thoughtless, demanding, or insecure), if you are basically happy, giving, thoughtful, accepting, and secure *most* of the time, you're well on your way to a rewarding love.

Love at First Sight

You see each other across a crowded room. Your eyes lock. Your hearts melt. Immediately you "know": you've found the one you've been searching for. It's "love at first sight"—the instant attraction people dream about. Love at first sight *is* possible (almost everyone has an anecdote to support the premise), but what is called "*love* at first sight" frequently turns out to be lust at first sight.

Looks undeniably play a part in such immediate attractions, and many times matter *too* much. All too often on my "LovePhones" radio show, I hear young women exclaim that they are in love because "he's so good-looking," and guys say "she's so hot"—and yet they don't really know or care enough about *who* the person really is.

Essentials

Surveys show that many people believe in love at first sight, although more *want* to believe it exists. On one TV show I did on the subject, half the audience at first said they believed in love at first sight, but by the end of the show, hearing horror stories of how some of these "fairy tales" turned out, three-fourths of the audience had changed their vote.

It takes time to determine how right or compatible a partner is for you. Real love develops slowly as you share and support one another through happy and sad times. My rule: Enjoy the initial thrill, but have at least six dates before you start seriously thinking he or she is really the "one." Even then, be cautious for the next six months as you observe your mate's character. Watch how he deals with family, friends, children, colleagues. Is she caring and responsive? Does he tell the truth? Observe her in times of stress. Is he there for you in an emergency?

Warning

Women, more often than men, fall too hard and too fast. So many women cry to me over the radio, "Everything seemed so perfect. Why hasn't he called?" I'll ask, "How long have you known each other?" "Just a few weeks" is usually the answer. After so little time, how can you possibly know enough to predict someone's behavior or explain their actions? Remember, love takes time!

So how do you deal with the butterflies in your stomach? On the other hand, how do you know if something that doesn't give you an instant rush is worth pursuing? Here are some tips:

➤ Enjoy the excitement of being turned on by a stranger, but don't expect too much at first blush.

➤ Don't dismiss a relationship that doesn't provide instant thrills.

➤ Take time to let lust mature into more lasting compatibility.

Stages of Love

One thing is certain about love: it changes! Love comes in stages. The first stage is not really love but attraction. If the attraction is accompanied by sexual thrills and excitement, we call it lust. In this "honeymoon" phase of blind bliss, you are usually obsessed with mystery and the desire to impress. You enter a fantasy world of idealizing the other person and imagining how perfect you are for one another.

The next phase is the testing period, where expectations are met—or not—and fears arise ("Is she really the one?" "Can this really last?"). You find out if you really enjoy the same things, if you can rely on one another, if you have the same level of commitment, and if you communicate on the same level.

If your relationship survives the testing period, you will enter a brief period of satisfaction where you'll feel that your fantasy of perfect love could indeed be fulfilled— until reality sets in. The more time you spend with your mate, the more opportunity you'll have to disagree with each other and see each other's flaws and imperfections. Inevitably, one of you might feel grumpy and disagreeable, or come down with some illness, providing a true test of your tolerance and ability to compromise.

You may also start to notice that his hair is thinning, her breasts are beginning to sag, she nags, he spaces out in front of the television. In this testing period, you have to learn to compromise, to accept imperfections, to reduce your expectations, to resolve your differences, and to develop a realistic view of your life together—either that, or you'll throw in the towel.

If your relationship weathers the test of time, you'll end up with more intimacy and commitment, and with the resolve to make adjustments to "make it work." During this time, love deepens, but lust may fade. This creates another challenge—that you not take your relationship or each other for granted. Researchers call this "companionate" or "conjugal" love, which is where you'll find the warmth of a long-lasting relationship.

Essentials

Some people forget or don't realize that the excitement and passion of new love may not go on forever—it either gives way to something more permanent, or the relationship ends. This may come as a real letdown to someone who fears "He must not love me anymore" when the lust stage runs its course. This can be the reason some people hop from relationship to relationship—to try to recapture the initial excitement or challenge of falling in love.

Too Young for Love?

The feeling of being in love can happen at any age. Steve is 16 and wants to know, "I met this girl and we want to spend the rest of our lives together. Should I dedicate my heart? Are we too young to know?"

Falling so madly in love that you think you want to spend the rest of your life together is a delicious experience. It *can* work, of course, even if you're young. You may marry your childhood sweetheart, but the chances are probably slender it will last. There's a lot of truth to the notion that you can't love someone else until you know and love yourself—and it is very hard for young people to truly know themselves. My advice to young people is to enjoy feeling love, but don't act on it prematurely.

When to Say "I Love You"

I usually say that when you are in love, you should feel free to say almost anything: "If it's on your mind, let it be on your lips." But many of us feel anxious about telling someone that we love him—and there are some legitimate conditions and considerations.

When to say I love you:

➤ When it's true

➤ When you want to get it off your chest

➤ When you've been wanting to say it a long time

➤ When you feel overwhelmed with gratitude for all that someone has done for you

➤ When it seems appropriate in the heat of passion (and you know you're not just carried away, or saying what you think she wants to hear)

➤ When you have your partner's full attention

Three little words—"I love you"—whether whispered or shouted from the rooftop, have such impact and significance. Many of us have fears about uttering these three little words—fears of feeling silly, of being rejected, or of being misunderstood.

But if you truly love someone, saying "I love you" is a risk you have to take. If you are concerned about what to say, start by expressing your appreciation or with a compliment: "I appreciate you for your support, (or strength, attentiveness, or thoughtfulness)." Then talk about your love in hypothetical terms: "If I could say I love you, without being afraid that you'd be scared to hear it, I'd say..." It's always a good idea to reassure the other person that you have no demands in return: "I want to say I love you, but it doesn't mean you have to say you love me back."

What if your mate has just told you he loves you? How should you respond? Obviously, with the truth. If you are not sure of your feelings, say, "That's wonderful. Let's take this slowly and see where it goes." If you are sure of your feelings, try, "I love you back" or tease, "I love you more." Express joy and appreciation: "Thank you for the beautiful gift of your love."

If you don't feel the same way, be delicate. Your answer may have an impact for a very, very long time. Never say: "I wish you wouldn't say that," "I don't love you back," "That's a bad idea," or "It's too late for that." You can kindly and dispassionately say, "That's such a nice thing to say," or "What a nice feeling"—something that clearly doesn't return the feeling but acknowledges it.

When *not* to say I love you:

➤ To force your mate to say or feel it in return

➤ When you're afraid your partner doesn't feel the same thing

➤ To get something from someone in return

➤ To convince *yourself* you feel it

➤ To prove to yourself you can say it

➤ To get someone to have sex

➤ Because you've always dreamed of saying it

➤ When you're not sure

➤ Because your mate has said he's in love with someone else

➤ When you don't have her full attention

➤ When you've barely met the person

Jumping the Gun

"What do you do when you think you love someone, but it might be too early to tell her?"

If the relationship is right, you won't need to play games—you'll be able to say what you feel. However, there is such a thing as jumping the gun. For instance, Eli had been seeing Rita for only two weeks when he told me, "I want to say 'I love you' to her. Is it too soon?" Of course, there is a chance that she feels the same way, in which case Eli's impulse would be welcome. But generally, two weeks is hardly enough time to get to know someone, much less love him. Early proclamations of love run the risk of making the other person suspicious of your intentions, burdened by your needs, and turned off by thinking of you (however unfairly) as insincere or desperate. It's safer to say, "I really like you a lot," "I feel tremendous affection for you at this moment," or "I'd really like to spend more time with you."

Examine what is behind your need to profess your love so soon (control, loneliness, or insecurity). Eli realized, "I don't have too many women notice me, so if one does, I have to say it to keep her because I'm afraid there won't be another." Eli needs instead to believe that the world is abundant—and that eventually the right person will come along.

Torn Between Two Lovers

I am always hearing from people who ask if it is possible to love two people at the same time. In almost every case, the person is asking for a specific reason—because of feeling torn between two lovers.

For example, Mitch called my "LovePhones" radio show to say that he is dating a woman he really cares for—she has a terrific career, is wonderful with his family, and makes him feel so comfortable. However, he still has feelings for his former girlfriend, and still sleeps with her on occasion—and finds the sex much more satisfying. While he loves his fiancée, he can't stop lusting after his old flame.

Many men and women find themselves split—they are physically attracted to one type of person, and emotionally attracted to another. While it is unreasonable to expect that one person will satisfy all of your needs, if you cherish and value monogamy, your happiness depends on finding a mate with whom you want to pledge exclusivity. It's a little tough if you're unable to merge these two competing sides of yourself (referred to as the "Madonna-Whore Syndrome" for men or the "Daddy-Don Juan Syndrome" for women). The trick lies in embracing and integrating your competing urges.

I encouraged Mitch to imagine his current girlfriend as being incredibly sexy, more of a "bad girl." She may also be looking for an opportunity or "permission" to express another side of herself. I also suggested to Mitch that if he couldn't work out his conflicts and integrate his competing desires, he might be wise to hold off on making any commitments, or to look for someone who's a better mixture of what he wants.

The Changing Face of Love

The beauty about love is that once you give yourself permission to feel it, you can experience it many times over—in different ways, perhaps, but in satisfying variations. You *can* always feel devotion, intense caring, trust, excitement, and spiritual connection.

Sophia recalled the first time she fell in love, with Rick: "I was the happiest girl on Earth. I felt I was doing exactly what I wanted, with the person I wanted." But they eventually broke up, and for years afterward she didn't feel the same way about anyone.

Sophia found that she kept comparing her new dates with Rick. "At so many other times with so many other guys," she said, "I always wished they were different, more like Rick." Finally, years later, she met Court. While she did not feel, as with Rick, that he was perfect for her, by this time she had changed her priorities. She wasn't looking for perfection, she was looking for someone to connect with on a deeper emotional level. Sophia called it "love" again, but the criteria, definition, and experience of it had changed.

Starved for Affection

Part of love is expressing affection. However, I often get calls from people who complain that their lover is not affectionate enough—or at all. People who think they are in love but feel deprived of affection are either so overly desperate and demanding that no one could possibly fulfill their needs, or, more likely, they sabotage themselves by getting into relationships that do not satisfy their need for affection. It's also possible that their styles are just different—one is more "touchy-feely," one more reserved.

But if you find yourself picking mates who withhold affection, it's time to ask yourself a few questions. Do you feel unworthy of love? Indeed, many women grow up with fathers who never hold them or say they love them. These women go on to choose men like their fathers, and then try to change them as a way of repairing the early hurt. Learn to recognize when you are trapped in such dysfunctional attachment, misperceived as "love."

All You Need Is Love

I frequently get calls from people asking, "Is it possible that if you love each other, you can overcome anything—different religion, background, careers?"

It is possible. You can be so committed that you can withstand all kinds of barriers and pain. Unfortunately, such devotion was more likely in the covered-wagon days, when people were hardier and more loyal. In modern times, both men and women all too often run when the going gets tough.

In addition, our society has not always nurtured and supported loyalty. It's enough to make you cynical. But I say you should not accept that. Do your part to spread love and keep good energy going. You *can* overcome any odds and find and create the magic called love, any way you define it.

The Least You Need to Know

➤ Our definition of love can change over time and with different experiences.

➤ Ask yourself important questions about honesty, loyalty, and thoughtfulness before determining whether you are really in love.

➤ Love at first sight may be only lust—but lust can sometimes develop into love.

➤ Love progresses through several phases, including attraction, testing, satisfaction, and "companionate" or "conjugal" love.

Chapter 16

HEY! COME BACK!!

Who's Afraid of Commitment?

In This Chapter

➤ How to tell when it's serious

➤ Rules for commitment

➤ Recognizing and dealing with men and women with "cold feet"

➤ Overcoming fear of commitment

➤ When you move too fast

I'm frequently asked, "How can I tell if she's the one? How do I know if this relationship will lead to marriage—or if I'm even ready for that step?" Commitment tends to progress in phases, but there are a number of clues that can tip you off as to where your relationship stands.

In the best case, you've both decided to dedicate yourselves to one another, to pledge your hearts for a lifetime of commitment. But what happens if your partner is not feeling exactly the same way? Or what happens if you're being pursued by someone, and you want to take things slower? Unfortunately, not everyone arrives at the commitment stage of a relationship at the same time. In this chapter, I talk about commitment, including how to spot "commitment phobes," and what to do if *you're* the one with cold feet.

You Know It's Serious When...

Single men and women often ask me how to tell if they really care for someone and are ready to settle down. Basically, if you're asking the question, you're still not sure. But here are some signs that can help you tell how serious you're getting, in two stages:

Stage I. You know you're getting closer to making a commitment when:

➤ You cancel dates with your friends because you'd rather be with him.

➤ You start saying "we" instead of "I" or "you."

➤ You answer on her behalf (for example, the waiter asks what you'd both like to order for dinner, and you know exactly what she'll want).

➤ You start gravitating toward couples instead of singles.

➤ You no longer keep track of all the single people you know or date.

➤ You find yourself more interested in romantic movies and love stories.

➤ You like hearing stories about others who have fallen in love.

➤ You no longer worry about her checking your answering machine or opening your drawers.

➤ You get tickets to some event and instantly think of taking her instead of your best buddy.

➤ You find yourself thinking of ways to please him instead of just yourself.

➤ You wonder about what furniture and belongings you'd both give up, or merge into your joint living.

Stage II. You know you're getting close to a proposal when:

➤ You would rather be with her than with anyone or anywhere else.

➤ You say you're tired of the single life and really mean it.

➤ You think more in terms of your future: how and where you will live and work.

➤ You have a newfound interest in weddings.

➤ You consider money differently—with an eye toward a house, for instance.

➤ You expose secrets you wouldn't tell anyone else.

➤ You enjoy fantasizing about what your children will be like.

➤ You really want your families to get along.

➤ You picture yourselves growing old, sitting on some porch in rocking chairs together.

If the majority of these signs seem to apply to you, consider becoming comfortable with the idea that you are one step closer to settling down and making love work. Take the next step and share these signs with your love mate for reassurance of where you stand in your relationship.

Rules of Commitment

Here are a few simple rules about commitment that, if kept in mind, will help you avoid a lot of heartache and frustration:

➤ Rule 1: Always believe him if he says he doesn't want to make a commitment.

➤ Rule 2: Believe it if she says she's never found Mr. Right. She's challenging you to try to fit the bill, but chances are you won't be "it" either. Do you really want to audition for this difficult role?

➤ Rule 3: Always believe him if he says he doesn't like discussing his feelings. You will be miserable in this relationship—and you're a fool if you think you can change him.

➤ Rule 4: Always believe her if she says she doesn't want to change. Don't take pity or feel challenged, although it's very tempting to think that you can show her a happier way.

Men With Cold Feet

"When it comes to commitment, a glacier moves faster than my boyfriend!"

"I have been with my boyfriend for three years and he refuses to discuss our future. I have asked him if we can talk marriage, but he simply won't. Am I wasting my time with him if he won't discuss the subject?"

> **Essentials**
>
> It was the complaint of the 1980s: men who wouldn't commit, men with cold feet, "Peter Pans" (men who just won't grow up) who loved to date but were terrified of settling down. While complaints about commitment seem to have leveled off, some "commitment phobes" still abound.

If you are trying to catch someone who doesn't want to be caught, you better decide how long you can continue the pursuit. But think about this: if you truly wanted a commitment, you would probably be with someone who was more willing to commit! Keep in mind my "Mirror Law of Attraction": we are attracted to people who reflect a part of ourselves. Women who find themselves with noncommittal men frequently have some unconscious motivation not to commit themselves.

Fence-sitters rarely change until they have to—that is, until they are faced with the loss of something they truly value. If you're running out of patience with a noncommittal mate, an ultimatum will certainly put him to the test. But be careful—once you make an ultimatum, you have to follow through or you lose credibility.

Warning
Ultimatums are risky. If you say to your partner, "Marry me or good-bye," be prepared to leave if your terms aren't met. Crying "wolf" only tells your partner that your word means nothing and that you are easily manipulated.

When a pattern continues for many years, it is often difficult to change the relationship unless *you* change. If you put up with a mate's continued ambivalence or distance, that's all you will get. The only way to find out what your mate's intentions are is to ask directly; and if you are reluctant to ask, you might ask yourself whether you really want to know.

Be wary if either of you turns love into a game of control. You'll know that's happening if one of you is pushing for a commitment, and the other resists because of *feeling* controlled. In that case, back off and give each other some time, until you can approach again out of true caring and not a need to control.

Women With Cold Feet

Men are typically pegged as the ones with commitment problems. But many women have cold feet too. For example, Stephanie told me: "As soon as a guy shows he cares about me, I brush him off."

If you see yourself in Stephanie's example, think about why you back off when men advance. Some women with commitment problems have low self-esteem. Remember the cliché, "I don't want to belong to any club that would have me as a member." It's important to value the people who see your worth. By brushing off people who like you, you are devaluing their opinion, and yourself!

Essentials
As men are becoming more comfortable making commitments these days, they are complaining more about women who don't commit. Women are realizing their own problems in this department, too.

Women with commitment problems may also be looking for a challenge. These women constantly need to test their attractiveness. If you fit this description, you have to start believing that you are desirable, and make the win as valuable as the chase.

Finally, some women, like some men who have cold feet, are afraid of being suffocated. Certain "commitment phobes" were smothered by parents who made all their decisions and influenced all their choices. Sometimes a fear of commitment is really a fear of repeating the same scenario—having a mate who is too attached and too involved, just like their overbearing parents. If you see yourself in this example, resist repeating the pattern. Feel more secure in your independence. Go out only with people who have their own lives and who will not try to live through or take over yours.

Essentials

Today, more and more women want to be parents—even if they don't have a man in their lives. According to a survey I analyzed for *New Woman* magazine, a whopping 40 percent of 16,000 single women said they would consider having a child on their own.

Tips for Recognizing Cold Feet in Men and Women

Here are some clues for determining whether your love interest has commitment problems:

➤ She frequently complains there are no good men "out there." (Hint: There are, but she attracts those who aren't ready for a commitment because she's not ready herself.)

➤ He looks—and finds—imperfections and faults in all the women he's gone out with.

➤ She tends to withdraw whenever she's pursued.

➤ He's a workaholic—too busy for a relationship.

➤ She says she wants a relationship, but her love history indicates that she doesn't.

➤ You're always doing the calling and pursuing. He never takes the initiative.

I Need My Space!

Having someone tell you "I need my space" is painful. It usually means that you want that person more than he or she wants you. But if you are the one demanding some space, you may be feeling suffocated by too much intimacy.

Remember I said that for any relationship to work, both people have to have similar needs for separateness or togetherness. If you and your partner are at different stages in your psychological development, you may have very different needs for intimacy—which can cause real problems in your relationship. If your partner is demanding "more space," get to the bottom of what he means. Does he really want to separate, or does he simply need a little breathing room? Sometimes, if you are able to leave him alone, his trapped feeling will subside, and he'll come back willingly.

For example, Diane had been dating Scott for nine months when he asked her for a little "space." She was devastated, because she really loved him with all her heart. But wisely, she stepped back and didn't call him. Within a few weeks, he called and the relationship got back on track.

Keeping Secrets

Some people run from commitment because they have a hidden shame or fear of rejection. Often this is the result of some secret (you never graduated from college; you have herpes; you once broke the law) that makes you feel as if you are just not good enough. What is the solution?

➤ Change your thinking, from "No one will love me if they know my secret" to get over your shame and fear, and decide that you deserve some happiness. If you do have a secret that will affect your partner, such as herpes, *discuss it now!* Remember, your partner has a right to know.

➤ Examine how you are using your secret or your shame to avoid or escape commitment.

➤ Trust your true love by showing him the real you—but only after you feel he's earned your trust and you know him well (after at least six months).

➤ Carefully select the right time to discuss your secret, and make sure your love understands you're revealing your secret out of concern for the relationship.

➤ Be prepared for possible disappointment or rejection. Not every one will be able to handle your secret.

Sabotaging Relationships

Along the road to commitment, many couples face dilemmas about faithfulness and other crises that sabotage the relationship. For example, Mike admitted, "I seem to have a problem staying faithful. Every time I have the opportunity to cheat with a beautiful woman, I can't stop myself." You will always be confronted by others you find attractive, but that doesn't mean you have to go after all of them (or *any* of them for that matter). It sounds as if Mike needs to feel that he *can* attract beautiful women—that his ego needs constant reassurance.

In John's case, his girlfriend is the one with the wandering eye. "My girl is always looking around, staring at attractive men. She compares it to admiring a piece of art. But I hate it, and I've told her that a million times. What should I do?"

Since John's girlfriend has heard and ignored his objections, there is not a lot he can do—except reassure himself that, after all, she *is* with *him*. Although looking is not the same as touching, if you've made your feelings known and they are being ignored, take heed. Chances are, she's gazing around for a reason (and it's not just art appreciation). She may not be ready to settle down, and is checking out other guys to see whether she's interested in pursuing someone else. If you're involved with someone who can't or won't stop looking around, despite your objections, take the hint and look for love elsewhere. You'll drive yourself crazy if you stay in the situation.

Constantly comparing a present love to an ex can be another way to sabotage your making a commitment. It's natural to compare your present lover to past loves. But remember, we often idealize old relationships, forgetting the pain, insincerity, and other flaws. While it's fine to indulge your private love history occasionally, don't overdo it. Put your energy and imagination into your current relationship—not into the past.

Overcoming a Fear of Commitment

If, in reading this chapter, you recognize yourself in any of the "commitment phobes," is there anything you can do to overcome your fears? The good news is yes, but as with any other significant change, overcoming your fear of commitment will take hard work—and a commitment to change! Here are some tips:

➤ Face reality. Realize that no one person will ever fulfill all of your needs (no one is perfect).

➤ Re-prioritize. Decide that focusing primary attention on your mate is something you value (rather than valuing playing around).

➤ Condition yourself. If you have a wandering eye, stop yourself every time you turn to look at other women.

➤ Examine your need to pursue others (for attention or proof of your desirability), and get those needs satisfied in other ways.

➤ Confront any anger or tension in your relationship directly with your mate, instead of escaping them by running to other relationships.

➤ Create a different love script, replacing the one of you as a swinging single with one of you as a committed partner.

Moving Too Fast

Before closing this chapter, I'd like to point out that not all commitment problems fall on the shoulders of the one resisting the commitment. In certain situations, one person in the relationship may be applying pressure too soon and may be trying to move the relationship along too quickly.

For example, Marie had recently met Joe, and within a few weeks had decided that he was the man of her dreams. At 34, she felt "Why waste time when you *know*?" But Joe felt no sense of urgency, and in fact was put off by her insistence. Marie seemed so hungry for attachment that it was scaring him away. In this case, Joe sensed that he was being cast in Marie's love script—and he felt that she couldn't possibly know *him* after only a few weeks. He was beginning to feel that it wasn't him that she loved, but rather the idea of being in love.

If your love interest is resisting your urge for commitment, examine whether you really are moving too fast. Think about whether you are truly in love, or are casting your mate in your love script without sensitivity to who he is or what he really wants.

Evaluate your pattern of choices. Do you constantly attract people who seem sensitive about commitment, who draw away, or who move too slowly? If you tend to move quickly in relationships, make this clear from the start. Explain, "If I really like someone, I tend to go fast." If your partner balks or seems to pull back, then you should pull back, too. Being sensitive to your own and your partner's needs for intimacy or separateness is the key to fulfilling both of you individually, and to finding a balance between you.

The Least You Need to Know

➤ Always believe it when someone tells you he or she has problems with or is unwilling to make commitments.

➤ Both women and men can have fears and resistance to commitment.

➤ Trying to change a "commitment phobe" is frustrating, if not downright impossible. Examine your need to attract these types of people.

➤ If you move too fast, wanting a commitment, you may not be truly in love but have a desperate need for attachment.

Chapter 17

The Dating Duo: Fighting and Jealousy

In This Chapter

➤ Why lovers fight

➤ The ten topics lovers fight most about

➤ Assessing your anger style

➤ Eight steps to stopping arguments

➤ Rating your jealousy meter

➤ Slaying the green-eyed monster

At some point in dating, you are bound to argue about everything from simple things like which movie to see to more complex issues such as handling finances. Believe it or not, arguing is part of any healthy relationship. It enables couples to determine what triggers each other's anger, how to handle the anger, and how to resolve differences. However, constant fighting can be a warning sign in dating. As the saying goes, anger is one letter away from "danger." If you can't agree early in your relationship, think of the trouble you'll have ahead, when life together gets more complicated.

Another element that can sabotage any relationship is that "green-eyed monster" we call jealousy. Jealousy can range from the superficial, for example, being envious of another person's body, job, or car, to the not-so-superficial—that your mate may leave you for someone prettier or richer. However, one thing that all types of jealousy have in common is that they breed on your own fears and insecurities. As with any other emotion, you can learn to control it or slay the monster on the spot with lots of self-esteem and confidence.

Top Ten Topics Couples Fight About

Being prepared for the pitfalls in a relationship can help you work through them. As soon as you notice the following common sources of tension in your dating, realize that it's to be expected. Then focus on the following solutions, rather than staying stuck in stalemates.

1. When to see each other

2. How often to see each other

3. Flirting with other people

4. Forgetting important dates

5. Being faithful

6. Who spends how much money and on what

7. How you spend time (watching too much TV, going out with friends)

8. The amount or type of sex you have

9. Being late

10. Family (when and whom to visit, their disapproval)

Anger Styles

Your style of handling anger and arguments can be explained in a manner similar to explaining your communication style (see Chapter 12). The two most common styles are withdrawing into the silent treatment ("He's mad and won't talk to me"), or expressing ("I have to talk it out to feel better"). Obviously, these two styles clash. Work on accepting and compromising, so both of you can have a chance to either cool off quietly or let off steam. Admit your style to each other, so you don't feel the other person is punishing or rejecting you (it's just their way). Then agree to take turns accommodating each other.

Why You Fight

There's always a deeper issue fueling a fight. For example, all of the top ten arguments listed earlier are smokescreens for the *real* complaints: "You don't think about me enough," "You don't love me enough," or "You don't care about me enough." Once you recognize the real feeling and address that real need, you can move toward a deeper intimacy.

Different Values

Joe called "LovePhones" with this complaint: "As a result of an accident that happened at work, I collected $45,000 in workman's compensation. My fiancée wants me to use the money as an investment in a house. But I bought a T-bird and plan to use the rest of the money to purchase other 'fun' things. Now we argue about it all the time and my fiancée even says that she's not sure she wants to be engaged to me anymore."

Joe and his fiancée obviously have different priorities. She wants him to buy a house as a sign that he's ready to settle down. His resistance and his types of expenditures may be a sign that he's just not ready to make that commitment. Instead of arguing about the "smokescreens" (what to spend the money on), Joe and his fiancée need to talk about each other's deeper needs and feelings.

Battles Over Control

Many fights are really over whether you or your partner needs to be the boss—if you need to make all of the decisions. If you tend to argue over silly things, you are most likely competing over who gets his or her way. It would be a real breakthrough if you could just stop when you notice a fight over these repetitive, meaningless issues and admit, "I just need to feel in control right now."

Misunderstandings That Stem From the Past

Many times people argue because they both just see a situation in a totally different way. We each wear our own special "glasses" through which we see the world. For example, Jim wants to simply go out with his friends and have a good time. Darla, his girlfriend, instead suspects that he's looking for another woman—what her ex-boyfriend did. Before starting an argument, examine your own personal fears as well as events that happened in your past. Are you really mad at the person, or just scared that the past may be repeating itself?

Fighting as a Turn-On

Some couples endure, or purposefully invite, the pain of fighting in order to enjoy the pleasure of making up. Arguing does stimulate physical arousal that can be channeled into sexual excitement. But beware of this motivation because it can erode your relationship. Find more constructive ways to spice up your passion for one another.

Getting Over Peeves

The best love is unconditional, such as the love mothers feel for their children. But when it comes to dating, you usually find something that eventually bugs you. As Roseanne's TV sister Jackie admitted to her new beau, "I bite off my nails and spit them across the room!" She may leave her shoes lined up on the floor, he may leave the milk carton spout open, or his dirty underwear lying around. Everybody has *something*—decide if you can deal with it!

Let others' habits stop annoying you by concentrating on improving yourself. If you need to make your date feel "wrong," examine how you need to justify any self-defeating generalizations you might make about men or women (for example, that men never do anything to help out around the house or that women always nag about what men don't do). Focus on the behavior without blowing it out of proportion. Consider whether the behavior is worth bothering yourself about. Some things are just not worth your time and energy; put the peeves in proper perspective and concentrate on more important priorities.

Constant Complaining

Mike is upset because his girlfriend picks on him about everything. "She yells at me for silly things, like wearing gray socks with blue jeans, or not closing the door behind me. What's going on with her?"

Unrelenting nags and complainers are either copying the way their parents behaved, or are dissatisfied with their own lives and are taking it out on their mates. Keep in mind that naggers only keep nagging because they aren't stopped. Tell such arguers firmly that they'll have to speak to you respectfully or not at all, and to hold their tongues when they're about to start petty attacks. Ask them to examine how they can turn their own life around to fulfill their dreams so that they don't take their frustrations out on you. If naggers and complainers felt better about who they are and what they do, they wouldn't focus on your inadequacies.

How to Stop Fights

Arguments have a certain pattern that leads to an escalating cycle of unexpressed needs, unfulfilled needs, and misunderstandings. Brandon and Sue hadn't made love in three weeks. Brandon lost his sexual desire because he lost his job and felt miserable. This caused Sue to feel rejected and undesirable. At a party one night, when Sue noticed Brandon talking to a pretty woman, she immediately felt threatened, and nastily called him "a pig."

To stop these types of arguments and prevent them from occurring in the future:

➤ *Nip problems in the bud.* Mountains grow out of molehills. Sue was already building up weeks of resentment and hurt since Brandon had been neglecting her sexually. She was ready to blow her stack. Talk about your needs or complaints when they're small and you first notice them.

➤ *Clarify behavior.* Hold off blowing your stack till you get the facts. The truth is, Brandon knew the woman from work and she was married. He had no intention of going out with her. Sue jumped to conclusions, given the colored glasses of hurt she was wearing.

➤ *Explain how each other feels and ask for support when necessary.* Brandon withdrew from sex and Sue without letting her know how he was feeling—leaving her feeling insecure and vulnerable to losing her temper.

➤ *Get to the bottom of what the argument is really about.* Ask the question "What am I *really* upset about?" On the surface, people seem to be arguing about money, time, household tasks, or sex, but they're really arguing about deep emotional needs that are not being met. If your girlfriend complains that you spend more time with your friends, she's really trying to say, "I need to feel important."

➤ *Say what you want.* Don't be afraid to express the real need you have and ask for what you want. If Brandon had asked Sue for support and Sue had asked Brandon for reassurance, they wouldn't have had the misunderstanding that they did.

➤ *Exercise self-control.* Before exploding, take a deep breath and hesitate one moment. Purposefully do something else—walk away, smile, even say you feel you're about to explode but don't really want to.

➤ *Correct irrational or negative thoughts.* Don't assume the worst before you know the facts. Usually, the other person is not trying to do you in, humiliate, shame, or embarrass you; they're usually just trying to cope with their own problems.

➤ *Look for relationship patterns.* Are you getting revenge for what others in your life have done to you? Look at deeper issues: Do you feel insecure or deprived in life in general and are you taking it out on this person or situation?

Jealousy Barometer

Jealousy consumes your self-esteem, sabotages your confidence, and ultimately scares any potential good catches away. But, as with any other emotion, if you recognize it and turn it around, you can harness it—for your dating success!

The following quiz will help you gauge your potential for jealousy. For each question, score yourself on a scale from 0–10, with 10 being the most true of you, and 0 being the least true of you. When you're done, add up your total score and record it at the end of the list.

Score from 0-10

____1. I worry that others get better dates or more dates than I do.

____2. I compare what I have to others.

____3. I wish I were like some other woman/man who dates a lot.

____4. I feel better when I think I have something or someone that another person might want.

____5. I tend to buy clothes or use language to impress other people.

____6. I date people who I think my friends would admire or envy.

____7. I'm insecure about how much my love interests like me.

____8. I pout or scold if I think my boy/girlfriend is looking at others.

____9. If my date flirts with somebody else, I freak out.

____10. As soon as I walk into a room, I gauge how I compare to others.

My total score:_____

What Your Score Means

If you scored 0-20, you don't have to worry about killing the green-eyed monster—you've already learned to control it. Most of us compare ourselves to others once in a while. This is okay as long as you keep your eye on your own ball, feel good enough about who you are, and use others as examples to motivate you to be your best. Sometimes even a tiny bit of possessiveness can make your mate feel that extra spark of being prized. A score of 20–50 is a warning that comparisons are eroding your confidence and that competitiveness is blinding you from your own potential success. A score over 50 is a danger sign. You are short-changing yourself by thinking you are less than others, comparing, or copying them rather than being yourself. This makes you act irrationally out of fear and insecurity, which further sabotages your dating opportunities and damages your self-esteem.

Slaying the Monster

Most of the quiz questions deal with comparison. Your ultimate goal should be to be yourself—constant comparison will just keep you from achieving this.

Of course, there are traits worth emulating, but they don't include having bigger breasts or a fancier car. Instead of focusing on superficial concerns, think about the following:

➤ *Often, what we envy in people is their confidence.* Work on developing your own. What we admire in others is often what we want for ourselves. Don't waste your time focusing on things you can't change—your height, for example. Concentrate on things you *can* change—your assertiveness, attitude, or self-esteem. Even if you don't have his big bank account or her 34C bra size, walk around with the confidence as if you do; you can have the feeling of having what you want.

➤ *Recognize the roots of your jealousy.* Did your parents always compare you to your siblings ("Why don't you get good grades like your brother?" "Your sister never gave us any trouble.")? Resolve that you don't have to live with the ghosts of the past.

➤ *Trace your insecurity.* Tasha's mother went through three divorces—no wonder she doubted her traveling boyfriend's fidelity. Knowing the *reason* for your feeling gives you more control over it.

➤ *Make a "life philosophy" fix.* You may think the "grass is always greener," but everybody's garden has patches of brown. If you wish you could snare a Prince instead of a frog, consider Princess Diana's reported depression, eating disorders, and dating miseries, shrouded in scandals and subject to palace and public disapproval.

Tip
In overcoming jealousy or envy, keep in mind the rule of the 12-step program to overcome addictions: God give me the courage to change the things I can change, accept the things I cannot change, and the wisdom to know the difference.

➤ *Refocus your thoughts.* When you feel pangs of jealousy, envy, or insecurity, refocus. Snap your fingers or use another action that interrupts your train of thought. Then let a new thought step in to replace the destructive one. Rather than obsessing that your boyfriend is attracted to another woman, turn your attention to what you can do to spark some energy between the two of you.

Confidence

Jealousy stems from insecurity and low self-esteem. Confidence slays the green-eyed monster, so if this is your problem, turn back to Chapter 6, in which I discuss self-esteem. Whenever you become flooded with doubts about your own self-worth, keep these tips in mind:

➤ *Do affirmations.* Immediately turn your mind to all the wonderful things about yourself. Even if you are not convinced about the truth of these good things at that moment, force your mind to think these things. After all, the "bad" or "critical" thoughts you have about yourself are no more true than these positive ones (the brain, like a computer, only knows what you put in it). It's like kicking a bad habit—force yourself to stop thinking destructive thoughts by substituting constructive ones.

➤ *Make "life philosophy" corrections.* Instead of believing that others having more means you have less, believe that other people have special qualities, and so do you. The more abundance around you, the more resources available to you.

➤ *Practice imaging.* Picture yourself on a first date; everything is going beautifully—you're smiling, the two of you are chatting comfortably. Review these scenes as if you were watching a movie in your head. The mental rehearsal makes it more likely that this will happen in real life.

➤ *Become the type of person you are jealous of.* Make the lifestyle for yourself that you envy in others. Tasha always feared that her boyfriend was going to cheat on her, and she imagined him having a fabulous time with any number of irresistible women. Deep down she wanted to be that "irresistible woman," desirable and leading an exciting life. Once she started concentrating on making that true of herself, she was more fulfilled in her relationship and herself.

Controlling the Monster on the Spot

Quiz questions 7–10 test how well you handle jealousy on a real-life date. You flunked if you are distracted by the idea that your date is about to leave you for someone else. If you are convinced that you are not good enough to hold someone's attention, you will probably convince this person of the same thing. Yolanda, for example, is always comparing herself to other women, telling her boyfriend that so-and-so is much more attractive, outgoing, and so on. Eventually she may convince her boyfriend that another girl *is* a better match—but more likely, she'll just push him away with her neediness and insecurity, and she'll lose him anyway.

You also flunk if you get so flooded with fury over a date's flirting that you fly off the handle. For example, Danielle told me, "At a party recently, I saw my boyfriend talking to another woman. I stomped over and made a scene, and dragged him away. The problem is, now he's not talking to me. What did I do wrong?"

Losing your cool is the worst thing you can do—you're allowing your jealousy to overwhelm your common sense. You may think you are showing the extent of your passion, but in the final analysis, your theatricality only reveals your insecurity. Do you enjoy losing control? Do you think it is an attractive quality? Will it get you what you want (attention, devotion)? Your answer to these questions should be "No."

If you feel yourself losing control, tap that stronger place inside yourself that communicates "I feel deserving, and I don't like that behavior." Take a deep breath at the moment and calm yourself down. Distract yourself with something that makes you feel good about yourself (do *not* flirt with someone else in revenge). What is the worst thing that could happen (that your boyfriend or girlfriend will leave you)? Reassure yourself that you can deal with the outcome of this situation, whatever it may be (you are not going to fall apart). Then calmly, when the two of you are alone, tell your mate what you saw and describe your concerns. Ask for an explanation of what was really happening (to see if you misperceived the situation) and describe how you felt when you saw the two of them talking.

For example, you might say, "I was really upset when I saw you talking to that woman. I felt embarrassed, jealous, and was totally afraid of losing you. Can you tell me what was really happening?"

Jenine did it the right way. When she saw Brian flirting with another woman, she felt flushed with anger and fear. But instead of rushing over to interrupt, she waited until the next night when she and Brian were sitting together on the couch watching a video. She brought it up in a positive context first: "I love the way we are together." Starting out being positive about the two of you allays defensiveness, reinforces your self-esteem, and sets the tone for working out any problems. Then in a more casual (non-accusatory) tone, Jenine reported what she'd seen, "The other night I noticed you were talking to Lisa, and it seemed pretty cozy. I was wondering if you could tell me what was going on inside you so I really know and I won't jump to conclusions." If you can, add reassurance, "I really want an honest answer. I don't want you to feel defensive or worry about my reaction."

When Brian admitted he found Lisa attractive, instead of flying off the handle, screaming, or throwing her glass of wine at him, Jenine said calmly, "That upsets me," and asked for more clarification, "What does that mean about our relationship?" That precipitated a conversation about their commitment and about how they both felt about fidelity.

While Jenine and Brian managed to have a balanced conversation and work through the jealousy crisis, not all of your discussions will work out this way. However, keep the following in mind: communicate and clarify your feelings. Give each other reassurance, to help you grow individually and as a couple. And remember, knowing the truth is always better than being consumed by jealousy and imagining the worst.

Are You Jealous of the One You Love?

The phrase "penis envy"—coined by Freud to refer to the feeling women have of being "less than" a man—has become politically incorrect and the concept has been challenged. Somewhere along the line, psychoanalysts conceded that men suffer from "breast envy" or "vagina envy"—feeling inferior to women because they lack the equipment to nurture and feed, or to receive pleasure through penetration. Critics have eschewed both concepts. But sexual characteristics aside, there's no doubt some men and women get hooked up with certain mates because they really wish they were them!

Rose is a prime example, as she told me: "My former lover was a personal trainer. I broke up with him because he was always flirting with the women he trained and I couldn't take it."

"You're really jealous of him, aren't you?" I asked her. She was surprised to be "found out," and admitted it. He had a gorgeous body, all the girls drooled over him, and he was cocky and confident. Rose wanted all that for herself. It is not uncommon for women (and some men) to date people whom they want to be like—they feel that if they possess the person whom they so admire, then they can vicariously have the lifestyle or qualities they admire.

Do you complain that your lover spends too much time doing things that don't involve you? Are you jealous of his friends? Have you tried to keep her from doing things that don't involve you? Do you try to involve yourself in everything he does? Do you criticize his work, yet think of him as perfect? Do you feel that he is "God's gift" but you are nearly invisible? Are you always imaging that others are trying to steal your lover away? If you've answered "yes" to any of these questions, read on!

Possessiveness

Irrational jealousy over a lover's friendships reveals your own insecurity. It is unreasonable to demand that your lover drop her friends—and it's cruel to ask a lover to choose between her friends and you.

If your lover is the jealous one, threatening to leave you if you don't drop your friends, ask him to examine why he feels threatened. Reassure him to the extent that it is possible, but then insist he back off. Tell him to stop living with ghosts of his past (past betrayals) and build his self-esteem, or he may really lose you.

> ### Warning
>
> Many jealous people put their lovers through "tests," which can backfire! For instance, Sara put a note on her boyfriend's car windshield, in which she pretended to be a secret admirer. When he didn't tell her about the note, she fumed, thinking that he was unfaithful and didn't love her. Or consider Laura, who was constantly telling her boyfriend to go out with other women, to get "experience." When he finally did as she asked, she screamed at him for betraying her. "But you made me do it," he protested. "I was testing you," she cried, "and you failed." Such tests are usually unfair to the other person, who is blind to your motives and whose actions you may be quick to misinterpret. Instead, ask directly for the reassurance you need.

Does Your Date Foster Your Monster?

It *is* possible that your jealousy is not self-perpetuated, but triggered by your lover. Some people provoke others' jealousy out of insensitivity, thoughtlessness, hostility, or self-protection (hurting others before they get hurt themselves). For example, Paula's boyfriend told her, "My other lovers were much more energetic in bed. Why aren't you?" Such comparisons are a sure way of making someone feel insecure, *and* less likely to respond sexually! Mates should build, not break, your confidence.

Refusing to Let the Monster Die

Steve's girlfriend, Saundra, gives him the third degree whenever he walks in the house. Recently, an old flame called, and Saundra lost it, insisting that they were seeing each other behind her back. When Steve brought Saundra roses to express his love, she snapped, "What, did your other girlfriend turn them down?" If your jealousy is making you behave irrationally, take a big step back. You are going to alienate your lover by constantly putting him on the defensive.

Focus on your feelings. Why are *you* so insecure? Has your lover given you any real reasons to doubt him? If so, why are you still involved in the relationship? Work on the problem so that it doesn't exist. Jealousy is unattractive, off-putting, irrational, and a surefire way of sabotaging all of your relationships. Rather than studying your mate for possible infidelity or petty indiscretions, work on your own self-esteem.

The Least You Need to Know

➤ All couples have arguments; it's *how* you resolve your differences that determines whether your relationship will last.

➤ Most arguments are smokescreens for the real complaints. Remember, deeper issues fuel a fight. Get to the real need and satisfy it; the real problem and solve it.

➤ Jealousy eats you up; celebrate others' successes and grow under their glow.

➤ Turn envy into personal evolution—to become the best you can be.

Part 4
Getting Intimate

In this section, I help you feel confident about saying yes or no to sex, while also helping you clarify your intentions and expectations.

Understanding and good communication are essential components of a strong relationship, but many people have trouble talking about sex and intimacy. The chapters in this section help you over this hurdle, and my safer sex guidelines give you the necessary signposts to help you make responsible choices.

Chapter 18

Sex and Love— What's the Difference?

In This Chapter

➤ Deciding when, whether, and with whom to be intimate

➤ Can friends become lovers?

➤ Having sex to get love

➤ What part sexual fantasies play

➤ Keeping the fires burning

➤ The new sexual trend

You have been on a few dates, and the two of you seem to "click." But now comes the tricky part—sex. No doubt about it, sex is complicated. For some people, sex is purely a physical act, undertaken for the purpose of arousal, release, and pleasure. But for many others, especially women and an increasing number of men, sex is making *love*; it involves an emotional connection, an act of giving and receiving affection and sharing feelings.

Essentials

Having sex with people we love and feel loved by is emotionally and spiritually fulfilling. And research indicates that it can also be good for your health. When you engage in sex, your body releases certain hormones and chemicals (including endorphins, the "pleasure chemical") into your system that have immune-enhancing effects. These physical and psychological effects make the act even more rewarding and desirable—and make the choice of having sex and with whom much more important.

Whether you are 15 or 50, sex without love poses problems. Before you take your relationship to the next step, think carefully about your own, and your partner's, feelings. While it is tempting to act in the moment of passion, remember that sex changes a relationship for good—often for the better, but not always. In this chapter, I help you sort out the complications so that you can deal with them before you act, so no one gets hurt, and sex ends up being a good experience.

Making the Decision

Obviously, the decision to have sex is a personal one. Some people (however unwisely) still choose to have sex without any emotional commitment. There are several criteria I strongly urge you to consider before making the decision to have sex. Hold off until:

➤ You really trust one another with your emotional and physical health.

➤ You are able to communicate openly about your needs and desires and how you feel about each other.

➤ You understand each other's attitudes toward dating and sex.

➤ You understand your own physical, emotional, and sexual needs.

➤ You have spent time together nonsexually.

➤ You have observed how she treats other people.

➤ You have observed how he behaves under pressure or in emergencies.

➤ You understand the consequences of having sex.

➤ You are willing to be responsible about birth control and safe sex.

➤ You've had at least six dates.

The First Time

Sharing yourself sexually for the first time is an important step, and one that should not be taken lightly. You will likely remember this encounter forever, and it may influence your feelings about sex and love, so make sure your first experience is a positive one. Rachel recently called "LovePhones" to say, "I'm 26 and have never been sexually active. I have a fear of sleeping with the wrong person. I want it to be special." The fear isn't necessary, but her concern that the first time should be special *is* warranted. Make sure your first lover is considerate, caring, thoughtful, and giving. Be proud, not ashamed, of being a virgin until then.

Men, too, have anxieties about their first time. For example, Barry called to say, "I'm 22 and still a virgin. I've met a girl who wants to have sex, but I'm really nervous. What should I do?" It's natural to feel silly, embarrassed, or ashamed about being inexperienced—especially when you think everyone else is sexually sophisticated. Don't try to pretend that you are experienced; share your nervousness, and appreciate your naiveté. A caring partner will appreciate your honesty and the opportunity to teach you. If not, walk away—this is not a person to trust with your intimate feelings.

You can eliminate some performance pressures by talking together. Agree to take it slow, and that things may not be as great as you both expect. Spend some evenings just exploring one another's bodies through massage. Give each other feedback on where and how you like to be touched, making a more natural flow into lovemaking.

Too many men and women express regrets to me about their first time—that they felt pressured into having sex, that it wasn't special enough. Don't do it just to "get it (virginity) over with." Think *before* you act, so you'll have no regrets later.

Saying No to Sex

It boils my blood when people feel pressured to have sex. It isn't just women. Men often feel pressure, too. It takes a lot of security to say no. But I urge you, if that's how you feel, say no! Don't worry about sounding foolish, being embarrassed, or ruining any spontaneity. It's better to be sure about such an important decision, so there are no misunderstandings and poor choices.

Valerie was so nervous about the issue, it even kept her from dating: "I get so nervous when guys ask me out. I keep thinking that somehow, sex will come up. It makes me so nervous that I never go out with anyone." Realize that YOU have control over what happens. Valerie's nervousness is extreme, and implies some sort of early trauma or bad experience. In any case, recognize that you can readily set the limits. At the beginning of a date, if you feel any pressure, spell out your intentions. Be direct. You can say something like, "I find you attractive and I want to go out with you, but I don't want to imply that I will jump into bed. That's a really important step for me that takes time."

Don't put yourself in compromising situations. If you have any doubts about a person, don't accept a date. But if you are out with someone who is more forward than you are comfortable with, make your feelings clear. You might even bring up the subject of sex in a very general way. For instance, mention that you heard something about casual sex on the radio or in the newspaper. State your opinions; put the issue right out on the table. For example, you might say, "I believe people should wait to have sex. They should care about each other. I'm simply not into casual sex." If your date becomes angry or loses interest, let him go. A person who doesn't respect your feelings on such an intimate issue is not someone to trust with your heart, body, or soul.

Ways to Say No

Saying no can be difficult. Here are some additional handy phrases to help make it easier:

> "I really like you, but I'm not ready for sex."

> "We have to get to know each other better."

> "Being intimate is very special to me and I have to trust the person first."

Using Sex to Get Love and Vice Versa

On my "LovePhones" radio show, I frequently get calls from women who complain that they are only having sex with their boyfriends out of fear of losing them. For instance, Jane called in and said, "I keep getting involved with men who sleep with me, but then won't call. What am I doing wrong?" Perhaps more surprisingly, I get similar calls from some men.

Too many people have sex when what they are really looking for is love. If you sleep with someone whose feelings are not the same as yours, you are bound to end up feeling hurt. It's a mistake to have sex with someone you don't really know with the expectation of receiving love, just as it's a mistake to mislead someone into thinking that you care when all you really want is sex.

My advice is to hold off having sex until you really know someone and what he wants out of a relationship. You can't possibly know someone's true intentions early in a relationship. If you find yourself jumping into bed too soon, examine your self-esteem and deeper emotional needs.

Some people (admittedly more men than women) love the thrill of conquest, and will "work" the relationship until they get what they want. After that, they lose interest. If you've ever been in this situation, you know how easy it is to blame yourself—for not being interesting, sexy, or attractive enough. Instead, recognize you were being used, and be wise to prevent it from happening next time.

For instance, Anita called and told me about a man in her economics class. "This attractive guy in my class flirted with me shamelessly and wrote 'I love you' on my notebook. He called me a few times and once we had phone sex. After that, he stopped talking to me. What's up?" It is very possible that this man either got what he wanted, or realized he wasn't going to get exactly what he wanted, so he pulled away. Anita should be glad this guy came and went so quickly. Also, I urged her to take responsibility for her own actions. After all, she engaged in sexual phone games with a man she barely knew. As the saying goes, if you cast your net too wide, you're bound to snag a few bad fish.

How Can You Tell if Someone Just Wants Sex?

As I mentioned in Chapter 13, the Virginia Slims Opinion Polls taken over the past 25 years reveal that women still complain that men treat them as sex objects. So now let's consider how you can tell if someone likes you for who you are, or is interested in just one thing—sex? Put him to the test: if you hold off on sex, what is his reaction? If he disappears, you know his intentions. If he sticks around, talk about your fears of being wanted only for sex, how having sex changes the relationship for you, and how you need to know you're cared for. Spell out the qualities that you value: listening, giving, and communicating.

Be wary of dates who

> ➤ Plant persistent sexual innuendoes in the conversation.

> ➤ Don't seem to listen.

> ➤ Have no history of long-term relationships.

> ➤ Make no or rare references to the future (phone calls or dates).

> ➤ Feed you challenging lines such as "You're the only girl I ever felt anything for" or "You could be the one to finally make me change my ways."

> ➤ Only call at the last minute or in the middle of the night.

> ➤ Agree to meetings only on their terms or at their request.

> ➤ Leave you feeling used, empty, or frustrated.

Using Sex to Manipulate

Having sex just to please or keep another person is not only damaging to one's self-esteem, it is manipulative and misleading. For instance, Sue's boyfriend lives in another city. She explains, "When he comes to visit, we make love but I don't always feel comfortable about it. But I don't want to do anything to make him think I'm seeing someone else. What should I do?" I suggested to Sue that she be honest, and if he is uncomfortable with her discomfort and decides to leave, perhaps the relationship was not on solid ground to begin with. Unless Sue expresses what she wants and needs, she'll never truly feel loved. Furthermore, by deceiving her boyfriend, she is not giving him a chance to really know her or please her if there ever was a chance for that.

Tara doesn't like certain positions in sex, but explains, "I do it because I know my boyfriend likes it and if I don't I'm afraid that he will find another woman who will." Let him. How do you think you "have him" anyway if you're sacrificing your self-esteem and self-respect just to keep him? Ultimately, the relationship is not going to work out because Tara's boyfriend will probably sense that she is desperate and willing to sacrifice her own self-esteem for his affection. As a result, he may start treating her poorly. Good relationships are built on honesty and trust, not dishonesty and manipulation.

Expecting Sex

Be wary of your expectations that a date will lead to sex. No one likes to be taken for granted or pressured. For example, Tom met Lisa while she was on a business trip in Florida. They hit it off, and he invited her back for a weekend, and even offered to pay for her trip. When she got there, he took her luggage into his room. Lisa freaked out and was upset that he assumed she would be having sex with him. The moral: Spell out your expectations, even if it seems forward or kills the spontaneity. Or better yet, don't have any expectations!

Just Sex

I'm frequently asked, "Is it possible to have a purely sexual relationship without any feelings being involved?"

Some people are just not looking for love or a long-lasting relationship; sex serves as a momentary thrill or satisfaction of an emotional or physical need. If both people feel the same way (and practice safe sex), no one gets hurt (like in the trend these days for "buddy sex," in which friends have sex but agree not to be committed to each other).

While such arrangements are possible when both people feel the same way, many people think they can pull it off only to discover that they really expect more or end up feeling more than they thought they would. Just as you should spell out your intentions about wanting to wait before becoming intimate, be equally clear if you go out with someone with the hope of having sex (and not much else). Say something like "I'm not looking for a commitment, so please don't feel hurt if I don't end up calling you or giving you what you want. Sex may not mean as much to me as it does to you." This is a bit cold, but it's certainly a fair alert.

I hope you come to see that the best sex is in the context of a loving, committed relationship. But if not, before you engage in an act that for you is devoid of feeling, consider not only your intentions, but also your partner's feelings. My suggestion is if you don't feel anything for the person you are sleeping with, but you know that person has feelings for you, move on before you cause a lot of heartache.

The best sex merges the physical act with an emotional and spiritual attachment. As one man I know put it, "She's the paint, I'm the brush, and the bed is our canvas, to create our beautiful painting of love."

The Sex/Love Split

After years of counseling patients and fielding calls on "LovePhones," I've heard from a lot of people who are confused about sex and love. In particular, I commonly hear the following two types of questions that are related to an important issue called "splitting."

The first type of question:

> "How come I can have great sex with a woman, but as soon as I start to develop feelings for her, I don't get turned on anymore?"

The second type of question relates to being torn between two opposite-type lovers:

> From men: "I like these two women: One is gentle and sweet and the other is a real tiger in bed. I'm torn. How do I decide between them?"

> From women: "I'm dating these two men: One would be the perfect husband and father—the kind of guy that my parents would love—and the other is a real exciting 'bad boy.' I wish I could mesh them into one guy, but I can't. What can I do?"

Separating sex and love can lead to an intriguing but disturbing dilemma referred to as the "Madonna/whore syndrome" in men or the "Daddy/Don Juan syndrome" in women. Here, the "sufferers" split lovers into either sweet, nice people or wild, sexy ones. Sex becomes desirable only with the latter, not the former.

While I frequently encounter this problem with married people, it also occurs with singles who are torn between two "opposite" lovers. For instance, Bill was enamored of Jill, a sweet, gentle woman who had all the qualities he wanted in a long-term mate. And she adored him and wanted to marry and start a family. The problem was, he found her boring in bed. Bill was also seeing Liza, a woman who had few of the qualities he valued for a wife and mother of his children, but who really turned him on sexually. Liza was fond of Bill, but wasn't interested in settling down. But every time Bill decided to totally devote himself to Jill, he ended up calling Liza for a "roll in the hay."

Men like Bill are compelled to seek a challenge, and often devalue the very people who most value them. They think they are looking for the "perfect" person who combines all of the values they supposedly want with the sexual attraction they crave, but in reality, they can't let one person be everything to them.

If you recognize yourself in Bill's scenario, it's time to retrain your brain. Rather than separating sex and love, insist on having one with the other. Take a look at your relationships: Do you stereotype men as either fathers or lovers, and women as either mothers or lovers? If so, look at your partners clearly. Are they really so easily pigeonholed? Allow your mate the opportunity to express both roles. Communicate all your fantasies, desires, wants, and needs (sexual and otherwise) and give your mate a chance to fulfill the many sides of you.

Admit that both sex and love are equally important and possible with one person. Discover that your lover is trusting, honest, steadfast, *and* a wild lover. These traits are not mutually exclusive!

Turning Friends into Lovers

Friendship is the best basis for love. So I find it charming when people ask me how they can change a friendship into a romance. It can be tricky—you have to be willing to take a risk that might put your friendship in jeopardy. Most people who admit they want something more would rather stay friends than risk losing what they have. But keep in mind that becoming romantic may not ruin the friendship; if you take the risk and your friend responds positively, it will strengthen it. And if your friend does not reciprocate your feelings, at least you know where you stand and can direct your energies elsewhere. Of course, it's up to you to gauge whether the potential rewards are worth the gamble—but I'd recommend going for it.

It can be tough to broach the subject of attraction with your friend, especially if you fear that your feelings are not going to be reciprocated. Remember the saying, "It is better to have loved and lost than never to have loved at all." Talk your feelings over, sharing your mutual expectations and fears. You could have the happiest experience of your life. One man posed the change this way. He told his friend: "Our friendship is over," and then, after a pregnant pause during which she was confused and nervous, he added, "Now, let's try being more than friends."

If it looks like you can't turn the friendship into love, it's up to you to control your longing, to keep the friendship close, but not intimate. As with any unrequited love or impossible situation, don't waste your energy wishing or hoping. Julie said, "I have strong feelings for a friend and I know nothing is going to happen between us, but every time I see him with another woman, I get jealous. How can I overcome this feeling?" As soon as the feeling overtakes you, switch your mind to planning or doing something for yourself. Focus on finding someone who can be both friend and lover. Figure out what you like about your friend and be open to someone else who possesses those qualities.

Who Makes the First Move?

Just as described in Chapter 8, more men today are relieved when a woman takes the initiative in sex, because it takes the pressure off them to always advance or perform. But men can also be a little intimidated by a sexually aggressive female. Tony was divorced four years ago and now is back in the dating game. "Are women really this fast now?" he asked me. "I like candlelit dinners, and they seem to want to get right to it!" At the end of Tony's date, the girl said outright she'd like to have sex. "I was so bowled over by such a bold female," he admitted, "that I was really worried about whether I could get it up for her."

While it may make you feel uncomfortable to know sex is expected of you on a date, *not* being approached can leave you feeling undesirable, frustrated, or confused. Cybil dated Howard six times, but complained, "He was a perfect gentleman, but I was jumping out of my skin, wanting him to do something. I was wondering if he was gay, strange, or impotent, and what was wrong with me." Courtney also complained, "I've been seeing this guy for three months and he's only kissed me. I can't help feeling he doesn't want me. I also don't want to be the one who does everything first. What's up?" Find out from him whether he is shy, inexperienced, or afraid of getting hurt. Explain that you feel uncomfortable being the initiator (but don't fall into sex-role stereotypes of expecting the man to make all the first moves).

If someone doesn't make a move, don't immediately assume you're not attractive enough. Find out what else is going on with that person (another relationship, inexperience, fear of rejection, embarrassment about themselves, their body, sex). Take a risk and state your own interest.

Cybil did the right thing. On her next date with Howard, she was open with him and said, "I've really enjoyed being with you, and I wonder why we haven't kissed, because we've had a great time and I wanted to kiss you." Thankfully, Howard was willing to be equally honest. He explained that he was afraid of making moves too quickly, and that Cybil might consider him too forward. Howard's openness about his fear, and Cybil's reassurance, were just the right triggers to give them permission for their first kiss.

How Important Is Sex?

Couples often fall "out of love" when the sex that was once good falters. For instance, Darlene called "LovePhones" and remarked, "Our sex life was great, but it's now so boring. I'm tempted to throw in the towel, or at least to have a little fling. My boyfriend doesn't seem to mind that the passion has cooled."

Every couple has to decide how important sexual compatibility is in the relationship. Lust and passion does tend to cool over time, and it often takes considerable effort to "keep the fires burning."

Essentials
A University of Minnesota study found that more than half of the students surveyed said they would move toward divorce if the passion ever went out of their marriage.

Warning
If you're just starting a relationship and the sex isn't satisfying or you're already thinking about straying, you're setting yourself up for failure.

Face your sex problems head-on. Do you have different sex drives, a sexual problem (such as premature ejaculation or inability to orgasm), or different preferences for positions, acts, or fantasies? Are you willing to work on the sexual aspect of your relationship? If not, then you should probably consider letting the relationship go. Sex doesn't have to be a top priority in your relationship, but if sex problems are driving you apart or pushing you to infidelity, then there are issues to be addressed.

Finally, examine your dating history. Do you have a pattern of sexual problems with partners? Is there a specific problem that keeps recurring? Are you choosing relationships that bring out this problem? Since sex is so personal, problems in that area can be a smokescreen for other troubles, such as fear of intimacy or commitment.

Many people take a lover's sexual problem personally. For example, when a man is having erection problems, the woman may feel it's her fault, that she's not attractive enough. Or if a woman is having problems with orgasm, the man may feel inadequate as a lover. Self-reproach or blame only makes the situation worse.

Different Sex Drives

Karen's boyfriend is ready for sex at any time, but she is not. She wonders, "Is there a chance for us?" Possibly. As with many couples, Karen and her boyfriend have different sex drives; no matter what's going on, he's ready, whereas her feelings are much more affected by her mood, the situation, how much time they have, and many other factors. Just as with other aspects of the relationship, decide how high a priority this part of your life is. Then, to make the relationship work, accept each other's differences and make compromises.

Some people have a naturally higher sex drive than others, but libido levels are related to many factors, both physical and psychological. This should reassure you that ups and downs are normal and do not signal the death knell of a relationship, and that changes and adjustments can be made.

Tip
Sex is not the only way of expressing love. Be creative; there are countless, warm, emotionally satisfying ways of communicating and sharing. Keep in mind that lack of self-esteem, loneliness, or boredom won't be cured by sex.

Essentials

Sex drives are affected by hormone levels that themselves can be decreased (by illness or medication) or increased. Research has shown that women who make love weekly have twice as many circulating hormones as those who have sex sporadically or not at all. Also, certain foods are reported to boost hormone production, especially those that are high in vitamin B-12, vitamin K, and zinc.

Fantasies

Many people worry about whether their sexual fantasies are okay. Of particular concern is fantasizing about someone else when you are making love to your partner. For example, Mike told me, "I fantasize about my friend's girlfriend when I'm with my own girlfriend."

Whether or not this is a problem depends on the reason for the fantasy. Sometimes, our fantasies have to do with things we want sexually that our partner isn't willing or able to give us. Other times, fantasies allow us to experience feelings that we don't feel free to express to our mates. For example, Mike was a virgin when he hooked up with his more experienced girlfriend. Thinking about someone else during sex with her was his way of making up for his inexperience, and for expressing his upset and jealousy about her other relationships.

If you are able to discover the purpose of your fantasy, you can decide if it is healthy or damaging to your relationship. In Mike's case, he needed to get over his anger toward his girlfriend and his insecurity about his relative inexperience. When he realized what was going on inside him, the fantasies stopped. In other cases, the fantasy can be helpful, to show you what you would like to do or feel with your present partner. Once you realize this, consider expressing, revealing, and sharing your fantasy with your partner.

Self-Pleasure

Engaging in self-pleasure (masturbation) is a natural act even when you're having sex with someone you're dating. Women who feel upset and inadequate after discovering a guy masturbating need to realize that, while it *is* possible urges are not being satisfied, it is also possible he just needs normal private time.

After-Burn, After-Glow

Many people, especially women, have complicated, intense reactions after having sex. Some fall into what I call "after-sex addiction"—becoming intensely attached to someone after having sex, even if you didn't care all that much for the person before. The experience of "giving your body" makes you feel more invested in the relationship.

Tip
Some men still seem to have difficulty expressing feelings of love during sex, but have less of a problem expressing themselves physically. In these cases, what seems to be insensitivity or obsession with sex is really a fear or inability to communicate verbally about love. These men should own up to their partner to prevent misunderstandings.

At the other end of the spectrum, other people retreat after sex, as Carla found out. "After dating Ken for a short while, we had sex. The next day, he didn't even want to talk to me. I still like him, and at least want to be friends. What's his problem?" If you really want to know, ask him. Don't waste one minute wondering, hoping, or torturing yourself. You may not get a satisfactory answer, since a person who retreats after intimacy may not be able to give you the response you need. But at least you've relieved some of your own anxiety by asking the question. Be prepared to let the relationship go if he isn't prepared for or receptive to your devotion.

Just as I mentioned about dating in general earlier in this book, having sex is an opportunity to learn about yourself and people. Always get feedback. Ask your partner, "What did our relationship mean to you? How do you feel now?

How do my actions affect how you feel? What did I do to affect how you acted?" Ask without implied criticism or demands. This means a magical combination of what I call "non-demand dating" (not expecting any response), and "informed dating" (learning from your experience). Your mate may be too immature, inarticulate, or inexperienced to answer you honestly, or he may not have insight into his own motives or feelings. But at least you know you've tried.

Spicing Up Your Sex Life

Kevin called "LovePhones" and said, "My girlfriend likes to role-play. One night she wanted to dress like a reindeer and make me Santa." I asked, "What would YOU like to be?" He answered, "I'd like to be a musician and have her be a groupie." My advice: Go for it!

Do you have a favorite fantasy "sex script?" Or is there a particular sex scene from a movie or book that turns you on? There is nothing wrong with imagining or acting out fantasies, as long as each partner is into the scene. Be creative. You have nothing to lose but your inhibitions.

Many people have idiosyncratic sexual desires or fetishes. For instance, Larry called "LovePhones" and said, "I really want my girlfriend to take nude pictures of me with her bra on my head." Carla called and said, "I get excited having sex when other people are around, like in the mall or parking lot." Fantasies and desires are very revealing. Think about your own; what do they tell you about yourself? How do your desires make you feel (safe, secure, risqué, rebellious, different)? If you're not hurting anyone, then it's fine to consider acting out your fantasies or indulging your fetishes. If, however, you are using this behavior to escape a real relationship and intimacy, reconsider and focus on some healthier activities.

Battles Over Control

Over the years, as the world has become more complex and daily life more stressful, I've noticed that more and more people tell me about their interest in sex acts involving dominance and submission. There is nothing wrong with playing "master and slave"—it can even be constructive, where one person is in control and the other takes orders. But the most extreme form of this behavior—*sadomasochism*, in which partners derive satisfaction from inflicting and enduring pain—is a serious disorder that reveals an inability to experience love, intimacy, and vulnerability. People who need to experience pain during sex are also usually numb to loving emotions. Furthermore, they may be so afraid to show their true needs for nurturing or love that they mask their needs with aggression. While some people may defend their indulgence in such activities, I feel most need professional help to release themselves to love.

It cannot be denied that even to less extreme degrees, couples get involved in power struggles in and out of bed. As Roman says, "My girlfriend acts like a drill sergeant. She bosses me around and doesn't listen. During sex, she tells me faster, harder. It's all for her. When she's finished, she rolls over and leaves me there." Roman has a female partner who behaves as many men do—selfishly! Roman needs to ask himself if he is looking for someone to control him, because he is afraid of being controlling himself. I suggested to Roman that he make control a deliberate game with his girlfriend—that he practice being the commander-in-chief for a change, and that they then take turns. Playing the extremes can be a helpful technique for couples to reach some kind of middle ground.

Keep in mind that whether you are straight, gay, or bisexual, the issues dealt with in this book all apply to you. The feelings, conflicts, and solutions are the same no matter who you are and with whom you get involved. But some questions that arise regarding dating are specifically related to sexual orientation, as many people ask me whether their actions or thoughts mean that they are gay or bisexual.

Bi-Curious: The New Sexual Trend

Bi-curious is a word of the 1990s—meaning those men and women who think they're basically attracted to the opposite sex, but who also feel intrigued about or have experienced sexual encounters with someone of the same sex. It has been said that the worst thing about bi-curiosity is that reading the personals takes twice as long.

As much as our society has come a long way in being more accepting of people with varying sexual orientations, there are still pressures both from outside and from within. I encourage everyone to value, trust, and accept themselves, but I hear so many men and women who doubt themselves and worry about their impulses and feelings.

Jim: "I've had a girlfriend for two years and I'm not gay, but I'm attracted to my best friend who is a guy. Why do I feel this way?"

Pat: "I love my boyfriend, but my best friend, who also has a boyfriend, kissed me one day. I had some feelings about it going further. What does this mean?"

This could mean that you're beginning to "come out" and realize your homosexuality, or it could also mean that, as in the case of about one in four men, you're at a point in your life where you are experiencing an attraction to the same sex. Think about what this person represents to you. Is he a mirror reflection of yourself (so attraction to him is a way to appreciate yourself); an image of the way you'd like to be (and therefore a sign of the qualities you should develop in yourself); a curiosity (that can also be quite normal); or just a natural attraction that you have always felt but suppressed?

Be aware of how acting on your attraction could impact your current relationship—always think of the consequences of your actions before acting on them. Every fantasy does not have to be acted out immediately; thinking it through can have value in its own right.

If you find yourself with a bisexual lover, you may face a dilemma like Craig: "I've been dating a girl for three years and she just told me that although sex is amazing with me, she also has a female lover. I can't share her. What should I do?"

You can't force a person to only be with you, no matter what sex that person's attracted to. If you don't want to share her, you'll have to let her go. However, don't think that your sex with her was inadequate in any way. The need for someone else, of whatever sex, is not about what you lack, but about her needs that you alone cannot fulfill, no matter how great the sex between you is.

The Least You Need to Know

➤ The perfect combination is having sex with someone you love, fulfilling both physical and emotional needs.

➤ Clarify your intentions and expectations about sex and love so that neither person is misled or disappointed.

➤ Feel confident about saying yes or no to sex.

➤ Understanding and good communication is essential for good sex.

➤ Accept your sexual urges, feelings, and desires; self-love is important for happiness within yourself and when choosing a partner.

Approaching Sex Safely and Sanely

> **In This Chapter**
>
> ➤ Making sure you don't get pregnant when you don't want to
>
> ➤ Safer-sex activities to avoid risk of disease
>
> ➤ Condom-sense
>
> ➤ Sexually transmitted diseases (STDs) to watch out for

Birth control and safe sex are topics that must be covered in a book on dating—especially in these times, when there are still so many unplanned pregnancies, and such risks of sexually transmitted diseases. If you avoid these subjects, you certainly are not ready for a sexual relationship.

With so much information available, there is no excuse for not being informed about issues regarding safe sex. Since the goal in love is to find a relationship based on honesty, openness, and trust, I admit that sexuality today is tricky business. You can't always accept someone's word that he or she is disease-free or using birth control. You must protect yourself—both from pregnancy and venereal disease. This chapter gives you the information you need to make informed choices and to stay safe.

Essentials

The 1996 Durex Global Survey of Sex and Condom Use of over 10,000 adults from 15 countries showed that of the factors considered most important when making love, protection against having an unwanted child was rated by only 16 percent of the respondents, not catching or spreading the HIV/AIDS virus was rated by 18 percent, and not catching or spreading other STDs was rated by only 5 percent.

The highest rated concern was satisfaction of self or partner, 27 percent and 37 percent, respectively. Women rated avoiding unwanted pregnancy as being more important than men did. Thailand and Germany were the countries most concerned about not catching or spreading HIV/AIDS.

Pregnancy Prevention

"Where do babies come from?" is a question little kids commonly ask. But you'd be shocked, as I am, to know how many adults don't understand the basics of how male and female bodies work, all of the activities and conditions that can lead to pregnancy, and the ways to prevent conception.

I get so many calls on "LovePhones" from men and women who are confused about the basics about reproduction. Many also have a sketchy understanding of birth control, and the risky behaviors (other than penetration) that can cause pregnancy. It seems that a lot of people need very basic and important information.

There are four basic types of contraception: barrier, hormonal, sterilization, and natural methods. Consult your doctor or a family planning clinic for specific information and for advice on the best method for you. Women as well as men should take responsibility for protecting themselves, and it's not a bad idea to use *two* methods to be doubly sure.

Barrier Methods

The barrier methods include condoms (for both men and women), diaphragms, and cervical caps. These methods are readily available and have no side effects (although an occasional person is allergic to latex or the spermicide used with diaphragms). These days, condoms can be purchased in almost any pharmacy and in many other stores as well. Buy only latex condoms, as the lambskin variety is not effective in preventing some diseases.

Diaphragms and cervical caps are available by prescription. Women must visit a gynecologist or family planning clinic to be fitted for these devices. When used with spermicidal jelly or cream, diaphragms and cervical caps are highly effective; although their effectiveness drops significantly without the spermicide. The message is obvious—use the spermicide.

Care should be exercised to ensure the effectiveness in placement and removal of these methods, and that requires being comfortable with touching your genitalia.

Warning
Never reuse a condom. Also, while you can leave a diaphragm in place for several hours (insert more spermicide if you have more sex), don't forget to remove it!

Hormonal Methods

Hormonal methods of birth control include the Pill, Norplant implants, Depo-Provera, and the IUD. All of these methods require a visit to a gynecologist or family planning clinic, and all involve some expense and have some side effects. These may include bleeding, headaches, depression, and changes in appetite or sex drive.

The Pill is highly effective when used properly, but some women forget and miss doses. If you have trouble remembering to take the Pill, consider Depo-Provera, hormonal shots that are effective for 12 weeks. Another option is Norplant, slow-release hormone capsules that are implanted directly under the skin (usually on the upper arm), that last a few years. If you want to get pregnant, the Depo-Provera shots can be discontinued, or the Norplant capsules can be removed at any time by a trained physician or other health care worker.

The IUD, which stands for intrauterine device, is available by prescription. Made of plastic or copper, the device is placed in the uterus where it thwarts pregnancy in one of two ways: either by preventing the egg from being implanted in the uterine wall or by preventing the sperm from fertilizing the egg. IUDs have endured some controversy and suffered in popularity, although many physicians consider them safe and reliable.

Natural Birth Control

Perhaps the least effective birth control methods are so-called natural methods, such as withdrawal, or planning sexual encounters according to the rhythm method, checking the woman's body temperature, or checking the consistency of the woman's vaginal mucus. Withdrawal requires that the man pull out of the woman's vagina before he ejaculates. This is problematic for at least two reasons: One, many men do not have this kind of control, and two, sperm is involuntarily released before ejaculation.

The rhythm method involves timing sex around a woman's cycle, avoiding times of higher fertility during mid-cycle or ovulation. The trouble is, some women have irregular cycles, or get sloppy about keeping track. Even if you're careful, you *can* get pregnant at any time during your cycle. If you are serious about avoiding pregnancy, think twice before relying on "natural" forms of birth control.

Sterilization

The last resort for most people of child-bearing age is sterilization (tubal ligation for women, vasectomy for men). Sterilization involves surgical procedures that should be considered permanent (although some men do have their vasectomies reversed). Unless you are absolutely certain that you never want children or you have the number of children you want, choose another method.

The Scoop on Sexually Transmitted Diseases (STDs)

I am continually amazed by the number of people who call "LovePhones" to ask about medical problems but who are too terrified or embarrassed to see a doctor. If you have any concerns about your health, put that embarrassment aside and get to the doctor right away. Many young people avoid seeking medical advice out of fear that their parents will find out. Your health is more important than your shame and fear of punishment. Use the opportunity to talk with your parents about sex, or request a private consultation with your doctor and be completely open about your problems.

An STD (sexually transmitted disease) is any disease acquired primarily through sexual contact. Most STDs are caused by bacteria, viruses, and other microorganisms. Some are hard to detect and all can lead to serious health problems (including infertility and death) if left untreated. Medical diagnosis and treatment is essential.

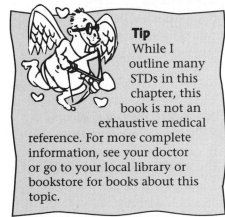

Tip
While I outline many STDs in this chapter, this book is not an exhaustive medical reference. For more complete information, see your doctor or go to your local library or bookstore for books about this topic.

Statistics indicate that 12 million *new* cases of sexually transmitted diseases are diagnosed each year, many in women and people under the age of 25. In addition, more than 50 million Americans currently suffer from STDs. That's about one in every four men and women. "Old" infections (gonorrhea, syphilis, and venereal warts) are resurfacing, and more than 20 new diseases have been identified in the past decade.

You might think that only people who are promiscuous are the ones accounting for these high numbers—but it's important to realize that it only takes *one* time having sex to be exposed to some disease.

HIV and AIDS

AIDS (Acquired Immunodeficiency Syndrome), caused by *HIV* (Human Immunodeficiency Virus), has forever changed the way we think about sex. By far the deadliest STD, AIDS is transmitted through body fluids such as blood and semen. An estimated 1 million Americans are infected, with the largest risk groups still composed of homosexual men and intravenous drug users. However, more and more heterosexual women and teens are infected every year. They put themselves at risk by thinking "It can't happen to me," and have unprotected sex or excessive sexual activity, and are uneducated about the risks. While treatment options now exist, there is no known cure for this disease.

AIDs has forced people to talk openly about sex, to think seriously about commitment and intimacy, and to put their health above instant sexual gratification.

Getting Tested

People fear getting tested for HIV, yet it is the only responsible thing to do in these times. Worrying is a waste of time. Take action and find out the facts. David was going for his results and panicked, "What if I'm positive?" Instead of just obsessing, suffering from what my friend Frank Hagan calls "Afraids," use this anticipatory anxiety to make yourself aware of dangers and to motivate yourself to behave more safely in the future.

Other Viral Infections

Genital herpes is a virus that produces blister-like lesions on the genitalia, buttocks, anus, and certain other areas. It can be present and contagious without symptoms, and is easily spread. While the symptoms, especially at first outbreak, can be treated with medication, the virus stays in the body. About 40 million American men and women have herpes. Condoms reduce the risk, but do not necessarily cover all the areas where the virus may be present. Also, oral herpes (cold sores on the mouth) can be transferred in oral sex to genital herpes. The stigma of having herpes must be overcome, and care must be exercised in sexual activity.

Genital warts (*human papilloma virus*), spread by anal, oral, or vaginal sex, produce hard fleshy bumps on the internal and external genitalia. Though usually harmless, they have been linked to certain cancers of the penis, vulva, cervix, and anus. While warts may disappear on their own, they may also be treated by a doctor, who can remove them by freezing, burning, using chemical solutions, laser therapy, or when necessary, surgery. The good news is that, unlike herpes, genital warts don't pop up again on their own.

Infectious *mononucleosis* (the "kissing disease"), caused by the Epstein Barr (herpes) virus, results in mild to extreme fatigue and fever that often lingers for months and requires a great deal of rest and stress reduction.

Bacterial Infections

Chlamydia, the most common STD, affects millions of people each year. This infection causes inflammation of the urethra, which can eventually lead to chronic pain and sterility in women and testicular problems in men. Many women experience no symptoms in the early stage of the disease, while in men, the symptoms are painful urination and the discharge of pus from the urethra. The disease is treatable with antibiotics.

Gonorrhea (commonly referred to as the "clap") has resurfaced in recent years with some drug-resistant strains. The bacteria lives in moist, warm cavities—such as your mouth, throat, rectum, and urinary tract (and cervix in women). Symptoms include frequent urge to urinate, painful urination, genital burning and itching, or unusual yellowish discharge from the penis or cervix. Fortunately, it can be treated.

Pelvic Inflammatory Disease (PID) occurs when a bacterial infection from an STD (gonorrhea or chlamydia), IUD, or other source spreads from the lower genital organs to the reproductive organs (tubes, womb, ovaries, abdominal lining), causing scars that prevent passage of fertilized eggs and complications leading to infertility or tubal pregnancy. Symptoms include a yellowish discharge, painful urination, spotting, fever, nausea, vomiting, and pelvic pain caused by swelling or tenderness in the cervix, uterus, or surrounding tissue, which are easily spotted during a routine gynecological exam. PID may be exacerbated by douching or use of intrauterine devices that force the infection further into the reproductive channels.

Syphilis is one of the more serious STDs, caused by the spirochete (a corkscrew) bacterium that can attack any body part. If untreated, it can progress to disability, dementia, and death. The infamous WWII epidemic was brought under control in the 1950s with the discovery of penicillin, but surprisingly, reported cases have doubled over the past decade (to 130,000 a year). The disease starts with chancre sores (pimple-like lesions) and if untreated, progresses to fevers, aches, and rashes, ultimately invading the eyes, heart, nervous system, bones, joints, brain, and other organs, leading to death in the final stage. A doctor's diagnosis (with blood tests) is necessary, since symptoms "mimic" other diseases such as heat rash and measles.

Fungus

Candidiasis, also know as a *yeast infection*, is caused by an overgrowth of a fungus that naturally lives in the vagina, mouth, and intestine of healthy people. As many women can attest, during periods of stress or after a course of antibiotics, the fungi can grow out of control, with symptoms including a thick, white, curdy discharge, itchiness, redness, swelling, and odor. While it is important to get an accurate diagnosis, yeast infections are readily treated with an antifungal medication that is now available over-the-counter at the pharmacy.

Parasites

Pubic lice (*crabs*) is one of the few STDs you *can* get from clothing, bedding, towels, and possibly toilet seats, as well as from direct sexual contact. It is cured by treatments such as Rid or Kwell, which you can get from a pharmacy. Make sure to wash everything carefully.

Essentials

STDs can "ping-pong"—partners can infect and re-infect one another continually. The reason is that one or both partners may be asymptomatic, so the disease may go unrecognized and untreated. This can happen with everything from yeast infections to herpes.

Safe Sex Steps

The safest sex, of course, is no sex. But short of abstinence, you can protect yourself by making responsible choices. First, avoid risky behavior and always use a condom. While condoms are not foolproof, when used properly they are highly effective in preventing most sexually transmitted diseases and pregnancy. Choose latex condoms, since they are sturdier and less porous than the lambskin varieties. Be wary of gimmicks such as flavored or colored condoms that are often made of inferior materials. Stick to condoms made by well-known and responsible companies (like Sheik, Ramses, and Trojan). Avoid oil-based lubricants such as Vaseline, since these products can damage the latex, causing it to tear.

Practice health-promoting behaviors—regular checkups, breast exams, and testicular exams—to detect any problems early.

Communicate thoroughly with your partners, and ask specific questions about their sexual history. Finally, never allow yourself to be talked into unprotected sex; "just once" is no excuse. Unprotected sex is like playing a game of Russian roulette.

I've often been asked, "If someone says he was tested for HIV twice and came out negative, should I believe him and have unprotected sex?" Absolutely not! Some people act as if a negative test gives them a license to go wild. That's absurd. Has your partner had sex since his negative tests? With whom? He could have been infected after the test. There are no exceptions—*always* practice safe sex!

Essentials

Remember that when you have sex with someone, you're having sex with all of that person's partners. That means if your partner is promiscuous, you could be having sex with many people!

235

Rating Safe Sex Activities

The challenge is to make these safer sex behaviors *VENIS* (very erotic non-insertive sex). Safer sex activities include:

➤ Dry kissing

➤ Hugging

➤ Frottage (rubbing against each other)

➤ Massage

➤ Mutual masturbation

➤ Solo use of sex toys

➤ Masturbation displays

➤ Watching sexy videos

➤ Telephone sex

➤ Cybersex (love messages on the Internet)

➤ Tantric sex (extended love-making techniques from the Orient that don't involve penetration)

Riskier activities include:

➤ Open mouth or deep tongue kissing

➤ Oral sex (with condoms or dental dams)

➤ Vaginal intercourse with a condom

➤ Anal penetration with a condom

➤ Urinating on unbroken skin

Unsafe sex activities include:

➤ Vaginal intercourse without a condom (even if pulling out before ejaculation)

➤ Oral sex without a condom (even if pulling out before ejaculation)

➤ Oral sex or vaginal penetration without a condom during a woman's period

➤ Rimming (tonguing the anal opening) without protection

➤ Anal sex without a condom

➤ Swallowing semen or urine

➤ Sucking blood or other blood contact from different body parts

➤ Sharing sex toys

Condom-Sense

I mentioned this earlier in this chapter, but it's worth repeating: Condoms are highly effective in preventing the transmission of STDs, but they must be used properly and consistently. Condoms *can* break, and they don't protect all body areas that might be infected (as with herpes).

Many men and women still have resistance to and questions about condoms that they need to overcome, as in the following examples.

Kristen: "My boyfriend wants to have sex, but he won't wear a condom because he says it doesn't feel good, and he'll lose his erection. He said he'll leave me if he has to wear one, and find a girl who doesn't care."

If he won't be responsible, by all means let him leave! As he goes out the door, remind him of phrases like, "If you really love her, wear a cover," or the more tongue-in-cheek, "Put a helmet on that soldier if he's going into action." Warn him of the dangers to himself too, and reassure him that he can always regain his erection if he loses it.

Peggy: "I had sex with an ex-boyfriend, and he didn't wear a condom. I have never had sex with anyone else, but I know he has. Could there be a problem?"

You bet! One slip-up is enough. You can't be careful yourself and sleep with someone who isn't. One young girl told a heartbreaking story on "LovePhones" of how she had sex for the first time and got infected with HIV. She shared a riveting poem to warn everyone:

> A tisket, a tasket,
> a condom or a casket.

Essentials

Statistics, unfortunately, show that not everyone is wise. Some estimates show that while approximately nine out of ten college students have sex, less than half use protection.

The 1996 Durex Global Survey of Sex and Condom Use showed that while Americans are seen by other countries as being the most willing to use a condom with a casual partner, they are actually only fourth in a list of countries (behind Thailand in first place) in which men always use a condom.

Carrie told me, "I've had sex with seven men and I thought I loved them all. Almost every one refused to use a condom. Why is it that men refuse to use condoms?" Many men claim that condoms reduce sensitivity. This is a terrible excuse. *A partner's resistance should not stop your insistence.* Be proud to be responsible. Learn to keep the condom handy, and to put it on efficiently (make it part of your love play). Learn to compensate for any physical insensitivity by attuning all your senses.

It isn't only men who may object to condoms; some women have similar resistance. They may dislike the thought of a barrier, enjoy feeling a man's ejaculation, or just be afraid of implying a man is not "clean." If you feel this way, examine your feelings to prevent them from interfering with smart behavior.

> **Essentials**
> Fortunately, women are taking more and more responsibility regarding condom use. The 1996 Durex Global Survey of Sex and Condom Use reported that among individuals practicing safe sex, condoms are carried by 70 percent of men and 56 percent of women.

> **Essentials**
> Besides condoms for men, it's important to consider barrier protection for women for safe-sex purposes. One method is a "dental dam." Imagine stretching a condom-like material in a rectangle shape over the vaginal area. (In a severe pinch, non-microwavable Saran plastic wrap can also be used.) Although this may seem unappealing, it clearly prevents skin-to-skin contact. Dental dams are not readily available in stores, but can be obtained in specialty shops like Condomania, or in women's sex boutiques like Eve's Garden (119 W. 57th Street, New York, N.Y. 10019).

Rules About Sexual Health

Smart sex in the 1990s requires that you:

➤ Protect yourself (through abstinence or condoms).

➤ Never make a mistake or allow an exception to safe sex practices.

➤ Ease up on using protection *only* if both partners were virgins when they met, or if both have tested negative for AIDS, and then had sex with each other exclusively.

➤ Talk about your sexual history. Say something like, "Before we have sex, we need to talk about diseases, safe sex, and our sexual pasts."

➤ Discuss what method you are going to use for safe sex.

➤ Find ways to enjoy intimacy other than through sex.

Unconscious Motivations

Our behavior is always influenced by our mind. Sometimes, though, you may not realize what deep motivations drive what you do—and this can get you in trouble. It's my job to help you become aware of these motivations, so that you can make smart and safe choices about sex.

Always consider your deepest needs and conflicts. For example, I was shocked to hear Diane tell me that her boyfriend insisted on having unprotected sex with her, even though she had genital warts, and that she readily agreed. He got the warts, too—and deep down, Diane was glad because she took it as a sign that he would stay with her.

Chris was going into the service and his girlfriend wanted desperately to become pregnant, even though Chris feared—rightfully—that they were not ready to start a family. I insisted he not let this happen just to please his girlfriend, and suggested she explore her deeper need: to prevent herself from being lonely while he's gone, or to ensure that they have a bond. Couples need to establish their bond *before* making a baby; those couples who become parents know the stresses that a child can put on a relationship.

The Importance of Being Honest

It's a moral and social responsibility to let your sex partners know about your health status. You do not have a right to put another person at risk, nor does anyone have the right to expose you to risk. There are plenty of stories about people flirting with the Russian roulette of disease. For instance, Roseanna told me: "I had unprotected sex with my ex-boyfriend, and he told me later that he is HIV positive. I've been tested, and I'm going crazy waiting for the results."

There will always be people who tempt fate by deliberately practicing unsafe sex. These people are depressed or angry and want to hurt themselves or others. For instance, Rich called "LovePhones" to say he had herpes. "I'm furious. I got it from some woman I slept with and I'm going to give it back to as many other women as I can. I don't care. I've been hurt a lot and now others can suffer along with me. I'm lonely and miserable, so why shouldn't they be?"

This vengeful attitude is dangerous and seriously disturbed. But you can't always tell who these people are. That's why it's important to practice safe sex in all situations. If necessary, let Rich's behavior scare you into safe sex practices.

It's a crime to deliberately spread the HIV virus. In some precedent-setting legal cases, such behavior is considered "assault with a deadly weapon."

With better public awareness and more organizations that are dedicated to public health, it's possible to get the information and support you need. For information on where to get more information about STDs, see Appendix B in this book.

The Least You Need to Know

➤ It's essential to be responsible about preventing unwanted pregnancies and sexually transmitted diseases.

➤ Abstinence and virginity are fine, but if you have sex, practice safe sex *every* time.

➤ Overcome any shame or embarrassment about speaking to partners or doctors about pregnancy prevention and safe sex.

➤ Get the facts, share your feelings, and stay safe.

Part 5
Starting Over

Rejection is never easy. Nor is dating after a long spell in a monogamous relationship. This section helps ease both experiences.

Everyone wants to be themselves, and to share with another human being. Honor that connection. Decide right now to do your part to make everyone you come in contact with feel loved. Thank everyone you date for what they bring to your life. Start with simple things, like "I want to thank you for taking me to that movie. I might never have seen it without your invitation." Even if you have had a less-than-perfect evening, say, "We may not be perfect for each other but I've still enjoyed our time together. You are a nice (special, interesting) person." Treat every date as an opportunity to see that there is value in every encounter.

Chapter 20

Handling Rejection and Breaking Up

In This Chapter

➤ Knowing when it's over

➤ The right and wrong ways to end it

➤ The "Frightful Five" blow-offs

➤ The nine phases of dealing with rejection

➤ Letting go

➤ Patching things up

Now that you've learned how to get a relationship going and make it work, it's time to deal with the flipside: getting out without falling apart.

"My boyfriend told me he loved me," Denise wailed, "so how can he turn around the next week and say he needs his space?" Easy. He meant he cared at one moment, but that didn't mean it would last forever. While it's never easy, and always disappointing, you must learn to move on when love ends for your lover but not for you.

The first and most important question you should ask yourself after a rejection is: Why waste yourself on someone who doesn't want you?

And if you are the one initiating the break-up, why waste time and energy for both of you? If you thought you were wild about someone, but are now having doubts, what do you do? What's the best way of disentangling yourself, while being both firm *and* kind?

Deciding to Break Up

In at least one relationship you'll have in your life, inevitably the day will come when you ask yourself, "Is this working?" or "How long should I keep at this before it's really over?" or "When's the right time to break this off?"

Only you can determine your limits of tolerance for working on a relationship. Some people look for instant gratification, and as soon as their needs aren't being met, they're out the door. Others hang on forever, hoping and praying things will get better. Neither approach is ideal, but it helps to know where you and your partner fit along this continuum.

Think of dating as a long road punctuated by traffic lights. Red lights signal danger, yellow lights require caution, and green lights mean keep going (but proceed cautiously since you never know when a car might run a red light!).

You know you are at a green light if your mate

➤ Has positive, close, friendly relationships with family, friends, and co-workers.

➤ Is responsible and trustworthy.

➤ Is a good communicator (listens and empathizes).

➤ Is open to commitment.

➤ Can express feelings and be intimate.

➤ Displays respect for self and others.

You're at a yellow light when

➤ You've been hurt by this person before.

➤ Many friends are giving you warnings or negative feedback.

➤ There is evidence of history of bad relationships.

➤ You recognize in yourself a pattern of attraction such that you always end up hurt.

➤ You fall in love too fast (without testing and observing).

➤ Either of you has a cheating past.

➤ The two of you are always talking about your ex-partners.

➤ You spend too much time just "hanging out" without doing anything meaningful.

➤ Your mate cancels or forgets dates.

➤ Your mate sends "mixed signals"—one minute you're great, the next you're ignored.

You know you're at a red light and it's time to put on the brakes when

➤ You're experiencing more pain than pleasure.

➤ You're being mentally, physically, or sexually abused.

➤ She betrays you or cheats on you.

➤ You feel used, abused, or foolish.

➤ He keeps secrets (like not revealing a home number or never inviting you over).

➤ She constantly blames, criticizes, or denigrates others (parents, friends, co-workers).

➤ Either of you has a lot of unresolved anger toward the same or opposite sex.

➤ There is a clear reluctance to commit (indicated by statements like "Marriage is a disaster" or "I'll never settle down").

➤ He is pushy, controlling, or obsessed with sex.

➤ Your friends warn you (unlike you, they're not wearing "love blinders").

➤ His life is dangerous (involves guns, drugs, illegal acts).

Excuses: Holding On When You Know You Should Let Go

Even when trouble is obvious, it can be tough to let go. I hear lots of excuses from people who are unable or unwilling to leave a relationship, including:

➤ *We've been together a long time.* For instance, Jennifer told me: "My boyfriend's cheating, and now he says he doesn't want to be with me as much as before, but I don't want to break up. We've been together for five years." It's natural to get attached to the people in our lives, but try looking at relationships as investments. If a stock is going down and your principle is dwindling, it's time to sell and cut your losses. You may also need to "reframe" the way you are viewing the situation. Instead of regretting all of those "lost years," think of what you've learned and of the valuable times ahead.

➤ *He (or she) was my first.* As Pam told me, "Its not working out with this guy I'm seeing, but I'm having a hard time letting go because he was my first." As I pointed out in Chapter 18, you'll probably always feel a special attachment to your "first," but you can't sacrifice happiness for sentimentality.

➤ *But I still love him (her).* Keisha explained, "I know I should stop going out with him—he cheats and treats me bad—but I still love him." Love yourself more, and treat yourself to someone who treats you well. You can always love the person, but that doesn't mean you have to be together.

➤ *I gave her (him) everything.* I recently talked to a guy who told me: "I really liked this girl and bought her lots of things. In fact, I just bought her a $50 sweater, and the next day she broke up with me! What can I do to get her back?" Save your money and your self-esteem and let an ungrateful and unwilling mate go. If someone clearly doesn't want you, regardless of your gifts, you're trying to buy love, a sign that you may be low on self-esteem. The result is disappointing anyway, as the other person usually ends up loving you less.

Sometimes we need a kick in the pants to get out of a really bad relationship. Laura told me, "My boyfriend drinks too much and has been unfaithful. When I tell him I want to leave him, he says he'll never let me go. He tells me that the problem is that I'm unhappy with my life, and I'm blaming him. Is it my problem?"

What *is* your problem, is that you are putting up with this man's psychological abuse and manipulation. His drinking, cheating, blaming, and threatening are sure signs that *he* is the one who is desperate, disturbed, and in need of help. Don't allow his threats to intimidate and paralyze you. Life is too precious to waste, so don't spend another minute being miserable and treated poorly. Be firm about your complaints, expectations, and intentions. Take action—get legal counsel or an order of protection if you think you need it. Insist that he get counseling, and get support for yourself (from friends, a therapist, or a 12-step program for people in relationships with alcoholics) to shore up your self-esteem. Then bless the guy and send him on his way.

Reading the Warning Signs

Most of us can tell if a relationship is going sour, but often we want to ignore even the most obvious clues. You've got to trust your instincts. Here are some telltale signs that you are about to get dumped:

➤ She stops returning your phone calls.

➤ He has endless excuses for why you can't get together.

➤ She displays affection less frequently (not holding you, not returning a hand squeeze).

➤ She talks about "me" instead of "we."

➤ He never talks about future plans.

➤ She ignores intimate talk ("I really like you," "We get along so well together") when you raise it.

➤ He's inattentive and distant.

➤ She's slowly removing all of her personal items from your house.

When you're smitten, it's easy to ignore signals that a relationship is going south. And it's natural to want to make the one you love love you—especially if that person considers himself hard to catch. Cathy's is a typical story. "I've been seeing this guy who lately has been rather indifferent and mean. I've also heard he's been seeing another woman. But I don't want to lose him. How can I get him to see that I'm the right one for him?"

Imagine hitting your head against the wall. Does it hurt yet? If it doesn't, would you hit it harder? When will it hurt so much that you'll be forced to stop banging against the wall? Consider emotional pain like that physical pain: When will your heart hurt so bad that you stop running after people who make you unhappy? Imagine that every time your heart is broken, your heart muscle gets chipped and torn. Be as protective with your emotions as you would be with your body.

Finally, I'm frequently asked if bad sex is a good reason to end a relationship. Yes and no. Bad sex is often just a smokescreen for other problems: lack of communication, lack of attention, unresolved hurt or anger, lack of trust, and more. Before condemning a relationship because of bad sex, carefully explore the reasons behind it. Having no sex is a warning sign that something is wrong, since it indicates a withdrawal from closeness, intimacy, and sharing.

Be Prepared

If the handwriting is on the wall—you sense it's over though you're not ready to admit it—how can you prepare yourself? For starters, ask for feedback. Be blunt; ask him if the signals you think you are detecting are the ones that he wants to be sending. If you have to force the conversation, you probably have your answer right there.

Prepare yourself for being alone by rekindling those friendships that you may have neglected during your relationship. Also, make an effort to make new friends that have no connection to the two of you. Protect yourself from constant reminders of your ex. If you and your soon-to-be-former lover have "your" special places, try going there with other friends to establish a new association in your mind. It is too easy to get sentimental about the restaurants, coffee shops, and even the corners where you used to meet. "Detoxify" these places, or after a few relationships you may find yourself without any place to hang out!

Warning

Most of us have heard one (or all) of these blow-offs more than once. I call them the "Frightful Five":

➤ "I love you but I'm not 'in love' with you."

➤ "I thought we both knew it wasn't going anywhere/was just sex."

➤ "There's no chemistry."

➤ "Let's just be friends."

➤ "I met someone else."

If you are handed one of these lines, don't beg or plead. Realize he or she wants the relationship over. You can ask for more explanation, but really what you want is to know it was once real, you once *were* loved, and still can be lovable. Hopefully you'll get some reassurance, but accept the end and move on.

Disappointing Dating Scripts: Making the Best of it

Bree was really excited about her date with Jason. She had her hair and nails done, bought a new outfit, and even bought some new things for her bedroom. She had been looking forward to the evening for weeks and was sure they would end up in bed.

They started the evening at the movies, where Bree put her hand on Jason's knee. When he didn't respond or return her touch, she began to worry. Outside, after the movie, he told her that his stomach was bothering him and he thought he'd just go home. Bree was disappointed, and felt foolish. Was Jason really feeling bad, or had she misread his flirting with her so heavily when they met? Whatever the case, Bree realized that her expectations had led to disappointment.

Bree had fallen into a common trap: "writing a script" for an evening without really considering the actual role of the other person. We write their part without thinking about their needs, expectations, moods, or plans. Bree wrote a script for romance with Jason. When the evening didn't go as planned, she felt horribly let down.

It's impossible to script every experience in life, because people are so unpredictable. And even if you could, would life be as interesting and compelling if you decided beforehand how everything would turn out? If things don't turn out as you plan, make the new events work *for* you. Instead of bemoaning Jason's unresponsiveness, Bree decided to welcome that Jason went home; it gave her free time and inspiration to start writing the novel she'd been thinking about for two years. See how you can "reframe" what happens—no matter what someone else does, you can turn it into something personally fulfilling.

When You Are the One to End it

Most of us know what it feels like to be dumped: the pain, humiliation, anger, and hurt. But the time may also come when you must do the dumping. Is it possible to minimize the other person's pain? Are there rules that govern breaking up?

Consider this scenario. As Paul described, "I've been dating Jill for a few months, and I really like her—as a friend. I recently met a woman I feel passionately about. Jill is terrific, and I know she loves me. What can I say or do to let her down easy?"

If you have ever been on the other side of the fence, like Paul, you will probably be sensitive to the following "DO'S" and "DON'TS" for breaking up with someone:

➤ DON'T break up over the phone (too impersonal).

➤ DON'T break up before a major holiday, anniversary, or any day important to the "dumpee" or the two of you (birthday, anniversary, Valentine's Day, Christmas, death of a parent)—an otherwise happy day will be tinged with pain, or an already painful day will become more unbearable.

➤ DON'T criticize or blame the person for what he may or may not have done.

➤ DON'T use one of the "Frightful Five" blow-offs, like "I love you, but I'm not in love with you" or "I never really loved you." These words tend to linger painfully.

➤ DON'T get wangled by guilt into changing your mind.

➤ DON'T hit below the belt, with phrases like "I just don't find you very stimulating" or "You were awful in bed."

➤ DO talk about it as a mutual decision ("It's right for both of us") to prevent self-blame on the part of the "dumpee."

➤ DO be respectful, giving the other person the opportunity to work through his feelings.

➤ DO reaffirm that there was something good between you (the "dumpee" often feels invalidated, as if her feelings never mattered or weren't real. She may need reassurance that the relationship *was* real, and that she really was cared for).

➤ DO remind the person of wonderful aspects of themselves (to boost his or her self-esteem).

➤ DO point out your own resistance and responsibility ("I'm not ready for a commitment," "I can't be true to someone yet"). The "dumpee" may try to reassure you, but stick to your guns and say "You deserve better." This may help prevent his self-blame and depression.

➤ DO accept being the "bad guy."

➤ DO spell out the terms of the separation clearly ("We shouldn't call each other") so that there is no room for misunderstanding.

➤ DO be firm. If you leave the door open even a crack, you are inviting the person to try to change your mind.

Remember the Golden Rule: "Do unto others as you would have others do unto you." This is a good time to put that rule into action.

Essentials

While women think that men have an easier time after a break-up, research shows that men may actually suffer more. When men get involved, they share otherwise repressed emotions. When they break up, they tend to keep their pain hidden, which often leads to physical complaints (fatigue, headaches, and so forth). Women, on the other hand, are more open about suffering, and tend to surround themselves with friends and family to help ease their pain.

Dealing With Rejection: The Nine Phases

If you are the one who is being dumped, be prepared for the "stages" of rejection. While the pain may be awful, each stage is part of the healing process. The stages generally follow the sequence described in the following bulleted list, but they can alternate with each other. Dealing with rejection is a lot like dealing with other kinds of loss, and the stages are similar:

➤ *The Denial phase:* "This can't be happening." During this stage you may find yourself waiting for the phone to ring, not believing that the relationship is actually over.

Solution: Acknowledge reality and acknowledge your feelings about it. Accept but do not dwell on shame and embarrassment, and all the "shoulda/woulda/coulda's" ("I should have known better," "I could have been sexier").

➤ *The Bargaining phase:* Driving yourself crazy, thinking that "If I get my hair cut," or "If I just let him have sex more often," or "If I don't call her for a week," he will change his mind.

Solution: There's only one solution: Accept that it's over.

➤ *The Loneliness phase:* Feeling as if no one understands or cares.

Solution: Surround yourself with people who *do* care, and who openly say so. Remind yourself often that you are loved.

➤ *The Heartbreak phase:* Feeling like your heart is really breaking. You may even feel pain in your chest, or want to throw up when you think of that person or if you see your ex with someone else.

Solution: You *can* go on. Rub your hand over your heart to soothe it. If you are feeling really bad, snap your fingers to interrupt the thought, and fixate on something that makes you happy. Do not drive yourself crazy with thoughts that your ex is blissfully happy while you're miserable. Only *your* experience counts, and only *your* efforts make you happy.

➤ *The Blame phase:* Pointing the finger at yourself or your ex for what each of you did wrong.

Solution: Decide that neither of you is at fault but that both of you are responsible for the break-up.

➤ *The Depression phase:* Feeling sad, worthless, and foolish. You may have trouble eating and sleeping, and you may imagine that you'll never find anyone to love again.

Solution: Allow yourself to feel your pain, but do not wallow in self-pity. Keep busy with exercise or projects.

➤ *The Anger phase:* Feeling furious for being rejected.

Solution: Allow yourself to experience the anger, but don't exaggerate it, or tack it onto all your past hurts. Don't let yourself become bitter.

➤ *The Acceptance phase:* Finally believing it's over. You no longer expect your ex to call, and you begin to feel at peace.

➤ *The Healing phase:* Getting your life back. You are now ready to go out with friends and to meet new people, and you are no longer dwelling on your ex.

Tip
Research has shown that it can take half the time of the relationship to get over losing it, and even then 10 percent of the pain remains. But it's different for everybody, and if you find yourself in turmoil after a year, or if you can't function (eat, sleep, work, etc.), get professional help.

Letting Go: The 18 Steps

Christina's is a typical story: "I've been dating Chuck for two years, and I really love him. A month ago he broke up with me, saying that he wanted to date other women, but I can't seem to move on. I can't picture myself with anyone else. He says he loves me, but that he'll never treat me the way I deserve. He keeps encouraging me to go out with other guys. What does all this mean? How can I get him back? He wants to be friends, but I only want to see him if I can get him back. How can I stop thinking about him all the time and get my life back?"

As the old song goes, breaking up is hard to do. But it's time for Christina to let go. It's the crucial step in moving on to a healthy life. The following list gives you some tips and exercises that can help with the process:

➤ *Practice thought-stopping.* It's normal to have recurring thoughts about your ex. One way to wean yourself is to decide on a specific time of day where you will give yourself over to the thoughts (such as nine o'clock at night, for ten minutes). If you find yourself obsessing at other times, force yourself to "change the channel" in your brain, or pick yourself up and do something constructive—take a walk, water the plants, clean out a closet.

Try this exercise: Think about your ex. Now think about being in love with someone else. Now think about your ex. Now think about getting a raise at work. Now think about laughing with a new friend. Now think about a pink elephant. See how you can control your thoughts?

In Japanese Morita therapy, you do not wallow in your feelings; you simply do what you have to do each day to function—and concentrate on those actions. You brush your teeth in the morning, you get dressed for work, and you talk to new potential mates. It's that simple.

➤ *Recognize the quality that you miss in your ex and find a substitute for it.* Focus on the qualities you liked in your ex. Was he funny? Great in bed? A good listener? Realize that these aren't such unusual traits—they do come along in other people, and you will encounter them more than once in a lifetime. Enjoy those qualities in other people or find other ways to enjoy them. Go to funny movies, or take up a sport yourself.

➤ *Instead of bemoaning the end, celebrate it.* In this technique, called "paradoxical intention," you wish the very opposite of what you *think* you prefer. Put on some music, uncork the champagne, jump up and down, and yell "Good riddance to bad rubbish!" Then honor your time alone.

➤ *Be your own cheerleader.* Remind yourself of all the good things about *you*. Make a list of those qualities and reread the list.

➤ *Call all your friends and have them reinflate your ego.* Get your pals on the phone and ask them to remind you of all your wonderful traits. Let them take your side. When Georgette was dumped, she called her best friend, who reminded her, "You are beautiful and smart and funny and fun to be with."

➤ *Understand the situation realistically.* Dee was devastated when her boyfriend decided not to leave his wife for her. He said he loved her, but was worried about his kids, his business, and his wife. If she had looked at the situation realistically from the beginning, she may not have been as devastated. While she shouldn't punish herself, she should have been prepared for the possibility.

➤ *Be realistic about dating in general.* While I certainly feel that you should pump yourself up, don't expect that *everybody* will love you.

➤ *Accept your responsibility, not as a way of blaming yourself, but to learn.* Go over all the sides of the story. Was he mean, cruel, insensitive? Blame him, and then face up to the fact that you pick men like that. For example, Francine realized she wanted Paul to be what he wasn't. She had overrated him and expected more from him than he was able to give, overlooking an obvious problem—he had said he wasn't looking for a commitment.

➤ *Reaffirm that you deserve to be treated well.* Remember how you would treat a child or best friend—you would be loving, protective, and reassuring. Treat yourself that way.

➤ *Do a "relationship review."* Recognize the patterns in your past relationships to prevent the same problems in the future. What type of person do you go for? What happened at every stage—who started the relationship, who made the decisions, what was the tone of the relationship (fun, sharing feelings, fighting), what did you do together (music, art, ideas, books, movies), who ended it? If you see a pattern that displeases you—you're always the caregiver, you try to "buy" love, you're frequently attracted to people who are already involved—make it a point to make changes.

➤ *Indulge in pleasure.* Make a list of things that make you feel good: getting a massage, listening to music, taking a walk. Indulge in these pleasures at least one a day.

➤ *Keep a sense of humor.* Research has shown that laughter strengthens the immune system. On this basis, seeing the lighter side of your situation is a positive step in your healing process. Imagine your ex in a silly situation, or go see a funny movie.

➤ *Feel empowered.* Consider that you *chose* for the relationship to be over. Even if you think *he* dumped *you*, consider that your energy helped create the outcome. Decide "I wanted it over." This is no more real or unreal than any other explanation.

➤ *Do deeper work.* Help the little child inside who is still hurting from past losses. Imagine yourself as this little child, and also imagine yourself as an adult protecting this child from being hurt, holding and comforting her.

➤ *Purge your anger.* Write your ex a letter, pouring out your hurt, disappointment, and anger—but *don't* send it. That's a good way to purge your feelings.

➤ *Rebuild trust.* Erica's dilemma is common enough: "My first love stabbed me in the back after I put my complete trust in him. Now I am wary of people and always protecting myself." Resist generalizing; not all men or women are alike. See each person as an individual. In your imagination, line up all those who have hurt you in the past and imagine throwing them in the garbage or picture them incinerating. Now you have a clean slate. Of course, trust gets shattered after you're hurt, but try to put the past aside. If you live in fear, imagining that people are not trustworthy, this is the reality that you will create. Accept the challenge of tuning your love antennae to people who are more trustworthy, and who are worthy of your trust.

➤ *Welcome your dreams.* As Brenda asked, "It's been seven months since my relationship ended, and I have constant dreams about the situation. What can I do to stop them?" Instead of seeing your dreams as obsessions, believe that your mind is trying to work through the pain on a deeper level.

Essentials

Researchers at a midwestern university helped women who were depressed over lost loves to use their dreams to heal their pain. All the women were having recurrent dreams of bumping into their ex and feeling devastated by the experience. The researchers trained the women to put a new ending on the dream, one where they walked away from the encounter smiling and feeling happy. Some women imagined they were with another man, others pictured being happy on their own. The women were told to review the script before going to bed, to set the story in their mind.

All the women felt better about coping with their loss using this technique, and the majority reported recovering sooner than they expected.

➤ *Repair your self-esteem.* Amanda's cry is typical: "My boyfriend left after two years. What's wrong with me?" Nothing. Not everyone can appreciate your value, but *you* need to continue to do so.

Warning

Some people are so distraught over a break-up that they talk or think about killing themselves or someone else. No one person holds the key to your self-worth. If your hurt and rage are this severe, or if your ex is threatening to hurt himself or you, seek professional help immediately.

Revenge

It's natural to want to anger, humiliate, and hurt the one who has hurt you. "I'd like to make her life hell, and make her suffer like I'm suffering," said Pete after he was dumped by Liz. "I'll get him for hurting me," Kaetlin vowed after Jorge cheated on her.

Don't waste your energy on revenge. As much as your ex might deserve your wrath, you are standing in the way of your own happiness by not letting go. To purge yourself of these feelings, tell your ex how mad and disappointed you are. But then take responsibility for yourself and move on. Be glad that the person is out of your life, and that you endured a bad relationship for three months instead of four.

Moving on can be especially difficult if you've helped a lover through a particularly bad time, only to have him leave you when his life got back on track. Try to be glad that this person's well-being is no longer your concern. But then look for patterns in your own life: Are you always the caretaker? Are you always on hand to "save" a lost soul? If so, be grateful that you've gotten this out of your system.

In my view, it is okay to indulge in fantasies of revenge (for a short while, anyway), as long as you don't act on them. Don't dwell on your ex. It is better to bless him, spread white light around you, and get on with your life. Remember, "Living well is the best revenge."

When Your Ex Refuses to Get the Message

You think you've done all the right things. You've leveled with your ex, telling her that your heart isn't in this relationship, and that it's over. But what if she refuses to get the message? Is it possible that you're sending the wrong signal?

Warning

Some people become obsessed when rejected. For instance, John's girlfriend continued to call, sometimes five times a day, for months after they broke up. When he didn't return her calls, she would show up at his house. John asked, "How do I get her off my back? I feel like joining the witness protection program."

It is very disturbing, and often frightening, to be pursued obsessively. Clearly, the woman's attachment to John went far deeper than their actual relationship, probably mirroring something in her family. Such an obsessive lover needs to be told she is a good person and cared for, but that your closeness is over, and that pursuing you is not acceptable. Insist that she get counseling. If such behavior persists, go to the police for an order of protection.

Be firm. Don't give in and get back together because of feelings of guilt. If you truly want to end the relationship, don't be tempted to sleep with the person "one last time." Any inconsistency in your behavior will be interpreted as a sign that you don't really want out.

On the other hand, what if the lover who recently left you calls and says she wants to see you? Be cautious. If she was so sure that the relationship was over, what has happened to change her mind? Is it loneliness, boredom, or a true change of heart? Proceed slowly to find out what she wants. When it comes to sex, be especially slow and cautious. Sometimes sex with an ex is good because you're free of commitment or problems, but a roll in the hay won't get you the love you want. Watch out for "yo-yo" lovers—the kind who vacillate between wanting you and wanting freedom.

"Why is sex always better after breaking up?" Sometimes it's easier for couples to have great sex when their commitment and relationship problems (arguments, miscommunications, angers) are put aside, and when they have dropped any expectations. Also, the tension of a breakup can seem to intensify passion. It's like the popular song goes: "The best part of breaking up is making up." But beware of starting arguments just to fuel your love.

Cutting the Cord

"Is it okay to keep in touch with an ex-boyfriend of three years if I'm now seeing someone else?"

"Is it normal to still have feelings for an ex?"

Both situations are "normal." Some people can totally sever a relationship and never see an ex again. Usually this happens if the relationship was fraught with pain and anger. But if you truly cared, you will always have a soft spot for that person. Past lovers are a part of your life and your personal history. In fact, at certain times in your life, you may feel an urgent need to get in touch. Often during major transitions (marriage, divorce, death of a parent or spouse, kids leaving the nest), people want to contact ex-lovers to be reminded of good times, or to resolve some issues. This connection can make you feel vital and acknowledged.

But before picking up the phone, think about what you are looking for. Review the relationship and what the person actually means to you. How did that person make you feel? What is he symbolic of? What were you going through in your life at the time (college days, your first job, junior year abroad, the prom)? Then, consider the other person. It might be that your call is the last thing that person needs right now.

Repairing the Hurt

What makes breaking up so traumatic? Often, there are many unresolved emotions and unfinished business. If you see an ex too soon, you risk triggering those unresolved feelings and fantasies, which will prevent you from moving on. But when the time is right, such reunions can also be a valuable opportunity to work through some unfinished business. Sometimes you'll discover that all of the feelings of unworthiness or rejection that you've been harboring are overblown. Such realizations allow you to move on to new relationships.

Don't rush a reunion with your ex—give yourself plenty of time for the wounds to heal. When you are both ready, get together and review what happened. Explain the things that hurt you, what you wanted, what you feared, and what you miss. With distance and a fresh perspective, any lingering pain may ease, and a new love may emerge.

Many of us entertain the fantasy of seeing an ex and having him or her say, "You were right all along. Take me back!" This would restore your feeling that you—and your love— mattered! It *is* possible for this to happen.

It happened for Didi. Didi had been very in love with Kirk when he left her. While she'd gotten on with her life, she still had feelings for him and always wondered "What if...?" Ten years passed, and after a serendipitous meeting, Kirk called. They got together and talked about their lives. He explained that he and his wife were "just friends." Their sexual relationship had long since died, even though the marriage was intact. Hearing this, Didi realized that the longing she felt for Kirk all those years was suddenly gone.

When Kirk left her years before, he fed Didi the classic line, "I love you but I'm not *in* love with you." Soon after their break-up, he fell "madly in love" with someone else. Now he was telling her that this love too had died, and his sex life was barren. It seemed like poetic justice to her. Kirk went on to apologize for hurting her, and to express his feelings of remorse.

Kirk's apology and expressions of regret were what Didi needed to deal with her residual pain. It helped her realize that she hadn't imagined his feelings for her, and that she was probably better off having Kirk as part of her past than part of her present.

Can't We Patch This Thing Up?

More often than not, when things go really sour, it's better not to look back. Getting back together will only work if both of you have worked on the problems that caused the relationship to founder. If you decide to give it another go, you both must also express your commitment to giving it a fresh start. Only under those conditions is it worth trying to patch things up.

Wanting to reconcile is a common dilemma: "When my boyfriend broke up with me I kept begging him to take me back. Why isn't he listening?"

You probably already know from previous chapters in this book that I'm no advocate of game-playing—if you have needs and feelings, express them. But I do think there is one time when you should hold back—when your emotional needs are out of proportion to the reality of the relationship. There's a big difference between saying, "I don't want to break up, I love you" and "I can't go on without you." The latter, acting desperate, pitiful, and "clingy," will only drive your lover away, since such desperation tends to trigger contempt and disgust (often because the person fears that your desperation may trigger his own). Your desperation also sends a clear signal that you are hanging on for your own needs—it is less about your true love for him than about your need to prevent feeling abandoned, and to play out your "love script."

Even if you have strong feelings for your ex, don't go crazy or make a scene. Imagine yourself surrounded by white light, being happy without the person. You *can* suggest reconciling, saying something like, "It would be nice to get back together." But don't put your life on hold, just leave the door open. Then pull yourself together, look your best, go out, and have fun. Your patience may pay off.

In letting your ex know you still care, don't make demands. People have to choose to be with you freely, not out of guilt, loneliness, or sentimentality. If your ex is asking you to do things as friends, take the bait only if you can control yourself. If you can't, keep your distance. As painful as it may be to say no, it will be less painful in the long run.

The Least You Need to Know

➤ Everyone faces rejection at some point in life.

➤ Someone may not love you, but *you* must always love you.

➤ There are predictable stages of dealing with loss.

➤ It's better to leave a bad relationship and get on with your life.

➤ You will survive any breakup, no matter how painful.

➤ "Living well is the best revenge."

Getting Back in the Saddle

In This Chapter

➤ Changing your old views

➤ Rebuilding self-esteem

➤ Dating when you have kids

➤ What will others think?

Each year, 1.2 million marriages end in divorce. That means 2.4 million people reenter the singles life again. Most have been married for about ten years, and about 70 percent will marry again. But making it work the second (or third) time around depends on how much you've learned from past mistakes and how well you've reassessed yourself and your needs.

The New You!

You deserve a life again! Being alone doesn't have to mean being lonely. Allow yourself to feel passion and give yourself permission to love again. Use the following guide to change your way of thinking.

Old Way of Thinking	New Way of Thinking
Restrictive: Dating is not for me	Permission: All possibilities are open to me
Punitive: I have no right to go out	Supportive: I have a right to enjoy myself
Fearful: I'm afraid to commit, get hurt	Confident: I can risk again, I won't make the same mistakes
Excuses: I have no time to go out	Freeing: I can figure out how to make love work

The loss or death of a spouse/lover is traumatic under any conditions, especially if the relationship has in many ways been good. Some divorced and widowed men and women feel so spiritually attached to their partner that they cannot move on to date others. Death is particularly traumatic because it can happen so suddenly.

To move on with your life, try a technique I call "completing unfinished business," in which you have an imaginary conversation with your ex or departed one and say all the things you wish you could have said when he or she was with you. Imagine asking for, and receiving, permission to go on with your life.

Rebuilding Self-Esteem

Being out of the dating game for a long time can make you feel insecure, frightened, and hesitant. "I've been out of that world so long," Jack said, "I have no idea what people do!" Many people struggle with guilt and feelings of being a failure. Take Leila, for example: "I couldn't make it work with Greg, so I'm really frightened to try again with someone else."

Parents negotiating child support and custody may have particular emotional conflicts (confusion, frustration, sadness, anger) at this time. Professionals have become particularly aware of the "father depression" that some men suffer from when they are saddled with child-support bills, but deprived of being with their children.

It is especially important for people who carry a lot of emotional baggage from the past to be aware of those feelings and try to prevent them from spilling into their new relationships. Recognize your fears and remind yourself that the past does not have to repeat itself. Reevaluate all your strong points (your character and your experience). Trust there will be people whose company you will enjoy and vice versa.

Single-Parent Dating

Alone again, you are entitled—when you're ready—to get back in the dating scene. Inevitably, you will have some practical concerns, and many fears and confused feelings: "When am I going to have time to date when I have children to take care of?" or "How am I supposed to be an example to my teenage kids when I'm playing the field also?" You will probably experience guilty feelings as well: "Will it upset my kids if I start dating again?"

These fears and feelings are all normal, and knowing that you're not the only one to feel this way can ease some of the pressure.

What About the Kids?

Of course you want to be a good parent. But consider yourself, too. Realize that your happiness will spill over into how you treat your kids and what example you set for them. It is important, however, to be prepared for all the feelings that your children may have in reaction to your dating.

Keep in mind that your children will always be upset about the new love in your life no matter how much they like him or her. Deep inside, children want their family back together again. Any newcomer is bound to be perceived, even subconsciously, as a stranger who is sabotaging their fantasy. It is crucial to understand this dynamic and recognize why your children may resent the new person in your life.

One way to deal with this is to introduce your kids only to someone who really matters to you; casual dates may only confuse them. Also, put feelings into words for children who may be afraid or unable to express themselves: "I know how disappointed you are that your father and I are not together and I understand why you may dislike my new boyfriend." Or, simply affirm the child's feelings: "It is normal to feel angry at me and my new girlfriend."

Tip
Most problems have practical solutions. If you need someone to baby-sit your kids, consider grandparents, your ex, friends, and neighbors.

You should also share some of your own feelings: "This is a difficult adjustment for me, too." And, reassure your child: "No one will replace your mother," or "No matter what, know I love you."

Tip

Ask about your child's feelings: "What do you think about (the person you're dating)?" or "How do you feel about me dating/having a relationship?" It's important to show that you respect your child's feelings, but do not let those feelings interfere with or rule your dating. Show that you are considerate of, but not controlled by, your child.

Warning

Some parents avoid the difficulties of dating by immersing themselves in their children. While this can be a welcome relief and offer joy and needed attention, such escape and living vicariously through children—or over-absorption in them—can be unhealthy for all concerned.

When a New Lover Meets Your Child

When you decide that it's time to introduce your new mate to your child, refer to your paramour in casual terms at first. For example, you might say, "I'd like you to meet a good friend of mine." Try planning an activity together. This not only makes the child feel included, but it also dilutes the anxiety of a face-to-face meeting.

Tip

In planning an activity together, make it playful. For example, go to a baseball or basketball game, shopping, or to the movies. Do something together in neutral territory first, outside of the child's home. This lessens the chances of the child feeling invaded or imposed upon at home.

Sleep-overs should be reserved only for serious relationships and only after your child has had opportunities to get used to your suitor's presence. Your child should also be told first that your relationship has taken a more significant turn. This shows respect for your child's feelings, and portrays sex as a very serious step in a relationship.

What Others Say

Others—friends, family members, co-workers—will always have their own judgments and opinions about you dating again. Some may sound ominous and scary: "You shouldn't be going out so fast, give yourself time to recover" or "No one's going to want someone with the baggage of kids." These opinions are just that—opinions. Remember, what others say is only a reflection of their own fears or experiences and does not have to be true for you. Take such advice with a grain of salt.

The New Lovers' Dilemmas

If you're about to date a single parent, but have never been married or had kids yourself, be prepared for differences in responsibilities and attitudes. Some couples adjust easily: Garth, a never-married man, was ecstatic that dating Barbara included a "ready-made" family with her two young children. Others face problems: Sue had a problem sharing her boyfriend with his ex-wife and little girl. She was resentful that he sees his ex-wife every other weekend, and feels threatened and left out.

Unfortunately, if Sue wants to continue dating her boyfriend, there's nothing she can do but accept her boyfriend's package: ex-wife and child. If you're in this same situation, it's important to discuss your feelings and get the reassurance you need. Also, don't waste time worrying about the ex; switch that energy to making your own relationship work. In addition, share time just with the child, so the two of you form a bond.

Where to Meet People

Review all the suggestions in Chapter 2 on where to find a mate. However, pay special attention to places that would draw other divorced people or divorced people with kids. Remember, meeting people in the same situation as you is just as important as meeting people with the same interests. This is especially true if you and the other person both have children, since each of you will understand the responsibilities and limitations that being a parent places on dating. Keep in mind that you can bring your child to any of the "hunting grounds." Children can serve as both company and ice-breakers for starting up a conversation.

Divorced men and women can find innumerable clubs and organized activities especially for them listed in specialty newsletters and community newspapers. Local religious centers are also a good resource. Playgrounds are particularly good places to meet other single parents. People there are usually free-spirited, which sets the tone for an anxiety-free meeting. Watching others play with their kids also gives you the opportunity to observe their kindness, thoughtfulness, and generosity. Other resources include children's events and activities (many are listed in local newspapers), school groups, and single-parent clubs.

The Least You Need to Know

➤ You're entitled to date and love again.

➤ Having children does not make it impossible to find dates, but make sure that new partners understand your situation.

➤ Kids will always want the family to be whole again—recognize this so you can understand your child's behavior regarding your dating.

➤ Only introduce your child to someone you're dating seriously—casual dates can be confusing.

➤ Friends, family members, and co-workers will have their own judgments about you dating again. Remember, what matters most is what *you* think and feel.

Fun and Revealing Exercises

In this section of the book, you'll find some fun and simple exercises designed to reveal aspects of your personality and love matches. Some are based on more extensive and even scientific methods that I have simplified here to make them easier to do and interpret. I have used many of these exercises in my therapy practice and workshops over the years, so I know you can learn from and enjoy them. Use them to gain a little knowledge about yourself and your date, and as a stimulus to get you to talk about yourselves, your interests, feelings, and needs.

Exercise 1: You in Your World

The purpose of this exercise is to explore how you see yourself in your world. I have done this exercise with thousands of individuals, couples, and families over the years. It's based on a psychological technique called "projective drawing," a well-researched and practical tool for estimating a person's view of themselves in the world.

Some people have a hard time expressing in words what they think and feel. But the way in which they draw a picture often offers clues about their inner feelings. Emotional nuances emerge from drawings, regardless of artistic skill.

Draw yourself in the drawing space at the end of this appendix. I'm purposefully not giving you any other specifics—don't worry about how you draw, just don't use a stick figure.

Interpreting Your Drawing

Keep in mind that the following interpretations are generalizations, so use them as a guideline only. Intensive professional analysis of drawings can take hours!

The page symbolizes your world. How you place yourself on the page indicates how you see yourself in your world. If you placed yourself in the middle of the page, it shows that you think of yourself as being at the center of your world. This could suggest that you are also centered (secure) inside yourself.

If you placed yourself off in the corner, it could mean that you need to improve your self-esteem and sense of importance. Placement to the left of the page suggests that you may be stuck in your past; to the right implies that you think more of the future. Drawing yourself at the bottom of the page suggests that you are "grounded" and feel more secure thinking about what's real and focusing on factual things and safe feelings; a figure at the top of the page can imply your enjoyment of fantasy and imagination.

How large did you draw yourself? A too-large figure (in relation to the page) can suggest confidence in yourself, a desire to stand out, or a degree of narcissism. If you are too self-centered, you need think of others more. On the other hand, if you drew yourself too small, it suggests that you may feel insecure or lost in the world.

This exercise should be fun and spontaneous. If you think too much about what you're doing, or try to guess the outcome and influence the interpretation, you ruin the validity.

Exercise 2: Your Real, Ideal, and Social Selves

The purpose of this exercise is to gain insight into what you think of as the "real you," as opposed to how you would like to be or what others think you are. This exercise offers clues about things that you would like to change about yourself. It also offers insight into the image you present to the world—which may or may not be the one you want to project. Finally, the exercise can help you integrate your three selves.

Describe yourself in the table on the following page. Use as many adjectives or phrases that come to you. Write these down spontaneously without editing them.

Me As I See Myself	Me As I'd Like to Be	How Others See Me
I am:	I'd like to be:	Others see me as:
_____	_____	_____
_____	_____	_____
_____	_____	_____
_____	_____	_____
_____	_____	_____

Interpreting Your Descriptions

Look closely at the adjectives you used in each column and compare the ways in which they differ. Connect any adjectives by drawing a line between them with a pen. The more similar the adjectives, the more comfortable and fulfilled you feel—your real and ideal images are in synch.

Review the adjectives in each column and put an "x" through the qualities you do not want to have. Imagine those no longer being a part of you. Now highlight with a highlighter or put a star next to the ones you like. Close your eyes and imagine yourself being this way—this makes it more likely that you will be.

Exercise 3: Body Talk

The purpose of this exercise is to show how body confidence is the key to self confidence. Look at your drawing from Exercise 1, or look at a picture of a male or female form in a magazine. Rate how positive or negative you feel about your various body parts (with 0 being very negative and 10 being very positive). Write the numbers on the picture.

If any part gets a rating below 5, have a "body conversation." Imagine what that body part would say to you and what you would reply in order to feel more positive about it. For example, describe what your arms/breast/penis/hips are saying to you. If you write, "I'm fat, please love me, I can't take the pressure," you might consider responding, "I love you anyway, don't feel bad, it'll be fine."

Exercise 4: Love Criteria

The purpose of this exercise is to identify your "love criteria"—the picture of who you are looking for and the qualities to which your love antennae are tuned. What qualities are you looking for in a partner—intelligence, attractiveness, or a sense of humor? In the following table, check the qualities you think you have, what you're looking for in a mate, and whether any of your past lovers had the qualities you desire.

Qualities	I Am...	My Past Loves Were...	I Want a Mate Who Is...
sensitive, caring			
thoughtful			
adventurous			
honest			

continues

Qualities	I Am...	My Past Loves Were...	I Want a Mate Who Is...
trustworthy			
easy-going			
fun to be with			
boring			
affectionate			
uncommunicative			
bossy			
shy			
sexy			
outgoing			
smart			
other qualities:			
_____			
_____			
_____			

Exercise 5: Blind Date

The purpose of this exercise is to gain a sense of your perfect image of a mate. Imagine you are waiting for your blind date to arrive. What do you picture the person looking like? What do you imagine talking about? How do you imagine feeling?

Exercise 6: My Perfect Vacation

Vacations are the perfect opportunity to experience your romantic vision and passion to their fullest. The purpose of this exercise is to help you focus on that image. Try getting a date to do this exercise, too; that way, you get a chance to see if your visions and interests are compatible.

Draw yourself and your date on the perfect vacation in the drawing space at the end of this appendix. Where would you be? What would you be doing?

Interpreting Your Drawing

Some people like vacations that are restful, with little activity and lots of opportunity to "chill out." Others prefer adventure and action. If you want to loll on the beach but your date wants to tour museums or ride the rapids, you may not be as compatible as you could be.

Exercise 7: What Dating Feels Like

The purpose of this exercise is to gain an insight into how you feel about dating. Draw anything that you feel inspired by when you think of "dating"—it can be forms, people, shapes, or whatever you like. Use colors if you can. Draw in the drawing space at the end of this appendix.

Interpreting Your Drawing

How do you *feel* about the drawing? Is the emotional tone dark (signifying sad feelings related to dating) or bright and light (happiness in dating)?

What are the shapes? Are they round (soft, cozy impressions of dating), arrows or bolts of lightning (excitement), zigzags (implying confusion or both negative and positive feelings), or sharp and jagged (suggesting hurt or angry feelings)?

Exercise 8: Writing the Movie of Your Dating Life

The purpose of this exercise is to show how you are in charge of your life by writing a movie of your dating life.

Elsewhere in this book, I share one of my favorite concepts with you—that you are in charge of the movie of your life. When people call "LovePhones" with questions about a relationship problem, I ask them to imagine a movie of their life. I ask, "What movie do you picture yourself in? What movie would your mate picture himself in? Do the movies have similar themes? Does your mate know the role you have cast him in?" Whether you realize it or not, you are always writing, directing, producing, and acting in all the roles of your life movie. Is yours a comedy or tragedy, an action adventure, or PG- or R-rated fare?

Jot down the following:

Title of the film:_____

Main characters:_____

Director:_____

Producer:_____

A summary of the plot, including critical scenes in the movie:

_____

_____

_____

_____

Interpreting Your Movie

Decide if your movie is the way things went in reality or the way you really want them to go. What is happening? Does the guy get the girl? Are they fighting? Is there tragedy?

If you like the scenes in your movie, you can rehearse them over and over in your mind to make them more likely to come true.

Have your date do the same and compare your movies. Do the plots overlap? He could be in an action adventure and you could be writing a romance story—if so, your love lives may not be on the same track. Tell him your story and see if he can enjoy playing a role in it.

Exercise 9: Shared Storytelling

The purpose of this exercise is to get you to weave a story together about your date that you both can enjoy.

This is one of my favorite exercises. I use it with couples to get them to focus on sharing a love story and working well together.

Throw out a line to start the story. Then your date adds a line. Take turns until you think the story is complete.

For example, he says, "We're having breakfast on our hotel terrace on the beach on the Greek island of Rhodos." She says, "I'm feeding you a champagne-dipped strawberry. Your fingers lightly glide up and down my thigh." He goes next.

Interpreting Your Story

Examine the story carefully. What actions did you add? What did your date add? Were your details sexual? Romantic? What feelings did you describe? Are your lines more emotive than his or vice versa? How well integrated is the story—did you start the story one way, only to have her shift gears? If so, you may be at odds, and frequently find yourself feeling alone in your relationship or often disagreeing. Or are you on a parallel track? If so, you both may have the excitement of adding new ideas to spark one another. Do you embellish one another's lines? This is good sign that you appreciate and support each other's real-life story.

If you find yourself somewhat at odds, are you both interested in getting in sync? Start another story and see how much better you agree on where the story goes. Doing this can help you learn to resolve differences and accommodate each other.

Exercise 10: Things I'd Like Us to Do Together

The purpose of this exercise is to discover common interests between you and your date.

Make a list of the things you like to do, and have your date do the same. Then go through your own lists and assign priorities ("1" for the thing you most enjoy, and so forth). Compare your list with his to see where you overlap. If none of your interests overlap, you may want to reconsider this relationship.

What I Like to Do	What My Date Likes to Do
_____	_____
_____	_____
_____	_____
_____	_____
_____	_____

Exercise 11: Be a Reporter

The purpose of this exercise is to help you focus on what you really want to know about someone to get better acquainted, and to help you be more assertive about speaking up and asking for what you want.

As a psychologist and former news reporter, I am used to asking lots of questions. This exercise helps you learn how to ask the right questions to help solve your dating dilemmas.

If you have questions about your date, or if you are wondering about a certain behavior, be a reporter. Interview the person, asking questions as if you were an objective third party doing a story about him or her, without any emotional investment or fears. Try not to jump to conclusions, do stay calm, and get the facts as well as the feelings. Ask simple background questions such as:

➤ Where were you born?

➤ Where did you go to school?

➤ What have you saved from your childhood?

Then ask fun questions such as:

➤ What's your favorite color?

➤ If you were an animal, what would you be?

➤ Who is your hero?

Then think of something that happened between the two of you that you wonder about, and ask about that:

➤ What did you mean when you said...?

➤ Why did you...?

➤ What were you thinking when you...?

Exercise 12: Your Own Personal Ad

The purpose of this exercise is to write a personal ad to clarify what you think you're looking for in a date, and to see how you would describe yourself.

In as many words as you like, write about yourself. Then describe the person you are looking for.

Examples of Personal Ads

Personal ads should let your personality shine through, and clearly state what you are looking for. So be honest and creative! Looking at samples of personal ads can help stimulate your own creative juices.

Here are some phrases that people used in their personal ads for a contest I hosted for *Details* magazine. I picked these samples because they represent some particularly vivid descriptions:

➤ "Jane Fonda look-alike seeks rich, well-heeled TV exec."

➤ "Prince or sheik sought. Into art and beauty."

➤ "Spring fever, into tennis and Sunday brunch, looking for love match."

➤ "Priceless '60s mint condition, presently garaged, looking for experienced driver to step on my accelerator."

➤ "Looking for well-built muscle man—not too kinky, but into body worship."

➤ "Into religion...I pray you come."

➤ "Likes to talk after you-know-what—no overweight, sweaty, or hygienically challenged persons, please."

➤ "Fifth Baldwin seeks Barbie with brains."

➤ "I admit I'll soon have to join Hair Club for Men."

➤ "By day I'm a mild-mannered businessman who does origami; by night I'm a winged creature who battles the forces of evil. If you're my damsel in distress, let me be your superhero."

Drawing Space

Drawing Space

Drawing Space

Resources

Clubs and Organizations

Single Gourmet
133 East 58th Street
New York, NY 10022

(212) 980-8788

Local clubs available in about 18 cities in the U.S. and Canada; contact local directory assistance. Offers dining events with mingling opportunities, often mixed with various outings such as theater, sporting events, or trips. Membership (initial, $75, renewal $40) includes newsletter and reciprocal membership in all Single Gourmet clubs. Plus cost of dinner or event.

Parents Without Partners
8807 Colesville Road
Silver Springs, MD 20910

(800) 637-7974

National organization with local chapters around the country. Offers activities for single parents of all ages with children. Membership fees (for example, $30) plus fees for some activities (for example, picnic, $3).

Outdoor Bound
18 Stuyvesant Oval
New York, NY 10009

(212) 505-1020

Outdoors and travel club offering various trips with varied activities from rafting to camping. About ten thousand people on mailing list. Membership fee $30.

12-Step Programs

Nationally available, contact your local directory assistance.

Based on the famed 12-step addiction model, these self-help groups offer frequent group support meetings for people with similar life issues ranging from alcohol or drug abuse (AA or DA) to overeating (OA) and love and sex addictions (LSA).

UJA-Federation
130 East 59th Street
New York, NY 10022

(212) 898-9100

National organization with local affiliates in various cities offering events, trips, courses; for example, Business and Professional Singles, Resource Line.

Christian Singles International
P.O. Box 3054
Harrison, OH 45030

(513) 598-2883

Maintains list of 150,000 people and claims 1,400 marriages. Lists personals and articles. Membership $29.95/year.

Book and Music Stores Offering Opportunities for Reading, Listening, Eating

Check local listings:

Borders Books and Music Stores

Barnes & Noble Bookstores

Media Play

Restaurant Chains

Check local listings:

Planet Hollywood

Hard Rock Cafe

Dating Services

Together
Corporate Office: 161 Worcester Road
Framingham, MA 01701

(508) 620-1115

Matches made on basis of questionnaire ("Compatibility Evaluation Guide") and in-depth personal interviews. Travel opportunities also available. Offices in 35 U.S. cities, London, and Toronto. Different membership plans (average annual cost about $1,000).

Visual Preference
74 North Maple Avenue
Ridgewood, NJ 07450

(800) 533-1712

After personal interview, matches made on basis of video or photo exchanges. Glamour makeovers for females included. Cost based on individualized program.

Great Expectations
255 Business Center Drive
Horfam, PA 19044

(215) 957-2780
Los Angeles, CA office: (310) 477-5566

Offices in about 50 cities (not including New York). Choices made by viewing videotapes of clients. Costs about $1,000 to $2,500 per year.

Conscious Singles Connection
243 West End Avenue, Suite 1504
New York, NY 10023

(212) 873-7187

Matches made by member profile through questionnaire and interview. Also has inspirational tapes, as well as guided Meditation for Singles to survive the holidays alone.

SoulMates
P.O. Box 8691
LaJolla, CA 92038

(619) 259-4321

Matches made by working one-on-one with a consultant, or by personal selection from a library of photographs and profiles, and voice mailbox system. Relationship skills seminars also offered. Of thousands of clients, a 70 percent success rate is claimed.

Field's Exclusive Service
41 East 42nd Street
New York, NY 10017

(212) 391-2233

On the basis of your answers on a questionnaire, this "marriage broker" gives you a list of people. Fee starts at $50 for three names and depends on the level of service.

Courses

New Life Expo
218 West 72nd Street
New York, NY 10023

(800) 928-6208

Symposium held in various cities around the country, consisting of 150 lectures, workshops, and exhibits on holistic health, alternative medicine, psychic phenomena, and environment discoveries. Admission $15 plus workshop fees.

Whole Life Expo
660 Venice Boulevard
Venice, CA 90291

(310) 396-7090

Expo held in various cities around the country (including New York, Los Angeles, Las Vegas, Seattle, and Santa Fe) with exhibits, speakers, and workshops on health, personal growth, and positive living. Admission plus workshop fees.

Learning Annex

New York office: 2330 Broadway
New York, NY 10028

(212) 570-6500

Washington, D.C. office: 1634 I Street NW
Washington, D.C. 20009

(202) 639-2000

Extensive curriculum of courses and events. Attendance about $29 for members, $39 for non-members.

YMCA/YWCA and YMHA/YWHA

Local chapters in various cities around the country. Contact local directory assistance. Offers support groups, courses, and activities on various themes from "How to Flirt" to "Letting Go and Moving On." Cost of events varies from $2 and up.

Magazines/Newsletters

New York Magazine and similar local city magazines at newsstands. Check events listings and personals.

Houston Single File
2476 Bolsover #608
Houston, TX 77005

(713) 496-DATE

Monthly subscription $20, call for similar magazines available in some areas.

General Services/Network

Dateline
257 Ely Avenue
Norwalk, CT 06851

(203) 866-6617 x137

Monthly subscription $21. Also offers other magazines, newsletters and singles services, referrals, and networking lists.

Travel Services

Richniks/Perks
362 West 23rd Street
New York, NY 10011

(800) RICHNIK

Offers social, recreational, and travel opportunities for singles.

HEDONISM

Book through travel agent for good prices.

All-inclusive vacation package to Jamaica, known for its almost entirely singles patronage and uninhibited atmosphere.

Club Med
40 West 57th Street
New York, NY 10019

(800) CLUB MED

All-inclusive vacation packages at villages around the world offering varied sports and activities. Sixty percent of travelers are single, median age 35; two-thirds are professionals. Membership fee plus cost of trip (week-long, over $1,000).

Information on Health Issues

ASHA (The American Social Health Association)
P.O. Box 13827
Research Triangle Park, NC 27709

(800) 230-6039
Or call the National STD hotline: (800) 227-8922

SIECUS (Sexuality Information and Education Council of the United States)
130 West 42nd Street, Suite 350
New York, NY 10036

(212) 819-9770
Fax: (212) 819-9776

For AOL members: **siecusinc@aol.com**
For other service members: **siecus@ibm.net**
E-mail: **SIECUS@siecus.org**
Internet Web site: **http://www.siecus.org**

Planned Parenthood Federation of America
810 7th Avenue
New York NY 10019

(212) 261-4300
Fax: (212) 246-1845 or (800) 230-PLAN
E-mail: **communications@PPFA.org**
Internet Web site: **wttp://www.ppfa.org/PPFA**

Alan Guttmacher Institute
120 Wall Street
New York, NY 10005

(212) 248-1111
Fax: (212) 248-1951

GMHC (The Gay Men's Health Crisis Inc.)
129 West 20th Street
New York, NY 10011

(212) 807-6664
Fax: (212) 337-1220
Internet Web site: **http://www.gmhc.org**

Dating Quiz

Take this test to see how good you are in the dating game and how to improve your
dating skills. The answers to this quiz can be found at the end of this section.

1. List the top three things that men say attract them to a woman:

   _____

   _____

   _____

2. List the top three things that women say attract them to a man:

   _____

   _____

   _____

3. Which of the five senses is the most powerful in attraction?

   Circle one:

   Sight   Taste

   Smell   Touch

   Hearing

4. If you were going to whisper sweet nothings in someone's ear, which ear would
   you whisper in?

   Circle one:

   Right ear   Left ear

5. What are the words that women most want to hear?

   _____

6. What are the words that men most want to hear?

   _____

7. What do both men and women (according to surveys) most want to hear?

   _____

8. What is the best way to "pick up" someone?

   _____

9. Where is the best place to go to meet someone?

   _____

10. How many approaches should you make before you give up on a dating prospect?

    _____

11. What's the best way to show someone you're interested?

    _____

    _____

12. How do you know someone's interested in you?

    _____

13. What is the best way to deal with rejection?

    _____

    _____

14. Who is the best date?

    _____

15. How many dates should it take before you know someone is "it"?

    _____

16. What is the best test of love?

    _____

    _____

17. List three qualities that make for the best-lasting relationship:

    _____

    _____

    _____

18. What is "condom-sense"?

    _____

19. Why do men roll over and go to sleep after sex?

    _____

    _____

Answers to Dating Quiz

1. Top three things that men say attract them to a woman (see Chapter 9).

2. Top three things that women say attract them to a man (see Chapter 9).

3. *Smell* is the most powerful sense in attraction (the messages go straight, and therefore quickly, from the olfactory bulb to the brain).

4. Whisper sweet nothings in the left ear to connect to the right (romantic) side of the brain).

5. Women most want to hear the words "I love you" and "You're beautiful."

6. Men most want to hear how good they are.

7. Both men and women (according to surveys) most want to hear their name.

8. The best way to "pick up" someone is to be yourself.

9. The best place to go to meet someone is where you feel comfortable, so you will shine. Other good choices: where energy is alive (sporting events, amusement parks, concerts).

10. Make three approaches before you give up on a dating prospect.

11. Show someone you're interested by admitting it, complimenting him or her, and making eye contact.

12. Assess someone's interest from his or her body language.

13. Deal with rejection by switching attention to what makes you feel good, and realizing that one hit in three is a good batting average.

14. You are your own best date.

15. Follow a six-date minimum.

16. The best test of love is going through crises together.

17. Qualities of best-lasting relationships (see Chapter 15).

18. Condom-sense is using one every time.

19. Men don't *have to* roll over and go to sleep after sex; they're tired, or have trained themselves that way, or they may want to escape intimacy.

Index

W

Y–Z

When You're Smart Enough to Know
That You Don't Know It All

For all the ups and downs you're sure to encounter in life, The Complete Idiot's Guides give you down-to-earth answers and practical solutions.

Lifestyle

The Complete Idiot's Guide to Learning French on Your Own
ISBN: 0-02-861043-1 • $16.95

The Complete Idiot's Guide to Learning Spanish on Your Own
ISBN: 0-02-861040-7 • $16.95

The Complete Idiot's Guide to Gambling Like a Pro
ISBN: 0-02-861102-0 • $16.95

The Complete Idiot's Guide to Hiking and Camping
ISBN: 0-02-861100-4 • $16.95

The Complete Idiot's Guide to Choosing, Training, and Raising a Dog
ISBN: 0-02-861098-9 • $16.95

The Complete Idiot's Guide to Trouble-Free Car Care
ISBN: 0-02-861041-5 • $16.95

The Complete Idiot's Guide to Trouble-Free Home Repair
ISBN: 0-02-861042-3 • $16.95

The Complete Idiot's Guide to Dating
ISBN: 0-02-861052-0 • $14.95

The Complete Idiot's Guide to Cooking Basics
ISBN: 1-56761-523-6 • $16.99

The Complete Idiot's Guide to the Perfect Wedding
ISBN: 1-56761-532-5 • $16.99

The Complete Idiot's Guide to the Perfect Vacation
ISBN: 1-56761-531-7 • $14.99

The Complete Idiot's Guide to First Aid Basics
ISBN: 0-02-861099-7 • $16.95

Personal Business

The Complete Idiot's Guide to Getting Into College
ISBN: 1-56761-508-2 • $14.95

The Complete Idiot's Guide to Terrific Business Writing
ISBN: 0-02-861097-0 • $16.95

The Complete Idiot's Guide to Surviving Divorce
ISBN: 0-02-861101-2 • $16.95

The Complete Idiot's Guide to Managing Your Time
ISBN: 0-02-861039-3 • $14.95

The Complete Idiot's Guide to Speaking in Public with Confidence
ISBN: 0-02-861038-5 • $16.95

The Complete Idiot's Guide to Winning Through Negotiation
ISBN: 0-02-861037-7 • $16.95

The Complete Idiot's Guide to Managing People
ISBN: 0-02-861036-9 • $18.95

The Complete Idiot's Guide to Starting Your Own Business
ISBN: 1-56761-529-5 • $16.99

The Complete Idiot's Guide to a Great Retirement
ISBN: 1-56761-601-1 • $16.95

The Complete Idiot's Guide to Protecting Yourself From Everyday Legal Hassles
ISBN: 1-56761-602-X • $16.99

The Complete Idiot's Guide to Getting the Job You Want
ISBN: 1-56761-608-9 • $24.95

Personal Finance

The Complete Idiot's Guide to Buying Insurance and Annuities
ISBN: 0-02-861113-6 • $16.95

The Complete Idiot's Guide to Doing Your Income Taxes 1996
ISBN: 1-56761-586-4 • $14.99

The Complete Idiot's Guide to Getting Rich
ISBN: 1-56761-509-0 • S16.95

The Complete Idiot's Guide to Making Money with Mutual Funds
ISBN: 1-56761-637-2 • $16.95

The Complete Idiot's Guide to Managing Your Money
ISBN: 1-56761-530-9 • $16.95

The Complete Idiot's Guide to Buying and Selling a Home
ISBN: 1-56761-510-4 • $16.95

Rap With the Idiots and Get a Free Gift

Okay...we're not smart enough to know what you're thinking, but we'd like to! Please take a few minutes to fill out the following information, and we'll mail you a gift in return.

Did you purchase this book for   Yourself   Friend   Relative

Other _____

Had you heard of *The Complete Idiot's Guide* series prior to your purchase of this book? ____Yes ____No

Have you purchased any other *Complete Idiot's Guide* titles? ____Yes ____No

If yes, what other titles do you own? _____

_____

For what other topics would you like to see *Complete Idiot's Guides*? _____

_____

How did you become aware of this book?

____Listening to Judy Kuriansky's "LovePhones" radio show

____Book was recommended by a friend or relative

____Saw it on the bookstore shelf

____Advertisement

____Attended a bookstore seminar with Judy Kuriansky

____Other _____

On a scale where 6 is extremely important and 1 is not at all important, please rate the following factors that influenced you to purchase this dating book.

	Extremely Important				Not At All Important	
Price	6	5	4	3	2	1
Like the way the information is presented in this book	6	5	4	3	2	1
Like *The Complete Idiot's Guide* series	6	5	4	3	2	1
Feel like an idiot when it comes to dating and think this book will offer great advice	6	5	4	3	2	1
Judy Kuriansky's expertise in this area	6	5	4	3	2	1

Please tell us something about yourself.

Age: ____Under 21   ____21 to 35   ____Over 35

Gender: ____Male   ____Female

Education Level: ____High school ____College

Would you like to be on our mailing list to receive the *Idiot's Newsletter*? ____Yes ____No

Thank you for your reply. We will mail your gift to the address you indicate below.

Name _____

Address _____

City, State, Zip_____

Mail this completed form to *Idiot's Guides*, c/o Macmillan Reference, Marketing Department, 1633 Broadway—6th Floor, New York, N.Y. 10019. Offer expires December 31, 1997.